OTHER WAYS
OF KNOWING

OTHER WAYS OF KNOWING

RECHARTING OUR FUTURE WITH AGELESS WISDOM

JOHN BROOMFIELD

Inner Traditions
Rochester, Vermont

Inner Traditions International
One Park Street
Rochester, Vermont 05767
www.gotoit.com

Library of Congress Cataloging-in-Publication Data
Broomfield, John.
    Other ways of knowing: recharting our future with ageless wisdom / John Broomfield.
        p.   cm.
    Includes bibliographical references and index.
    ISBN 0-89281-614-7 (alk. paper)
    1. Nature—Religious aspects. 2. Knowledge, Sociology of. 3. Science—Philosophy. 4. East and West. 5. Spiritural life.   I. Title
    BL65.N35B76 1997   97-7876
    121—dc21   CIP

Printed and bound in the Canada

10 9 8 7 6 5 4 3 2 1

Text design and layout by Kate Mueller
This book was typeset in Caslon and Galahad

Distributed to the book trade in Canada by Publishers Group West (PGW), Toronto, Ontario
Distributed to the book trade in the United Kingdom by Deep Books, London
Distributed to the book trade in Australia by Millennium Books, Newtown, N. S. W.
Distributed to the book trade in New Zealand by Tandem Press, Auckland
Distributed to the book trade in South Africa by Alternative Books, Ferndale

To Jo Imlay

for her journey is my journey,
and this book is hers as well as mine.

Contents

Acknowledgments

I am deeply grateful to the many people who have helped with *Other Ways of Knowing*. Regrettably it is not possible to acknowledge each individually, but I wish to thank the following especially.

For their shining example of how to combine passion for things of the mind with a life of spiritual service: Joanna Macy, Flora Courtois, His Holiness the 14th Dalai Lama, Willis Harman, Father Bede Griffiths, Karan Singh, and Huston Smith.

For financial assistance for my writing and for earlier years of research: Laurance Rockefeller, Ellen Ghilarducci, Tides Foundation, American Institute of Indian Studies, Australian National University, Massachusetts Institute of Technology, University of Michigan, and National Endowment for the Humanities.

For support in my search for funding: Anthony Low, Leo Marx, Roxanne Lanier, Sidney Lanier, and Elizabeth McCormack.

For widening my understanding of Indian spirituality: Ajita Ranjan Mukherjea, Amita Chakravarti, Bachoo Roy, Lily Roy, Ed Dimock, Judy Kroll, Gangadhar Sharma and family of Naggar, and my hatha yoga teachers at the Ann Arbor Y.

For teachings in Tibetan Buddhism: the rinpoches and yogis of Khampargar Monastery, Tashi Jong.

For shamanic teachings: Michael Harner, Sandra Ingerman, Angeles Arrien, Barrett Eagle Bear, Antonio Nuñez, Zaida Nuñez, Te Hata Ohlson, and Mana Cracknell.

For the gift of Martin Buber: Margaret Bearlin.

For insights in holistic health and the new sciences: Max Heirich, Ron Chalfant, Henryk Skolimowski, Michael Shallis, Fritjof Capra, Rupert Sheldrake, and my colleagues in the Program in Science, Technology, and Society at M.I.T., especially Sharon Traweek, Evelyn Keller, David Nye, and Martin Krieger.

For seeding ideas and encouraging me in new directions: Colleen Lundy, Jeremy Tarcher, Michael Toms, Justine Toms, Bill Kautz, faculty colleagues, teaching assistants, and students at the University of Michigan, particularly Anne Epstein, Philippe Uninsky, Kira Stevens, and Pete Becker (whose scholarly generosity is a model to academe); and faculty colleagues and students at the California Institute of Integral Studies, particularly Ralph Metzner, whose avid search for new understandings surrounded us with innovative thinkers.

For their professional excellence, empathy, and responsiveness, which made the production of this volume an unqualified pleasure: the staff at Inner Traditions International, particularly my editors, Rowan Jacobsen, Jon Graham, and Anna Chapman.

For helping me keep a sense of proportion: all the good people along the way with the sense of humor to laugh at me and themselves; and the earth and the animals, who have shown me how much I have to learn.

In this regard, I owe most to my family: Jo, Kia, Rai, and Sam the shaman spirit. Jo has my profound gratitude for her companionship in exploring the mysteries we both treasure; for her good judgment that has saved me from many errors; for her skills as a writer, editor, and gentle critic; for her patience and understanding; and, above all, for her integrity and rich gift of love.

Copyright Acknowledgments

"Little Songs for Gaia" from *Axe Handles* by Gary Snyder. Copyright 1983 by Gary Snyder. By permission of Gary Snyder and North Point Press, a division of Farrar, Straus, and Giroux, Inc.

"By Frazier Creek Falls" from *Turtle Island* by Gary Snyder. Copyright 1974 by Gary Snyder. By permission of New Directions Publishing Corp.

"1," "11," and "73" from *Tao Te Ching* by Stephen Mitchell. Translation copyright 1988 by Stephen Mitchell. By permission of Harper-Collins Publishers, Inc.

"Seeds Are the Ticket to Ride" by Tony Basilio from *Noetic Sciences Review*. By permission of Sereta Basilio-Lewis and *Noetic Sciences Review*.

"On Returning to Religion" by William Barrett from *Commentary*, November 1976. By permission of *Commentary;* all rights reserved.

"The Boy in the Bubble" by Paul Simon from *Graceland.* Copyright 1986 by Paul Simon. By permission of Paul Simon Music.

Introduction

Take heart! Humanity is wise and, in its rich diversity, possessed of vast reservoirs of creativity, inspiration, and spiritual energy with which to meet the challenges of the new millenium. Be of good cheer, for this is an intentional, life-enhancing universe with love as its vital force.

You and I have great work to do. In the twentieth century humans have been hell-bent on acquiring new knowledge. In the twenty-first century we must have the wisdom to save ourselves from the effects of this knowledge.

Our problem is complex, but its core can be simply stated: In the modern West we have made the serious error of equating our way of knowing, which we variously call science and history, with all of knowledge. To put it another way, we have taken a thin slice of reality and mistaken it for the whole. Happily, there are other ways of knowing.

At a time when many despair about the fate of the earth, my purpose with this book is to bring you the good news that the necessary wisdom is readily available from many sources: From the sacred traditions of our ancestors. From the spiritual lives of our own and other cultures. From spirit in nature. From the deep knowledge of healthy processes embedded in our own bodies. From feminine ways of being. From contemporary movements for personal, social and ecological transformation. Unexpectedly, even from the apparent source of our current crisis: science itself.

> Reason sets the boundaries far too narrowly for us, and would have
> us accept only the known—and that too with limitations—and live

1

in a known framework, just as if we were sure how far life actually extends. As a matter of fact, day after day we live far beyond the bounds of our consciousness.[1]

Carl Jung

A Parable from Polynesia

When my British ancestors sailed into the Pacific in the eighteenth century, they encountered a people whom they called Polynesians, who spoke one language even though their island homes were separated by thousands of miles of ocean. The Polynesians told of great voyages of exploration undertaken by their ancestors hundreds of years earlier. They explained that their navigators had relied upon an intimate knowledge of star paths, the habits of migratory birds, and the varied patterns of light and motion of ocean waves and currents. The pilots who guided these ancient voyages had the capacity, they said, to rise in spirit above the masthead to see far beyond the horizon. In crises, when even these skills proved insufficient, guardian spirits might be summoned in the form of birds, fish, dolphins, whales, or sea dragons to point the voyagers to their destinations.

The early European explorers were awed by these accounts, but to their rationalist successors in the increasingly scientific climate of the nineteenth and early twentieth centuries, the claims of ancient Pacific voyaging seemed far-fetched. Quite apart from the tall talk of guardian spirits and seeing over the horizon, how could stone-age illiterates like the Polynesians have accomplished in their primitive canoes what even a modern navigator as renowned as Captain James Cook, in the Royal Navy's finest vessel, could do only with the aid of compass, sextant, chronometer, and log?

The question remained: How did the Polynesians come to be settled on islands scattered over an area of ocean as vast as modern China and Russia combined? My high school textbooks in New Zealand in the 1950s gave this answer: Sad to say, those heroic voyages recorded in Maori song and story were, in reality, pathetic mistakes. Polynesian canoes out fishing or making short journeys between neighboring islands had been caught in storms, and a few lucky boatloads, swept by winds and the notoriously strong Pacific currents, ultimately had drifted to re-mote, unsettled lands such as Hawaii, Easter Island, and New Zealand. The book illustrations, reproductions of Victorian paintings, showed the haggard castaways summoning their last strength at the sight of land and salvation.

The story is instructive because it illustrates nicely how the scientific mind responds when confronted with apparently anomalous cultural or natural data. In the modern West we have a number of well-rehearsed and persuasive answers in such situations:

- If we cannot do something with our advanced techniques and mechanical devices, other peoples certainly could not.
- If they did possess elements of "real" knowledge, they must have stumbled upon them, because they did not have our scientific method of systematically recording observational and experimental data.
- Matter is the only true reality, so nonmaterial causal expla-nations are superstitions, not science.
- Proof requires quantifiable measurement.
- Where otherwise inexplicable patterns are observed, in human behavior as in nature, random chance provides the answer.

In a nutshell: Things are unknowable except as we in the modern West know them.

Postscript: The last twenty-five years have produced a scientific change of mind about the Polynesian voyages. First, archaeologists un-earthed the remains of ancient Polynesian outriggers almost as large as the ships that carried Europeans into the Pacific. No fishing canoes these.

Then, in the 1970s, when the distribution of Polynesian cultivated plants, traditional tools, and ritual designs was mapped by computer, the statistical frequencies eliminated random chance as a possible explana-tion. Similarly, improved knowledge of Pacific currents and wind streams led to computer simulations of the likely lines of drift of out-riggers lost on the high seas, and few of them coincided with the routes between the main island groups in Polynesia. It would have been virtually impossible for castaways to wash up on the shores of Hawaii, Easter Island, or New Zealand.

Meanwhile, scientists studying exceptional human abilities in laboratories in the United States and Europe uncovered startling evidence of "remote viewing": the human capacity to "see" places and events far beyond the range of eyesight. Finally, there was the "discovery" of living Polynesians and Micronesians who still possessed traditional navigational skills, and with their guidance, some of those amazing long-distance voyages without the aid of mechanical instruments were replicated in the 1980s.

Why did it take us two hundred years to believe what another people told us was true? "Things are unknowable except as we know them." Until we could find a way to plot the elements of the Polynesian account onto our conceptual grid (history and science), we could not verify them (accord them the status of truths).

In making this observation, I am not implying that our civilization is unique in excluding understandings that do not fit our conceptual schema. I am, however, drawing attention to the fact that all too often in the modern West we have rejected the learned experience of other cultures, including that of our own forebears, only later to discover that this experience contains invaluable resources.

We cannot continue in this way. Given the scale of the problems we confront as we enter the twenty-first century, we no longer have the casual luxury of waiting another two hundred years to learn from the wisdom of others.

This being so, let me ask you to consider what we should do about the one remaining element that science cannot verify in the accounts of the ancient Polynesian voyages: the navigators' reliance on spirit guides. Having been proved wrong in our skepticism about the rest, are we wise to continue to dismiss this as superstition?

Central Themes

This parable from Polynesia introduces the three main themes that will intertwine throughout the book. The first is an examination of the structure and underlying assumptions of our modern historical and scientific understandings of reality. The second is an exploration of other ways of knowing available to us from the diverse cultural experience of thousands of human generations. The third is a search for sources of spiritual enlightenment in nature.

Let us nurture other ways of knowing, treasuring the fact that their strengths and limitations will be different from those of science and history.

1

DANCING WITH THE PAST

What Is History?

Science is our culture's pride and joy, but this chapter is about history. Not many of us can claim to be scientists, but we are all historians. Historical reasoning is fundamental to modern Western thought. In our everyday lives, all of us use interpretations of the past to explain the present.

History is commonly understood to be the record of human experience. The historical method, together with the scientific method, which was developed concurrently, is generally credited with providing us in the modern West with a capacity to trace human development unrivaled by other civilizations.

It indicates our confidence in the accuracy of our record of the experience of our species that we use the word *history* for both human activity in the past and its study. "History speaking" was the greeting with which Kingsley Amis' pompous fictional professor answered the telephone in the movie *Lucky Jim*. Those of us who are professional historians try to be less presumptuous, but we do offer our writings as accurate recreations of the past.

As a card-carrying member of the guild, I must warn you that we historians misrepresent our trade. By failing to make explicit the limitations of the historical method, and the limits of history itself, we reinforce the comfortably narrow view of human experience maintained by our civilization. Don't worry if this statement seems too cryptic. I'll elaborate.

The Present Shapes the Past

History is not a set of facts fixed in the past, simply awaiting proper selection and ordering. History is the *present* perception of past events. There is no history apart from the "historian." The observer and the observed past are inextricably entwined.

> History is lived forwards but it is written in retrospect. We know the end before we consider the beginning and we can never wholly recapture what it was to know the beginning only.[1]

Most academic historians, I am sure, would agree with this elegant statement by Veronica Wedgewood of the difficulties we face in writing "objective" or "detached" history, and most would place the same emphasis on our knowledge of ends before beginnings. Unfortunately, this obscures a crucial point: There is no fixed or determinate *end*. Current perceptions change, and with changing perceptions the "endings" are redefined. As a consequence, history is rewritten endlessly.

Nor is there a single history. If we accept the premise that history is the present perception of events in the past, we must acknowledge a corollary: Numerous histories result from diverse present perceptions of differently remembered pasts.

> The great battle in American history was the Battle of Little Bighorn. The Indians wiped out the white men, scalped them. That was a victory in American history.[2]

Eugene O'Neill's interpretation of Custer's last stand is not the textbook version—it is not accepted white man's history—but it was the perception of the Sioux victors at Little Bighorn, and it is the history accepted by the descendants of Sitting Bull, Crazy Horse, and their warriors.

Academic historians have a ready response to this. They are carefully trained to pay scrupulous attention to differing views of participants and to reconcile or incorporate them in the historical account so as to provide a composite view. I believe their argument is untenable, resting as it does on the supposition that human events and their perception are separable. They are not. Each participant's comprehension of an event is part of the event itself. Human consciousness shapes action, and actions have meaning only through human perception.

Participants' comprehensions of the "same" event are diverse and frequently irreconcilable. Many years ago the ethnohistorian Bernard S. Cohn, in a brilliant short article entitled "The Pasts of an Indian Village," traced the widely divergent histories maintained by different castes in a small north Indian community. These groups had coexisted for centuries, but they had lived (experienced) different histories. They did not share a common past.[3]

We can understand the statement "There is no single history" in another sense. Human experience of an event, even one person's experience, is more like a kaleidoscope than a set image. The past contributes shapes and colors to the kaleidoscopic pattern, which is then continually shaken and rearranged by later experience.

"The point is that past events grow. They are not finished," comments Jane Roberts.[4] For instance, the Watergate break-in might indeed have gone down in history as "a third-rate burglary," as White House spokesperson Ron Ziegler wished us to view it, if Richard Nixon had promptly destroyed those incriminating tape recordings. A later decision not to destroy the White House tapes—a decision in no way mandated by the events of June 17, 1972, at the Watergate Hotel—fundamentally affects the historic value we place on the earlier event. In a very real sense the present shapes the past.

I compared historical experience to a kaleidoscope. Here is another visual analogy. Some years ago a colleague at the University of Michigan, video artist Richard Manderberg, developed a technique to enable a dancer to dance with an image of herself on a videoscreen as she had danced a few seconds earlier. As she fitted her movements to this "old" dancing image of herself, Manderberg was able through the controls of his master screen, on which the combined images were shown, to vary the colors, vary the size of the "two" human figures, and make one or the other (the "historic" or the "contemporary") apparently approach or recede from the viewer.

Here, I believe, is a metaphor for history more apt than the one to which we are accustomed. Individuals and whole cultures are forever dancing with shifting images of their pasts. Our consciousness and actions are always choreographed to our histories. Present and past dance *pas de deux;* they move continually, the colors, the relative size of the forms, and their proximity to the viewer (the "historian") perpetually shifting in value.

History and the Human Experience

Having reconsidered two of our culture's generally accepted understandings of history—the discrete separation of past and present and the existence of a unified past—let's now consider the possibility that history as a methodology has a limited ability to give us a satisfactory comprehension of human experience.

To illustrate this, here are two stories of travel in the Arctic. One concerns the celebrated U.S. Navy aviator and explorer, Richard Byrd, who made the first airplane flight over the North Pole on May 9, 1926. His achievement was marked by his rapid promotion to admiral and his elevation in the history books to a place of honor alongside the other U.S. polar hero, Robert Peary, "discoverer of the North Pole, April 6, 1909."[5] Byrd's historic journey was accomplished in the most favorable spring weather, and he took advantage of the twentieth-century technologies of the internal combustion engine, the radio, and support ships of the U.S. Navy.

The second story concerns four Cree families—adults of both sexes, children, and dogs—whose two thousand mile journey in uninhabited northern Quebec and Labrador in the 1950s was described to a Montreal court by one of their number, Stephen Tapiatic, as nothing out of the ordinary.[6] Close to the Arctic Circle for five months in the depth of winter, they canoed and walked on snowshoes over an equivalent of the distance from one side of Europe to the other, living off the land and using only knives, axes, fishing tackle, rifles, and (most critically) ten thousand years of their people's experience in traveling through the North American Arctic—and unnumbered earlier centuries in Siberia.

Our history records Byrd and Peary as pioneer explorers. The Eskimos and other Native Americans who preceded and assisted them, and whose skills eclipsed or at least matched theirs, go nameless. Their experience has only a shadowy place in history. In part this results from ethnocentrism, but the professional historian in good conscience will point to an additional problem: the existence of historical documentation in the first case and its absence or extreme paucity in the second.

Before we weigh this argument, let's consider another story. In 1980, I traveled from California to Western Australia on one of the new breed of high-tech ocean freighters. For six weeks between the ports of the Asian mainland and through the islands of the South Seas, this computerized marvel was guided by satellite transmissions that continuously gave position fixes and provided weather data to its automated navigational equipment. The Norwegian officers were especially pleased with the new satellite surveys of the ocean currents, which enabled the vessel to speed its voyage with the greatest fuel economy by sophisticated changes of course to take advantage of favorable currents.

Our mariners had finally caught up with the first settlers of Oceania, the Polynesians and Micronesians, who had sailed back and forth across the Pacific for three thousand years. As mentioned in the introduction, their navigational skills without magnetic or mechanical aids—in particular their ability to ride the currents—were so "advanced" that until recently most Europeans and Americans refused to believe that theirs were more than chance voyages. This despite the available evidence of origin myth, saga, genealogy, geographical knowledge, and even demonstrated navigational ability. These island peoples were nonliterate, their experience largely opaque to history.

Which holds true for the vaster part of human experience. *Homo sapiens* has walked this planet for as many as two hundred thousand years. Our erect forebears may have preceded us by four or five million years. Consider how miniscule is the portion that is recorded history: Four thousand years is the figure often used—and that's stretching it!

In the face of this realization, how do we as supposedly enlightened moderns avoid an overwhelming sense of loss and consequent ignorance?

By our concentration on the detail of the recent past, that thin sliver of human time for which we have historical records. We do this buoyed by the confidence that the experience of "early man" was but a prelude to our own; that our development—the progressive accumulation of knowledge and skills—places us at a more advanced level.

This is the cultural evolutionary model, the application to human society of Darwin's familiar theory of biological evolution. In the cultural as in the biological model, the core belief is that the direction of development is from the simple to the complex: that human society has evolved from tiny bands of wandering hunters and gatherers, using mere sticks and stones for tools, to the great nation-states of the present day, with their ingenious high technology.

You will recall, I am sure, the dramatic representation of this belief in the opening sequence of the movie *2001: A Space Odyssey*: the apes discovering that a bone could serve as a tool and throwing it high in the air, where it metamorphoses beautifully into a starship.

This modern mythology, like all myths, has a kernel of truth. We should be cautious, however, of accepting without question a neat packaging of the vast story of humanity that places contemporary Western civilization so conveniently at the pinnacle of evolution. The theory permits some comfortable deceptions. For instance, having accepted as a first principle that development is from the simple to the complex, we can discount the need for detailed knowledge of the diversity of cultural forms and substitute for it a linear sequence of developmental stages, each one a step up the evolutionary ladder. In order to establish this cultural progression, we are encouraged to disregard as irrelevant the techniques of earlier humans that we no longer command.

Perhaps most damagingly, the model relegates to a position of inferiority twentieth-century contemporaries whose skills for environmental adaptation are markedly different from our own. It classifies them as cultural survivals from an "earlier" stage, "living echoes of our own primitive past," as the Kalahari Bushmen were described in the television program *Wild Kingdom*.

The absurdity of such condescending attitudes toward "primitives" is revealed by a quick look at the Bushmen. They are desert and semi-desert peoples of southern Africa, diverse bands of hunters, herders, and horticulturalists, who live in a land so harsh few of us could survive more than a few days. Their superb knowledge of their natural environments and the strength of the community structures that sustain them command our respect.

Cultural evolutionary thinking dumps the Kalahari Bushmen and others like them on the scrap heap of history. Manipulating the time line to deny whole cultures full participation in the present is obvious sleight of hand, but dismayed at this as we may be, we should recognize that, in a sense, history is a grand illusion, an intellectual mirror trick. As noted earlier, the proof of the superiority of modern Western civilization is said to be its possession of the historical method, along with the associated social and natural sciences, which give us the capacity to accumulate knowledge systematically. Earlier humans "lacked" this method. They were "prehistoric." Thus, *our* limited capacity to comprehend their experience, resulting from the limitations of the historical method, can be advanced as proof of *their* inferiority. They failed to produce the historical documentation we need.

The Limits of History

In the words of Hans-Georg Gadamer, "It is not really we ourselves who understand; it is always a past that allows us to say: 'I have understood'."[7] History—modern Western civilization's way of constructing a past—provides us with a framework of understanding by denying discontinuity. We make sense of reality by insisting upon unbroken linear sequence.

Time, as we understand it, is a line, existing in only one dimension and flowing in a single direction. Events are fixed points on this line of time, and causation is understood as the sequence of events. Cause and effect are related as past and present.

So fundamental to our civilization is this perception of sequential causation in unbroken, one-dimensional, onward-flowing time—history, as we call it—that we think it is natural reality. It is scientific—our truth. Other cultures' ways of understanding time, if incongruent with ours, may be attractively quaint but must be fundamentally wrong.

History (or science, if you care to give it its other name) leaves no room for the possibility that our construction of reality, our way of knowing, is limited.

We may not think we know it all, but we do believe that *logically* there is nothing to prevent us knowing it all, given the power of our investigative techniques. "The method works," declared Lewis Thomas in *The Medusa and the Snail.* "There are probably no questions we can think up that can't be answered, sooner or later, including even the matter of consciousness."[8] On the pervasiveness of this sort of reasoning, Gadamer comments: "The concept of knowledge based on scientific procedures tolerates no restriction of its claim to universality."[9]

In fact, linear time and sequential cause and effect are merely two of the patterns we have constructed in order to make sense of reality. Like all such explanatory patterns they are simplifications of the universe, which, in its inconceivable vastness and complexity, is always threatening to overwhelm the limited capacity of the human organism to comprehend. In Loren Eiseley's lyrical words:

> One exists in a universe convincingly real, where the lines are sharply drawn in black and white. It is only later, if at all, that one realizes the lines were never there in the first place. But they are necessary in every human culture.[10]

Our civilization's construction of reality, our way of knowing, like that of every other civilization, is limited. It is an approximation, a crude sketch map to one section of the cosmos, and we must not mistake it for the cosmos itself. It is but a semblance of reality.

Every cartographer knows that any map she draws must exclude most features of the landscape and that the scale of those she chooses for representation must be systematically exaggerated. The result is useful for defined and limited purposes, even though it is a distortion not to be confused with the landscape itself. All explanatory systems necessarily distort. All concepts are proximate. "As far as the laws of mathematics refer to reality, they are not certain," Albert Einstein warned us, "and as far as they are certain, they do not refer to reality."[11]

If this is a hard lump to swallow, here's an even less palatable one: Our systems of understanding, which are the constructions that enable us to have knowledge, also set limits beyond which we cannot know. They are like the horizon on the ocean: an invisible barrier to a world unseen. Human perceptions, no matter how powerful, elegant, and self-consistent, are bounded and thus bound us. "The limits of my language mean the limits of my world," wrote the Austrian philosopher Ludwig Wittgenstein.[12]

The paradox that our way of knowing is the very thing that constrains our knowledge is considered a truism in the philosophical traditions of Hinduism and Buddhism. In the words of Sri Aurobindo: "Human knowledge throws a shadow that conceals half the globe of truth from its own sunlight." Indian folk religion says the same thing in a more earthy way. There are many tales of Hindu deities who descend from heaven to enjoy the delights of sex. Paradoxically, to gain this experience the Absolute must take on the limitations of gender—female or male.

It is exceedingly difficult for us in the modern West to accept the proposition that our way of knowing is a constraint. Why? In part, because paradoxes are anathema to our dualistic, either/or system of reasoning. In part, because of the absolutist pretensions of modern science, i.e., the conviction that our scientific method is of a different order from all other human systems of understanding. Science, we have been taught, is a clear window on an external reality that is unaffected by our observations.

Combine this belief with the linear view of time, and it becomes easy to see why we customarily understand history as a discrete entity fixed in the past, unaffected by either the differing perceptions of historical actors or later observers.

The Unconscious of Knowledge

> What counts in the things said by men is not so much what they
> may have thought or the extent to which these things represent
> their thoughts, as that which systematizes them from the outset.[13]

You will, I hope, have observed that what I am trying to do is probe below the surface of our culture's spoken and written words for "that which systematizes them from the outset." The phrase is Michel Foucault's. He also wrote of

> a *positive unconscious* of knowledge: a level that eludes the consciousness of the scientist and yet is part of the scientific discourse . . . rules of formation, which were never formulated in their own right, but are to be found only in widely differing theories, concepts, and objects of study.[14]

It is important that we bring to consciousness, as well as we can, these "rules of formation" that systematize our civilization's ways of knowing. Otherwise, it will be difficult for us understand how we have set ourselves apart from our ancestors and most of our non-Western contemporaries. Until we can do that, we can scarcely hope to learn from their wisdom. This, I believe, we must do in order to have a future. Let's look at some of the ways in which we have separated ourselves from other civilizations.

The first observation is that a linear sense of time sets the modern West apart from all earlier civilizations, except those Semitic traditions—Judaism, Christianity, and Islam—from which the concept is derived. Most of the great civilizations at one stage or another did toy with the idea of time as a one-directional flow, and some retained this concept as an alternative possibility, but nowhere did it become as dominant as it has in the modern West.

In a popular 1960s ballad, Joni Mitchell likened time to a merry-go-round. "We are captives on the carousel of time," she sang, "And go round and round and round in the circle game." Many cultures, including folk culture in the West itself until well into the twentieth century, understood time and history in this way: as cyclical, composed of rhythmically patterned recurrences, long and short, overlapping one another in the manner of the seasons, the phases of the moon, the tides, day and night. "Round and round and round in the circle game."

Time was not metrically even, nor was it always of equal value. Full and empty time, thick and thin, malevolent and beneficent was punctuated by festivals and natural calamities. For some peoples there were times when the dead and the living walked together. For others the dead and the unborn were always with the living because past, present, and future were concurrent (as we might say), or, to put it another way, there was only the continuous present. Time had many dimensions, but they were simultaneous, not sequential.

"Those who have a cyclic view of time are easily able to accept the convention of historic time, which is simply the trace of the turning wheel." By contrast, John Berger continues: "Those who have a unilinear view of time cannot come to terms with the idea of cyclic time: it creates a moral vertigo since all their morality is based on cause and effect."[15]

Another deficiency of an explanatory system that relies wholly upon sequence to understand causation is its inability to accommodate simultaneity. Unlike cultures which recognize a multidimensional present, we have no way of explaining the mutual influence of simultaneously occurring events. For us there must be a past cause for any present effect. This remains for our culture an established fact of nature despite more than half a century of experimental evidence from particle physics indicating that a theory of sequential causation is insufficient to explain the behavior of subatomic matter.

The challenge posed to our commonsense assumptions by anomalies now appearing in many areas of the natural sciences is something we shall explore at depth in later chapters. Suffice it to say here that quantum mechanics and chaos theory in the physical sciences, and the hypotheses of morphic fields and the holographic brain in the biological sciences, all suggest that we should take coincidences (causeless interactions) more seriously than we customarily do.

From time to time all of us experience extraordinary conjunctions of events, or words and events. We may mention an old friend we haven't seen in years, only to run into him later that week. Or we need a piece of information, and on the same day the newspaper has an article on the subject. We commonly shrug these things off as "mere chance," but the frequency with which we resort to jokes and laughter in the face of these perplexing occurrences betrays the discomfort we feel.

Our word *coincidence* acknowledges that we recognize something more than mere concurrence or conjuncture, but it carries none of the weight of its equivalent in some languages outside our civilization, such as Balinese, Javanese, and Malay, where the word for *coincidence* also means "truth." This is a fascinating area to which I'll return in chapter 6 when we look more closely at time.

People in cultures that pay close attention to coincidence know the intrinsic power of numbers for good and ill. So, it appears, have most humans for the past several millenia. It is ironic that we who dismiss numerology's "superstitions"—lucky seven, ill-fated thirteen, and the like—reserve our highest deference for numbers, the foundation of our "exact" sciences, which we regard as the distinguishing characteristic of our civilization. Most of us, for example, feel more comfortable in asserting a fact if there is an accompanying statistic to cite as proof. We do not, however, consider this reliance on verification by quantification as ritualistic in the manner of the ancient systems of numerology.

I began the last paragraph with an intentionally provocative statement: that people in those cultures "know" the intrinsic power of numbers for good and ill. The implication of such phrasing is that I share this view of reality; otherwise I would surely have said: These people "believe" that numbers have intrinsic power for good and ill. People can *know* only that which is real; or, to put it more exactly, we will attribute knowledge to them only if their perception of reality matches ours.

This emphasis demonstrates how our way of knowing inevitably places restrictions on our knowledge. Let's look more closely at the contrasting cultural understandings of number. We *know* that our mathematics are a powerful tool. We know also that other cultures have believed certain numbers and combinations of numbers had magical power. What we *cannot know* is how it is to know (experience) reality in that other way.

If this seems perplexing or absurd, reverse the proposition and discover how familiar it really is. We are quite accustomed to the assertion that ancient civilizations did not and could not share our scientific understanding of reality. For instance, peoples who relied on numerology, astrology, spirit worship, and distinctions between beneficent and malevolent time were prevented from developing a rational, scientific understanding of sequential cause and effect. They could not know how it is to know (experience) reality scientifically, the way we do.

To this you may justly respond: But we are not like them; we have a knowledge of history; they did not. Ah, but that's the point precisely: We are not like them. Even though our history allows us to peer in upon their exotic constructions, the fact of the matter is that we do understand reality historically—as a line of sequential cause and effect—and we cannot, by this means, know how it is to know (experience) reality in a nonhistorical way. Though we may have thoughts about these other ways of knowing, it is (to return to Foucault) our historical understanding "which systematizes them from the outset."

The Word

Many aspects of our historical consciousness were not shared by earlier humans, nor are they shared by millions of our twentieth-century contemporaries. Consequently, much of their experience is extremely difficult for us to penetrate. For instance, most ancient civilizations did not share our conviction, essential to the enterprise of history, that a human lifetime is of importance in the cosmic scale. Why record human scurryings and attribute weight to our words and actions, if our stay on Earth is but an infinitesimal moment among countless eons?

Significantly, the modern discipline of history was developed in the late eighteenth and early nineteenth centuries when educated European opinion reckoned the world to be no more than a few thousand years old, with human history starting at the creation. By contrast, our current scientific wisdom tells us that, although *Homo sapiens* arrived two hundred thousand years ago, this is late in the day compared with other forms of life whose fossils are dated as far back as three and a half billion years, appearing perhaps a billion years after the formation of the Earth and possibly eleven billion years after the Big Bang.

Pause for a moment to contemplate the vastness of these time dimensions, and consider whether there is not good sense in the Hindu view of a single human lifetime, or even several human generations, as fleeting and insubstantial. We are able to take history seriously only by scaling time down to human dimensions.

Being so exclusively human centered (more accurately, male human centered), the story of the past that we value is not the same as that which was of significance to our ancestors. Our history provides for modern Western civilization a view of reality alien to those who recognized other living creatures—and goddesses, gods, and spirits—as occupying places of prominence in their world. It is the consciousness of these ancestors that informed human experience down the long millenia, and our narrowly focused man-history is a barrier to our empathy with that experience.

My former Michigan colleague, Frances Reid, a Sioux, recounts how shocked she was in her first weeks in elementary school to discover that her white teacher was innocent of the fact that trees have lessons to teach us. Interspecies communication, at the heart of Native American life and of many other peoples, does not loom large in standard American or European school curricula or in our history books. For our culture it is not real.

The modern West is also idiosyncratic in its conviction that it is possible to study the world without changing it; that we can write history without making it. This is a supposition dismissed as an absurdity in other civilizations. Our ancestors knew, as do most of our non-Western contemporaries, that words, even unverbalized thoughts, are invested with power, and that the specialists in words—shamans, witches, medicine men, priests, lawyers, bards, and genealogists (guardians of myth: historians)—are awesome and dangerous. Robert Graves quotes an ancient Irish triad: "It is death to mock a poet, to love a poet, to be a poet."[16]

There must be sacred sanctions on the specialists in words, for there can be no pretense that their utterances leave the world unshaken.

In the beginning was the Word,
and the Word was with God,
and the Word was God.

John 1:1

In the beginning there was a word.

Tao Te Ching

"OM"

What is the lesson for historians? That we cannot, in the cloak of the detached and objective observer, take refuge from responsibility for the power we wield to create a past for our civilization: a code of symbols by which experience is shaped and interpreted.

Nor can we take refuge from responsibility for the power we wield to destroy other codes of meaning. This is no hypothetical proposition. History, the sibling of European imperialism, has laid waste to alternative modes of constructing reality.

Before the coming of *pakeha* (white people), Maori knew that their land was a gift of the angling skills of Maui, the trickster demigod. The story was told and retold with the greatest pleasure, generation after generation.

For the longest time Maui didn't raise a finger to help his older brothers with the fishing, but his wives, humiliated by his laziness, finally forced him to get some tackle. In doing so he exceeded even his customary outrageous behavior. He violated the *tapu* (sacred sanction) of an ancestral grave to take his own grandmother's jawbone for a hook.

The brothers wouldn't have this troublemaker in their canoe, but Maui stowed away, emerging once they were well out to sea. A terrible row ensued, with the brothers refusing Maui any bait. Never at a loss, the rascal punched his own nose. Wiping the blood on the ancestral jawbone, he immediately hooked the largest fish ever seen. It almost swamped the canoe, and Maui was able to haul it up only after intoning a powerful chant.

At last the giant fish was on the surface, and Maui left to make an offering in gratitude to the gods. Disregarding his instructions not to touch the fish, the brothers tried to cut it up. It thrashed wildly about as deep gouges were hacked in its flesh, and these have remained as the jagged, irregular shapes of the land into which the dying beast was transformed.

Te Ika a Maui and *Te Waka o Maui*, the fish and canoe of the Maori's primordial hero, passed into history as the North and South Islands of a land named New Zealand after the home country of Abel Janszoon Tasman, the seventeenth-century Dutch "discoverer" of these shores. The great fishing voyage of Maui and his brothers is reduced by history to a tale told for the amusement of children.

On the other side of the globe, the Cree of Canada provide another example of a society under assault from history in a different way. For thousands of years hunting was the core of Cree culture. It gave them a livelihood in their harsh, subarctic environment. Hunting governed their settlement patterns and their seasonal movements. It furnished the feasts that bonded their communities, and its rituals were the core of their spiritual life.

The land was divided into territories, each territory belonging to one hunter, who was intimately attuned to the animals of the place and to the hunting spirit. From them he learned when and where he and his group should hunt, which animals to take and which to conserve, what should be done to honor the prey, and what should be given in repayment. The Cree say it is the animals who possess the land and define the territory. When they moved, the hunter moved with them. Traditionally, the territory was not a fixed area of land. It was shaped and reshaped in the flowing bond between animal, human, and hunting spirit.

The deeper this communion, the more powers—*metew*—the hunter possesses. *Metew* comes from years of toil on the land, but it comes as well from the drum, through which the hunter converses with the hunting spirit. When it is time for him to give up hunting, he passes his drum and with it the territory to a younger hunter.

It is critical for the maintenance of Cree culture that a worthy successor be chosen. He must be a man who has worked with the old hunter and knows the territory well. Commonly, he is a son or other male relative, but the crucial factor in the choice is not human kinship but the rapport between the younger man and the animals and the hunting spirit. The successor must be someone who knows his proper place among the great forces of nature.

Over the past two generations it has become difficult for old hunters to find a suitable man to receive the drum. Increasingly, since the 1940s, Cree children have been taken from the bush to missionary and Canadian state schools to be taught the chronicle of the European settlers' triumph over "Indian" resistance in the struggle to open the North American wilderness for "development." In the history books native peoples are portrayed as backward, superstitious, even savage. There is an inevitability to their passing from the stage of history, and in the texts they are already people of the past tense.

Cultural inferiority is the lesson these children learn. Little wonder they become ashamed of their Cree heritage. They are encouraged to speak English rather than Cree, and few get home for more than a month or two each summer. Many grow to adulthood without ever spending a winter hunting season with their families in the bush. By the time they leave school, most prefer city life and store-bought food.

Among those who do return are some who come as government bureaucrats to maintain the new registers of hunters, replete with maps that fix permanent boundaries for the hunting territories and show the "unoccupied" lands available for white Canadian enterprise. These documents have no place for the animals and the hunting spirit. The hunter's discourse with the drum is being silenced by history.[17]

Likewise, in Australia the rocks and hills of the ancestors, the spirit and flesh of the Aboriginal people, are desecrated and forgotten as the Great Dreaming is dispelled by history. Addressing a planning conference for a history of Australia to celebrate the bicentenary of European settlement, Marcia Langton spoke for the Aboriginal people:

> Most of this country has been taken from our people in a little over 190 years of colonisation. . . . In tandem with the theft of our land, has been a cultural repression denying us an identity in Australian history.
>
> The Aboriginal technique of telling history is a particular cultural form, as valid as any other, including white historiography. Our tradition is an oral one, and the recital of our past takes place within a linguistic and cultural structure as yet largely misunderstood by white historians.
>
> In the same way that white people would not tamper with the structure and form of the *Iliad*, the *Odyssey*, Chaucer's tales, or Shakespeare, Aboriginal people do not want our oral history to be tampered with. Overzealous white historians and editors have altered the structure and form of Aboriginal stories, myths and oral records to make them more comprehensible to a white audience, but have thereby made them incomprehensible to Aboriginal audiences. . . . When the cues, the repetitions, the language, the distinctively Aboriginal evocations of our experience are removed from the recitals of our people, the truth is lost for us. The form and structure will not be passed on to others and they are denied

the right to look after their heritage and in turn pass it on. . . .

We are ultimately responsible to "our own mob," and not to the discipline of history nor the white concept of knowledge. . . . Aboriginal people know what can be passed on and to whom. This responsibility to family, kin and community is keenly felt. Our relations will edit and correct our versions of history and participate in the version of our histories which will be passed on to our children as our set of truths.[18]

At this juncture I hear protest from my guild sisters and brothers: History is just as capable of recording the brutalities and injustices suffered by the victims of imperialism as of recording the victories of the imperialists. A valid point. But history inflicts a more fundamental, structural damage that can be tempered, but not undone, by well-intentioned efforts to redress the balance of content. Recall Foucault: "What counts in the things said by men is . . . that which systematizes them from the outset."

The Europeans who came with diseases, guns, and other technological wizardry, bureaucratic regiments, and administrations to destroy the societies and polities of the non-Western world came also with history, that peculiar and powerful mode of systematizing experience that characterized other symbolic codes as fairy tales.

The combined effect of subjugation (for which historians provided the justifications) and the disintegration of culture was a devastating "loss of inner continuity." The words of psychologist Stanley Keleman, speaking of old people whose perceptions of life after death are dismissed as fantasies, apply equally well to the experience of people in colonial cultures in collapse:

> They describe a place, a feeling, a particular kind of reality. And you call it a fantasy! What you're really saying is that their description doesn't fit your perception of what the world is like. What you've done is put that person outside of your frame of reference, and say that their world doesn't exist. You turn their perception into an hallucination. That's a terrifying position to any person . . . since it teaches them to reject their own perceptions. . . . The result is a loss of inner continuity that is fearful.[19]

To injury we have often added insult with our self-congratulation: that by providing history for nonhistorical peoples, we have rescued for them their "forgotten" past!

A More Humble View of History

We must adopt a more responsible and humble view of history, as of science. History is not "the past," the landscape of human experience. It is interpretations of fragments of that experience, maps drawn to differing projections and inevitably incorporating varying distortions, which serve as a guide in *present* belief and behavior. As such, history is inescapably political.

By failing to insist upon the historian's detachment from "present politics," am I leaving no room for scientific history, the disciplined, self-critical task of documentary verification and exegesis? On the contrary, I agree with my old teacher Keith Hancock that "history, as an activity of the mind, stands or falls with the fidelity of historians to their own well-tested rules of good conduct."[20]

History is one form of discourse on experience—one among many—and, within their domain, historians are no less constrained by conventional procedures of selection and arrangement and the culturally sanctioned canons of proof than those who "speak the past" in other cultures. Within their discrete domains of discourse, the puppeteer of *wayang kulit* (Javanese shadow play) and the poet debater in *kabigan* (Bengali musical verse tournament) work to rule in interpreting evidence. No bard dispenses with responsibility merely by denying detachment.

But is there any point in doing history if it is merely a partial and distorted projection of human experience, and moreover a destroyer of other codes of meaning?

This second issue, history as destroyer, is a great problem and concern for me. While I have no logically satisfactory answer, I will hazard a couple of imperfect ones. In the first place, history is the chief mode of discourse in our civilization and as such is the very stuff of politics. As feminists have rightly emphasized, struggle in Western societies involves writing and asserting the histories that have been denied. History *is* present politics. Marcia Langton again:

> Aboriginal contributions to Australian history have fundamental cultural and political purposes. We are reclaiming our right to identify and define ourselves. Central to this aim is the prevention of cultural theft.[21]

Ah, there's the rub! How do we from the West find a way to explore other cultural traditions without engaging in pillage or destruction? "We cannot use the spiritual heritage of other peoples as though we are importing raw materials," cautions the Iranian historian of religions Seyyed Hossein Nasr. "There has to be give as well as take."[22]

The French anthropologist Claude Lévi-Strauss observed that culture contact creates an unavoidable paradox:

> The less human societies were able to communicate with each other and therefore to corrupt each other through contact, the less their respective emissaries were able to perceive the wealth and significance of their diversity.[23]

There must be two-way communication for mutual benefit, with the "emissaries" of various cultures meeting as equals with mutual respect. And the meeting must be of hearts as well as minds. This book is devoted to the search for such open-hearted meetings.

To return to the first point: History provides only a partial view of human experience. This gives me no trouble. Partial and blurred perceptions are all we humans have to work with, given the limitations of our organism. The fact that history resembles all other human observations of our universe—fleeting glimpses of fragments of reality—is no reason to discard it. "Our life is a faint tracing on the surface of mystery," writes Annie Dillard.[24] To accept this is wisdom, not despair.

> [François Mianscum of the Mistassani Cree] had left his bush camp only a few days before he appeared in court. "When I was told to touch the book, my first reaction was to wonder what this book is for," he said. "Until I was told to touch it, the book, so that I could speak the 'truth.'"

In the courtroom the round-faced, cheerful François, deeply serious as he was asked if he would tell the truth, the whole truth and nothing but the truth, placed his hand on the Bible. Before answering he began to talk to the translator. After some conversation the translator looked up at the judge and said: "He does not know whether he can tell the truth. He can tell only what he knows."[25]

2
THE FRAIL HERO AND THE SMALL DEMON

Straight Lines and the Demon

Once upon a time my friend Pete Becker, University of Michigan linguist, was a student of *wayang kulit,* Indonesian shadow puppet theater. He was told that *wayang* controls power gone amuck: madness, demons, disease, and stupidity. "By nature all these are sources of chain-reacting, linear power, which accelerates by repeating more and more of the same."

His perplexity about how *wayang* could exercise such control evoked the explanation from a Balinese friend that it was like the doors on his island, designed "so the demons can't get in." A few feet inside any entrance in Bali is a flat wall or screen, placed so one cannot go straight in but must pass right or left.

> Demons and people possessed or amuck move in straight lines, not
> in curves like normal human beings. [In *wayang*] the music and
> shadow play move round and round and keep the demons out.

Then Pete's friend "paused and laughed heartily, and added, 'As you might say, demons think in straight lines.'"[1]

When I first read this account, I was on a fellowship year at M.I.T., at work on a critique of the idea of progress in science and technology.

This struck me as an apt metaphor for the demon that possesses us in the modern West: "chain-reacting, linear power, which accelerates by repeating more and more of the same." "Demons think in straight lines," the man from Bali had said. This inspired the following notes in my journal, February 28, 1982:

> I look up from Pete's paper and through the window I see a panorama of concrete, brick, metal and glass, all divided neatly into lined segments. I see a crane, taller than any of these buildings, constructed as a maze of lines, with its most important functional part, the cable, a straight line reaching to the ground. In front of the building, below the crane, there is a row of trees. At least I am accustomed to think of it as a row, though from where I sit I am not at the correct angle to see the trees lined parallel to the wall. Power and telephone lines are strung along the road, which itself carries the dotted dividing line I used recently as a metaphor for time—linear time.
>
> The parking lot is painted with lines, and the cars, in obedience, wait in reasonably neat rows. It looks orderly, and I am reminded that we are accustomed to equate social order with linearity. We speak disparagingly of people getting "out of line." The presence or absence of rows tells us, with one glance at a crowd photo, whether people are orderly or simply milling about. The mob is distinguished from the officers of the law as much by the presence or absence of lines, as by that of uniforms.
>
> The school days of our children, whom we seat in rows, are occupied with instruction in the arrangement in lines of symbols, as well as material objects. We sometimes rate their intelligence, or judge their sanity, by testing their conformity to the cultural norms of linear perception. This data is said to show that the "spatial perception" of males is superior to that of females, which explains (we are told) why the latter are less well adapted to the demands of our techno-scientific culture.
>
> A map of the Pacific on the wall beside me provides a study in linear representation. I see the "imaginary" lines marking the equator, the tropics, and the coordinates of latitude and longitude. There are the "real" lines dividing land and sea, and the dotted indicators of the margins of continental shelves and oceanic troughs. There are twisting lines of arrows for currents, and bold straight lines for airline routes. The map, as also the pictures on my office

walls, are neatly bounded by rectangles and hung in line with the horizontals and perpendiculars of ceiling and walls.

I have on my desk a copy of James Watson: *The Double Helix: A Personal Account of the Discovery of DNA,* which is full of linear diagrams of molecular sequence, not so different from the segments of that crane silhouetted against the Cambridge skyline. "In physics the basic order has for centuries been that of the Cartesian rectilinear grid." The writer is the theoretical physicist David Bohm who continues:

> In the development of new ways of using language, the Cartesian coordinates—three perpendicular sets of uniformly spaced lines—played a key part. . . . To use coordinates is in effect to order our attention in a way that is appropriate to the mechanical view of the universe, and thus similarly to order our perception and our thinking.[2]

> This morning's edition of the *Boston Globe* carried a headline: "Scientists tracing new evolutionary path." Below were lines on a time grid to illustrate the development of apes and humans. I am reminded that we have developed scientific instrumentation, e.g. seismographs, electrocardiographs and radar screens, to give similar linear, visual representations of natural processes.

When I wrote this in 1982, I was firmly convinced that we had boxed ourselves in with our scientific perception of a segmented material reality. "Lines mark boundaries," I noted, "and the bounded objects are linked by lines into a functional system. Embedded as the line also is in our sense of time and causation, it is hard for us to think of process without directionality. Purpose for our civilization means advance, becoming—not simply being. "Demons and people possessed or amuck move in straight lines, not in curves like normal human beings."

The Battle in the Forest

In June 1989, a sabbatical to India gave me the chance to return to my writing, and now there was a new science book on my desk. It was full of stunningly beautiful, flowing images that seemed to bear no relationship to the earlier rigid diagrams. The book is called *Chaos,* and it reveals that something startling is happening in science. The author, James Gleick, writes in his prologue:

> Where chaos begins, classical science stops. For as long as the world has had physicists inquiring into the laws of nature, it has suffered a special ignorance about disorder in the atmosphere, in the turbulent sea, in the fluctuations of wildlife populations, in the oscillations of the heart and brain. The irregular side of nature, the discontinuous and erratic side—these have been puzzles to science, or worse, monstrosities.[3]

Synchronistically, my own interior and exterior landscapes had changed equally dramatically in the seven years that had intervened between Cambridge and my retreat in India. Now as I wrote, I looked out across a deep Himalayan valley, studded with Hindu temples and Tibetan Buddhist *gompas*. Straight lines were few and far between: the roof ridges of some of the more recently constructed houses, the power lines, and the water pipe running to our house across the hillside from a spring. Significantly enough, the pipe was blocked, and electricity flowed only intermittently. The demons here were kept at bay!

And what of the linear demons back at M.I.T.? Contemporary science is in upheaval. The battle is joined, but as yet there is no resolution.

> In every Javanese *wayang* the frail hero, Arjuna, meets a small demon, Cakil, in the forest. Because they are who they are, they fight and Cakil dies—but not forever: he will be killed over and over again in each *wayang.* Arjuna and Cakil live in different conceptual worlds. When they meet, "two worlds, two epistemologies coincide for a moment. . . . Each epistemology—each category of being—exists within a different concept of time, and all the times are occurring simultaneously."[4]

This is the situation in contemporary science, and, as in the *perang* (the battle scene) in *wayang kulit,* it is a moment of riotous clamor and exciting confusion—"thick time." In the late twentieth century, we are undergoing a scientific revolution as profound as that which occurred three hundred years ago to usher in modern Western civilization. "When paradigms change, the world itself changes with them," Thomas Kuhn tells us.[5] He also warns that paradigm shifts do not come easily.

They are tenaciously resisted by the scientific establishment, which defends a way of seeing the world and of practicing science in it.

We need to understand what is being defended, for it is our way of seeing the world, *our* reality, that may die in the *perang*. And that could be damned uncomfortable if we don't know what's going on.

The Saga of Classical Science

"Where chaos begins," James Gleick writes, "classical science stops." What is classical science?

To state it most broadly, it is the foundation of our modern confidence that we can dominate nature and shape the environment to our advantage. This in turn rests on the conviction that we can obtain an increasingly accurate understanding of the laws by which the universe operates. Because of the consistency of the workings of the giant cosmic machine, its basic functional principles can be ascertained by systematic observation and experiment, which arm humans with predictive power.

The universe, in classical terms, is understood to be composed of particles of matter, and humans are set apart from material nature by their unique capacity for self-reflective consciousness. Mind and matter are distinct. Not consciousness but the laws of physics direct the material world. Thus, humans can observe and measure without altering the state of nature.

> I do not think it matters much to the fortunes of man what abstract notions one may entertain concerning nature and the principles of things. . . . For my part I do not trouble myself with such speculative and unprofitable matters. My purpose, on the contrary, is to try whether I cannot in very fact lay more firmly the foundations, and extend more widely the limits, of the power and greatness of man.[6]

The writer is Francis Bacon, and it is to Bacon and his contemporaries of the seventeenth century that we customarily give credit for the origins of classical science. From his statement it is evident his interest was to extend human power, a concern that remains central to modern science. Bacon's objective was "the relief of man's estate," the improvement of human welfare. Guided by science, history was to become "a journey of accumulation to increase and multiply the revenues and possessions of man."[7] This was to be achieved by increased power over nature: "For whensoever man shall be able to call the creatures by their true names, he shall again command them."[8]

There are assumptions here that have remained important to classical science. First, there is the dualism of the separation between "man" and "the creatures." Humans are seen as standing apart from nature and are thus able to identify, categorize, and name the objects, animate and inanimate, that are nature's elements. Objects set apart from ourselves are capable of being manipulated—or destroyed—for presumed human advantage.

Second, Bacon's phrase "to call the creatures by their *true* names" assumes a set, natural order in the universe, existing "out there," to be discovered and properly categorized.

To Bacon's younger contemporary, the French philosopher René Descartes, this suggested, as a central task, the establishment of foundations of scientific certainty. As the proof of existence, he proffered his now famous logical proposition: "I think, therefore I am." In so doing, he elevated human reason to a position of supremacy. All is obtainable by reason and analysis, he declared. "There can be nothing so remote that we cannot reach to it, nor so recondite that we cannot discover it." As a corollary, Descartes reinforced the other great dualism of modern Western thought: the separation of mind from matter.

He also encouraged the segmentation of thought that our culture subsequently has come to value so highly. His search was for "a method for finding out the truth," and he was convinced he had discovered it in the form of rigorous categorization. He explained: "The distinct is that which is so precise and different from all other objects that it contains within itself nothing but what is clear." Reality should be carved up into discrete conceptual categories, delimited sharply from one another.

For science to be certain, nature was also required to be uniform and its laws invariable. Rejecting out of hand the possibility of God's intervention in the natural world, Descartes postulated a mechanistic, physical model of reality. He argued for reductionism in science: a concentration on the search for basic elements, the fundamental constituents of the universe. "If anyone could know perfectly what are the small parts composing all bodies, he would know perfectly the whole of nature."9

Descartes was convinced that the perfect analytical method could be developed, and it was in numbers that he saw the possibility for exact science. Brilliant mathematician that he was, he set in place another characteristic of scientific Western civilization: validation by quantification. Given the force of his contributions, it is not unreasonable that classical science is often called the Cartesian system.

In early seventeenth-century Europe, there was a spurt in mathematical innovation, and scientific attention was increasingly directed to problems amenable to calculation. The concept of reality as measurable was encouraged by the growing appeal of mechanistic explanations of nature: the universe as clockwork. By this time many European towns had public clocks, and given the familiarity of these and an increasing array of other mechanical objects, it is not surprising that people found an analogy between the machine and nature attractive.

Philosophers reinforced the tendency by espousing an atomic theory, which reduced the entire fabric of the universe to minute particles of senseless matter. This was a radical departure from the understanding, which had held sway since ancient times, that everything in the cosmos is imbued with purpose and forms an intelligent universe, filled with matter, visible and invisible, and guided by spirit in a grand harmony of motion. Nonsense, said the atomic philosophers. Particles are "dead" and "stupid," movable but not themselves capable of motion. Most of the universe is empty, and lumps of matter hurtle through this wasteland of space, pulled by the magnetism of other lumps.

Late in the seventeenth century, the English mathematician Isaac Newton combined these theories with the latest observations in astronomy to produce a general theory of gravitation. His new schema offered an explanation encompassing all motion, terrestial and celestial; science had tied the universe together again. For most of us in the twentieth-century West, the Newtonian system is still the underpinning of our perception of reality.

The idea of empty space had confirmed the fragmentary view of nature, according to which the universe is not continuous substance, a single living organism as Aristotle (along with the ancient Chinese and Hindu philosophers) had thought, but a collection of separate parts held together as a machine by mutual gravitational pulls.

The framework of classical science was in place. To this the eighteenth-century rationalists added the plank work of the positivist human sciences, convinced that a perfect predictive system could be developed that would encompass even the workings of the human mind.

The nineteenth-century evolutionists, Charles Darwin in the vanguard, completed the edifice with their overarching materialist theory of the development of nature that gave a competitive, probabilistic explanation of the diversity of life forms. If the inorganic world was a collection of separate parts held together by gravitational pulls, the organic world was revealed to be a collection of separate species locked in a fierce struggle for a share of scarce resources. Aggression was the law of nature, and the one test of fitness was survival.

Such is the tale of classical science—a tale oft told, for like all classic tales it serves as an origin myth, justifying and directing contemporary practice. It is a saga, with its legendary male heroes whose exploits hold lessons for those of the present day who aspire to emulation. Respecting the power of this myth for our civilization, I have been careful in my recounting to retain its traditional form, as much to emphasize its didactic purpose as for the information it contains.

I should add that none of the ideas that compose classical scientific thinking went unchallenged, however. Some of the criticisms seem devastating, none more so than those of the late–eighteenth-century German philosopher, Immanuel Kant, who demonstrated logically that objective knowledge is not possible. But science, like any good religion, was not to be undone by mere demonstrations that some of its central tenets were fallacious.

Scientific Articles of Faith

By the beginning of this century, there was a solid corpus of received belief undergirding classical science. These scientific articles of faith, as I call them, are worth summarizing because they still direct the practice of most scientists of the present day.

1. Matter is real. All else is a product or reflection of material interactions.
2. There is an external material reality independent of our consciousness.

3. Observed separations between objects or individual organisms have reality independent of the human observer, i.e., nature's categories are not human fictions.

4. The observer and what is observed are separate. Thus, scientific observation does not significantly affect the behavior of natural phenomena.

5. The universe has rationally systematic, unchanging laws accessible to human intelligence. Therefore, humans ultimately should be able to know it all.

6. Each scientific discovery reduces the unknown.

7. Knowledge not susceptible to rational, quantifiable proof is suspect. To carry this belief to its logical extreme: Only that which can be counted is real.

8. The human species, being uniquely possessed of self-reflective consciousness, is separate from and superior to other life forms.

9. We can significantly alter the relationship of other life forms to our species, not through interaction with their consciousness but through the reorganization of matter.

10. The world can be improved by the human reorganization of matter.

11. Human advantage can be achieved at the expense of other life forms.

12. There is no sacred area off limits to science, except perhaps experimentation on nonconsenting, living humans.

13. The parts explain and control the whole (organism, planet, universe) and not vice versa.

14. The best explanation of a phenomenon is the simplest.

15. Given an approximate knowledge of a system's initial conditions and an understanding of the relevant natural principles, the approximate behavior of the system can be calculated.

16. No communication or physical effect can take place faster than the speed of light.

17. Time is unidimensional, unidirectional, and metrically even, except at the quantum and astrophysical extremes.

The only item on the list that would not have been found a hundred years ago is the final phrase: *"except at the quantum and astrophysical extremes."* In that seemingly innocuous qualification is the whispered intimation that classical science in our century may be coming apart at the seams.

Twenty Questions

The eminent American nuclear physicist John Wheeler, one of the team that worked at Los Alamos to build the first atomic bombs, likes to shock audiences with a parable of the new physics.

He recounts how he once gave a novel twist to Twenty Questions. (As you may know, this is a parlor game in which one player chooses a word, and others have to guess it in no more than twenty questions, to each of which the word-chooser responds only "yes" or "no.") On this occasion, when it was Wheeler's turn, he decided not to pick a word but to let it emerge from the questions. Unaware of this, of course, the other players proceeded with their guessing as though a word had already been chosen. Wheeler, for his part, was completely free to answer "yes" or "no" to the first question put to him, but thereafter gave responses consistent with each of his prior answers. He, and unwittingly his co-participants, became more and more tightly constrained by the pattern formed by questions and answers. Ultimately, before the twenty questions were exhausted, the group had guessed the "correct word"—or, if you like, someone had proffered a word that fit the pattern created.

Such is the way of the world, Wheeler tells his audiences. The "word" is not picked in advance, as classical science would have us believe. This is not a "fixed law" universe. Rather, the "word" is created over and over again from the exchanges of innumerable signals between innumerable participants. Mutual self-consistency is the only requirement for the game's maintenance.

But is this really new? Wasn't Charles Darwin saying virtually the same thing a century and a half ago, to the scandal of those who believed in a universe created complete in one fell swoop?

The difference is that the Victorian evolutionists agreed with the physical scientists of their day in separating mind from matter. Material circumstance, not consciousness, gave direction to natural selection. But for John Wheeler and those contemporaries who share his view of the implications of quantum mechanics, the distinction between mind and matter is no longer clear-cut.

> May the universe in some strange sense be "brought into being" by the participation of those who participate? . . . The vital act is the act of participation. "Participator" is the incontrovertible new concept given by quantum mechanics. It strikes down the term observer of classical theory, the man who stands safely behind the thick glass wall and watches what goes on without taking part. It can't be done, quantum mechanics says.[10]

What is quantum mechanics? Simply expressed, it is the theory developed to explain results produced by attempts at subatomic measurement.

The realization at the end of the nineteenth century that the atom could be split resulted, in the classic Cartesian manner, in a search for subatomic particles, which, being indivisible, would prove to be the fundamental building blocks of the universe. This search, which continues, has produced results so startlingly inconsistent with classical physics that they are difficult to express in common language, shaped as it is by Newtonian concepts. "Those who are not shocked when they first come across quantum theory cannot possibly have understood it," said one of its creators, the Danish physicist Niels Bohr.[11]

Consider these paradoxes:

The basic operation in classical mechanics is the accurate measurement of the position and speed of movement of objects, in order to predict their future state. For subatomic particles, however, no way has been found to combine these measurements. The process of determining the particle's position somehow obscures its velocity; similarly, when its velocity is measured, the position is blurred. It's as though the particle were saying: "Choose! You can have one or the other, but not both." By classical standards this should eliminate the possibility of prediction, and indeed, that proves to be the case for individual particles.

Quantum mechanics is an acknowledgement that fully accurate prediction is not possible at the subatomic level. It substitutes mathematical formulae, applicable only to aggregates of particles (whole systems), which provide no more than estimates of the *probability* of various potential outcomes. The accuracy of these estimates, which is remarkably high, can be understood by an analogy to the flip of a coin. A single flip randomly produces heads or tails, but a succession of flips always gives an approximately 50–50 split.

With the introduction to science of what the German physicist Werner Heisenberg named the "uncertainty principle," the hope of achieving a fully deterministic model of the universe had to be discarded, however reluctantly. Albert Einstein, although a major contributor to quantum mathematics, signaled his refusal to accept the implication that the universe runs on chance with his famous retort that God "does not play dice."[12]

God may not, but something seems to be toying with us at the subatomic level. According to the laws of classical physics, waves (carriers of energy) and particles (material objects) have properties that are mutually inconsistent and exclusive. This is not true at the quantum level. Depending on the way in which an experiment is devised, subatomic "matter" behaves more like a wave or more like a particle.

The astounding fact is that particles seem not only to vary their "responses" according to how scientists frame their "questions," but also to assume a definite form *only* in response to those questions. To put it another way, the scientist's action in measuring the particle plays a role in its manifestation. Hence John Wheeler's conjecture: "May the universe in some strange sense be 'brought into being' by the participation of those who participate?"

Strange indeed. In classical mechanics any object moving from *a* to *b*, or altering its state from *x* to *y*, can be traced through intermediate positions or states. Not so a subatomic particle. It is at *a*, then instantaneously at *b*. Similarly, it is *x*, then instantaneously it is *y*. This "quantum leap," as it is called, prevents any causal connection being established. It is not possible to say that *a* moved to *b*, or *x* became *y*. In classical terms, such statements require observation of intermediate positions or states, which imply the passage of time. But the quantum leap, being instantaneous, does not require time, thereby rendering meaningless distinctions between past, present, and future.

Nor does it permit the statement that a particle has continuous or ongoing existence. Because of the absence of observable intermediate states, it is fully consistent with the evidence to say that particles a and x disappear, and particles b and y are created. But what then becomes of our notion of a substantial, enduring material reality? These subatomic particles are supposed to be the basic building blocks of the universe, and yet they are playing fast and loose with their own (and our) sustained existence as matter. Does this mean the Gautama Buddha was right, three millenia ago, when he taught that we go into being and out of being every instant, constantly recreated?

Quantum mechanics also undermines our commonsense understanding of cause and effect, and in so doing pulls down another pillar of classical physics. This is the principle, known to physicists as "locality," that two separated objects can affect one another only by the transmission of signals (energy or matter), with time required for the transmission to cross the intervening distance. On this rests our understanding that causation is sequential: from past to present, and present to future. What then do we make of the fact that a subatomic particle will change its motion instantaneously in response to a corresponding change in a particle with which it was earlier associated, no matter how far apart the two now are? Let it be emphasized: The particles are at a distance from one another when the motion of one is altered, yet the effect on the other is simultaneous.

John Bell, who gave his name to the theorem describing this interconnectedness, said:

> Non-locality means that we cannot discuss the different parts of space independently. Yet we cannot get hold of whatever connection there is between the two different regions of space. The latest theory that I am playing with in interpreting this non-locality involves the idea that time runs independently at different points in space. I can't explain it to myself, so I can't explain it to you.[13]

Don't blink yet. What about antimatter and antiparticles? Yes, this is subatomic physics, not science fiction. Faced with evidence of the creation of energy from nothing, quantum physicists have factored into their equations "virtual" particles, or antiparticles. "Unlike real particles, they cannot be observed directly with a particle detector," we are told by Stephen W. Hawking, Lucasian Professor of Mathematics at Cambridge University. But "we now know that every particle has an anti-particle, with which it can annihilate. . . . There could be whole anti-worlds and anti-people made out of anti-particles. However, if you meet your anti-self, don't shake hands! You would both vanish in a great flash of light."[14]

What's It All about, Alfie?

> *Modern physics has uncovered a view of the world that is utterly fantastic and non-intuitive and incredible.*
>
> Alan Lightman, M.I.T. astrophysicist

Answers within the Classical Framework

Given these seemingly revolutionary discoveries, what do practicing physicists make of the implications for our general understanding of reality?

A large number, perhaps a majority, say this is not their concern. They are physicists, not metaphysicians. A typical response is the one given at the University of Michigan a few years ago by Gordon Kane, a professor of physics, when asked whether his discipline should concern itself with the existence of a "real world" outside physics. "Not at all," he replied. "Physicists haven't addressed that question in twenty years."[15] Francis Bacon must have applauded from his grave: "I do not think it matters much to the fortunes of man what abstract notions one may entertain concerning nature and the principles of things."

Bacon, we may recall, had a more practical concern—"to extend the power and greatness of man"—and a similar justification is usually given by today's scientists. Stephen Hawking explains:

> Because the partial theories that we already have are sufficient to make accurate predictions in all but the most extreme situations, the search for the ultimate theory of the universe seems difficult to justify on practical grounds.[16]

However anomalous quantum mechanics may be in classical terms, it works. Hawking continues:

> Indeed, it has been an outstandingly successful theory and under-
> lies nearly all of modern science and technology. It governs the be-
> havior of transistors and integrated circuits, which are the essential
> components of electronic devices such as televisions and comput-
> ers, and is also the basis of modern chemistry and biology.[17]

Hawking, I must hasten to add, is not one who avoids speculation on the broader meaning of the new physics. He acknowledges the incon-sistencies between quantum mechanics and existing theories of gravita-tion, but like many of his colleagues he is confident that a unified theory will soon be found to incorporate both. "There are grounds for cautious optimism that we may now be near the end of the search for the ultimate laws of nature."[18]

The Classical Framework Discarded

Descartes, you will remember, argued that for science to be certain, these laws of nature must be uniform; they must apply to all parts of the universe. The hope of a unified theory rests on the same logical premise, but there is another school of contemporary scientific thought willing to discard this plank of the classical system.

Its proponents maintain that the universe is a hierarchy, with differ-ent physical laws in operation at each of its separate levels. As the scale changes, so do the rules of the game. Hence, there is one physics for the infinitely small (quantum mechanics), one for the macro-world of everyday existence (classical mechanics), and one for the astronomically large (the general theory of relativity). The central task of natural sci-ence is then redefined as the search for the mechanisms that connect these various levels.

A much more radical step away from classical physics is taken by those who suggest that rather than multiple levels within a single uni-verse, there are actually multiple universes.

This hypothesis is offered as a solution to the conundrum posed by the probabilistic nature of explanation in quantum mechanics. For any quantum event, there is a large number of possible outcomes, and prob-ability theory says that all must have occurred at some time and all will occur again. But some of the logical possibilities are never observed. Where then are they occurring? Perhaps in parallel universes that our measurements do not penetrate.

Those who saw Tom Stoppard's play *Rosencrantz and Guildenstern Are Dead* will have an advantage in grasping this intriguing concept. They will recall that the protagonists in the comedy are continually flipping a coin in the hope it will turn up tails, but always it is heads. Of course, there is no logical reason why such an unbroken run should not happen to any player of the game, given that each flip has a 50–50 chance of producing heads, but Rosencrantz and Guildenstern are painfully aware that in our universe this does not occur. They are understandably reluctant to face the logical conclusion: that they are in another universe—in their case, beyond the grave.

Multiple levels within a single universe, or multiple universes? Neither, answers another group of scientists. In an equally radical departure from the classical structure, this school of thought joins John Wheeler and his "Twenty Questions" in asserting that this is a universe made up as it goes along.

The logic of this position rests both on quantum mechanics and evolutionary cosmology. In the first instance, its proponents point to the ephemeral quality of subatomic particles: At its basis the universe is being created anew every instant. To this observation, they add the argument that if indeed this is an evolving cosmos, why should its governing principles not evolve along with everything else?

Ah, but surely there's a catch: If the universe is made up as it goes along, how can we explain our scientists' success in replicating experiments and predicting so accurately the occurrence of natural phenomena?

An answer can be framed in these terms: Though this is not, as classical science taught, a "fixed law" universe, there is a powerful tendency toward repetition because the process is one of innumerable exchanges of innumerable signals. In general, the transmissions that have proved to be possible in the immediate past are the ones most likely to occur in the immediate future. They have cut grooves, so to say. Prediction is thus seen to be a statement of the statistical probability of recurring connections. It is not a statement that a particular event must happen or will continue to happen.

"If the evolving regularities of nature are not governed by transcendent laws, then could they not be more like habits?" speculates the English biologist Rupert Sheldrake. "If nature is habitual, then well-established phenomena will indeed appear to behave as if they are governed by transcendent, changeless laws."

With new phenomena, however, the case is different.

> An essential feature of the evolutionary process is that new organized systems come into being . . . for example the appearance of a new kind of molecule, or crystal, or plant, or instinct, or piece of music. In so far as these things are truly new, they cannot be explained in terms of a simple repetition of what has gone before.... If memory is inherent in the nature of things, the phenomena will not arise in exactly the same way on the first or thousandth or trillionth occasion. . . . This possibility means that we can no longer take for granted the conventional assumption that all scientific experiments should in principle be exactly repeatable.[19]

The Cheshire Cat's Grin

A few paragraphs back in explaining the tendency toward repetition in nature, I used the terms *recurring connections* and *transmission of signals*. This terminology reflects the shift of focus in twentieth-century physics (first in Einstein's theories of relativity and then in quantum mechanics) from separate objects to the exchanges of information between objects that knit them together into whole systems—"the pattern which connects," to use Gregory Bateson's phrase.[20]

Werner Heisenberg used similar words to describe the conceptual revolution he and his fellow quantum theorists have wrought:

> One sees that one has now divided the world not into different groups of objects but into different groups of connections.... The world thus appears as a complicated tissue of events, in which connections of different kinds alternate or overlap or combine and thereby determine the texture of the whole.[21]

Faced with the realization that the form in which subatomic particles manifest is a response to the scientists' experimentation, Heisenberg also wrote:

> Natural science does not simply describe and explain nature; it is a part of the interplay between nature and ourselves; it describes nature as exposed to our method of questioning. This was a possibility of which Descartes could not have thought, but it makes the sharp separation between the world and the I impossible.[22]

Which, in turn, eliminates objectivity in its classical sense.

This suggests another answer to the question: If the world is made up as it goes along, how can we explain successful scientific prediction? Our predictions are themselves signals, part of that web of communications of which existence is composed, and as such they play a role in shaping the future. If reality is not independent of us, then the future is not independent of our expectations. The conscious intent of the experimenter affects the behavior of the physical matter under observation.

> *"Is it the flag that moves,*
> *or is it the wind that moves?"*
> *"No," answers the Zen master,*
> *"it is the mind that moves."*

Mind and matter are not distinct. Yet another classical mainstay is ripped out: the belief that there is an external material reality independent of our consciousness.

Let's face it: René Descartes was wrong. Perfect knowledge of the whole of nature is not to be obtained from knowing perfectly what are "the small parts composing all bodies."

> Rather, what should be said [wrote David Bohm] is that wholeness is what is real, and that fragmentation is the response of this whole to man's action, guided by illusory perception, which is shaped by fragmentary thought. In other words, it is just because reality is whole that man, with his fragmentary approach, will inevitably be answered with a correspondingly fragmentary response.[23]

After four centuries of the reductionist pursuit, "what stands revealed," in Annie Dillard's words, "is the Cheshire cat's grin."[24] At what was thought to be the bottom of the heap, down in the subatomic, "particles" are revealed to be systems of communications, interactions, and patterns of movement rather than solid objects.

> One has to view the world in terms of universal flux of events and processes [says Bohm]. The new form of insight can perhaps best be called *Undivided Wholeness in Flowing Movement*. This view implies that flow is, in some sense, prior to that of the "things" that can be seen to form and dissolve in this flow.[25]

To Give Birth to a Dancing Star

> *I tell you, you must have chaos in you*
> *to give birth to a dancing star.*
>
> Nietzsche

The enticement to you to join me on this ramble through the thickets of the new physics was a quote from James Gleick: "Where chaos begins, classical science stops." I owe you an explanation.

Chaos is an emerging, interdisciplinary field bridging the natural and social sciences. It employs the new computer-aided mathematics of fractal geometry to study systems so complex that they previously defied scientific analysis. Examples are earthquakes, landforms, weather, disease epidemics, fluid turbulence, wild animal and plant populations, crystals, and snowflakes.

Its proponents claim for chaos theory a place beside the theories of relativity and quantum mechanics as the third scientific revolution of the century. What are the grounds for this grand claim? Here are just three of the many that are advanced.

First, chaos destroys the classical assumption that from an approximate knowledge of a system's initial conditions, combined with an understanding of the relevant natural principles, the system's approximate behavior can be calculated. That assumption is undermined by the simple but previously disregarded fact that in complex systems tiny differences in input can quickly become overwhelming differences in output.

This has been dubbed the "butterfly effect." A butterfly stirring the air with its wings in Peking today could (we might fancifully suppose) affect storm patterns over New York next month.

"Sensitive dependence on initial conditions" is the formal name given the phenomenon. It deals another blow to reductionism by revealing how inadequate is the isolated study of a piece of a system for understanding the whole. Fortunately, by providing new models and mathematical techniques, chaos is encouraging more scientists to look at global systems, thus drawing them out of the narrow confines of their disciplinary specialties.

It is also making some of them more modest in their claims for predictive applications of scientific knowledge. Gregory Bateson alerted us in *Mind and Nature* to what is now accepted wisdom among chaos theorists:

> [There are] large classes of phenomena where prediction and control are simply impossible. . . . Under tension, a chain will break at its weakest link. That much is predictable. What is difficult is to identify the weakest link before it breaks. *The generic we can know, but the specific eludes us.*[26]

Second, chaos forces a redefinition of "chance" and "randomness." It reveals that underlying apparent chaos is a deep, ordered structure from which, in an instant, a highly organized system can emerge. This has profound implications in many areas of science, among them Darwinian evolutionary theory, where an assumption is made that the existence of random data indicates that the underlying process is random. Chaos theory suggests that such an assumption is untenable. "God plays dice with the universe," says American physicist Joseph Ford. "But they are loaded dice. And the main objective of physics now is to find out by what rules they were loaded."[27]

Last, this new field demands the acknowledgement that chaos is creative: that disorder, rather than order, is generative. "We know now that nonequilibrium, the flow of matter and energy, may be a source of order," write Ilya Prigogine and Isabelle Stengers, European chemists and philosophers of science. "This . . . leads to a new concept of matter, matter that is 'active.'"[28]

The Perang

Prigogine has written elsewhere: "For most of the founders of classical science—even for Einstein—science was an attempt to go beyond the world of appearances, to reach a timeless world of supreme rationality. But perhaps there is a more subtle form of reality that involves both laws and games, time and eternity."[29]

> In every Javanese wayang the frail hero, Arjuna, meets a small demon, Cakil, in the forest. Arjuna and Cakil live in different conceptual worlds. When they meet, "two worlds, two epistemologies coincide for a moment. . . . Each epistemology—each category of being—exists within a different concept of time, and all the times are occurring simultaneously."[30]

Such is the situation in science today. Even though the arguments for the new sciences seem persuasive, it is perhaps easier now for us to see why there is such resistance from a majority of scientists to bolting from one epistemology, one concept of time, to the other. Like all of us, they are people of their age and culture. "When paradigms change, the world itself changes with them." Such fundamental change is not easy for any of us, ironically least of all for the profession whose labors have created this awkward, though profound, moment.

By and large, classical science works. It produces usable results. Why throw it all away because some doubts have been raised about how it fits into a broader metaphysics?

I recall a conversation during my year at M.I.T. with Professor Arthur Miller of the Harvard Physics Department, in which he stated that the source of science's immense achievement was its success in detaching segments of natural reality for examination. When I commented that we had had warnings from other cultures, such as the Native American, that such segmentation was a source of potential disaster, he replied adamantly, "Science is only possible in this way, and we must have science."

Quite understandably, the practitioners of classical science are convinced of its importance. They are imbued with its saga, and it is they who have inherited the mantle of its early heroes. During their rigorous educational initiation, they are drilled in the "scientific articles of faith." The practice of classical science is often fun, and it always fills the day with meaningful activity. Not only are its practitioners convinced personally of its importance, but they also have convinced the society at large. They are respected and highly rewarded. It is a secure, orderly world of straight lines, firmly ruled by scientists themselves.

They also have been phenomenally successful in embedding their straight lines into powerful and persuasive technologies. The source of my despair those years ago at M.I.T. (what more fitting place for this angst than the Massachusetts Institute of Technology?) was the realization of how our technologies box us in conceptually.

These highly sophisticated tools to help us handle the world around us have been constructed according to our dominant perceptions. Their patterning conforms to our civilization's general patterning of reality, and in turn it reinforces those patterned perceptions. This can be seen most clearly in our medical technology, where the machines produce symbolic representations of a particular cultural understanding of the human body, health, disease, and death.

Given the classical, mechanistic view of nature, we are disposed to rely on machines to establish "fact," believing them to be objective and therefore more credible than subjective human experience. We are encouraged to consider the information they give more trustworthy than that of our own senses. Scientific instruments, we have been taught, produce "hard" data. Those data—not surprisingly, considering the metaphysical specifications to which the instruments were constructed—appear to confirm our belief that nature, and our patterning of it, are one and the same.

The technologies persuade us (and most especially their creators, the scientists) that our civilization has made tremendous advances in knowledge and the consequent ability to control nature. The eagerness with which our gadgets are sought after around the world seems to give independent confirmation of these beliefs.

Fortunately, our civilizational "cybernetic loop" is not closed completely. There are other human cultures, past and present, whose patterning of reality challenges and often contradicts the understandings of classical science. "May God keep us from single vision and Newton's sleep," cried William Blake. To which we can add: Bless the patient and persistent voices from inside and outside Western civilization that have continued to urge us to respect other ways of knowing.

Speaking from the vantage point of a French village, John Berger is one such voice:

> Closely connected with the peasant's recognition, as a survivor, of scarcity is his recognition of man's relative ignorance. He may admire knowledge but he never supposes that the advance of knowledge reduces the extent of the unknown. This non-antagonistic relation between the unknown and knowing explains why some of his knowledge is accommodated in what, from the outside, is defined as superstition and magic. Nothing in his experience encourages him to believe in final causes, precisely because his experience is so wide. The unknown can only be eliminated within the limits of a laboratory experiment. Those limits seem to him to be naive.[31]

How can we make sense of this assertion that the advance of knowledge does not reduce the extent of the unknown?

One answer is suggested by Berger: in the "recognition of man's relative ignorance." Given the extent of human limitations in proportion to the overwhelming complexity of the universe, any advance of knowledge can be no more than a drop in the ocean of ignorance. As English biologist J. B. S. Haldane told us, "The universe is not only queerer than we suppose, it is queerer than we can suppose."

There is another possible answer: The advance of knowledge cannot reduce the extent of the unknown because reality is not independent of us. As our knowledge changes, the world changes. When we gain new knowledge, we reshape our concepts, thereby altering the communications—the flow of signals—to our fellow humans, other life forms, and the rest of the whirling stuff of this cosmos. "The pattern which connects" is changed, and our knowledge becomes outdated. New knowledge creates new mysteries, and thus will it always be.

Like John Berger's peasant, we will be wise to give up our belief in final causes. We also will be wise to heed the warning of the friend from Bali against chain-reacting linear power, which accelerates by repeating more and more of the same. Then we may learn to move not in straight lines, but in curves like normal human beings.

When the frail hero, Arjuna, meets the small demon, Cakil, in the forest, "two worlds, two epistemologies coincide for a moment. . . . Between each of these epistemologies there may be—and usually is—a confrontation and a *perang,* a battle. No one ever wins conclusively, but rather a proper balance is restored."[32]

3

THE LEGEND OF
THE GREEN EARTH

"Do we walk in legends or on the green earth in the daylight?"
asked a Rider of Rohan. "A man may do both," said Aragorn.
"For not we but those who come after will make the legends of
our time. The green earth, say you? That is a mighty matter of
legend, though you tread it under the light of day."

J. R. R. Tolkien

A Beckoning Mirage

Science and history are the dominant myths of the modern age, linked
by a common epistemology of time. With the claim they assert to universal validity, they have held us spellbound. They and they alone, we
have been taught, are the keys to both past and future. We have failed
to recognize their role as mythic systems and have not understood that
mathematics, the esoteric language of the sciences accessible in its farther reaches to few even among the initiated, is the sacred symbology
of a faith.

"We only recognize the myths of others," the Indian scholar of religions Raimundo Panikkar observes wryly.[1] But all of us on this green
Earth, in the light of day, walk in legend and myth. We live by the tales

we tell. Our universe of understanding is metaphor. "Our immediate awareness of reality consists of images," Carl Jung said. "We are living completely in a world of images, and we have the greatest trouble in saying anything valid about the objective reality of things."[2]

We must be mindful of our imagery, for it *is* our world. We must be conscious of our mythology and ask whether it is apt for our times. We must take heed that the tales we tell enhance the life of our universe.

Classical science and history will not suffice as the mythologies of the twenty-first century. Forged in the era of European expansion and imperialism, these are myths of domination, focused on mechanisms of control in a segmented universe of separated objects. They have drawn their power from a more ancient myth of the West: Judeo-Christian millenarianism, the legend of the coming of the Messiah to bring a thousand years of peace and abundance. Modern science assumed the mantle of the Savior, albeit offering a salvation secularized, and the idea of progress gave history a trumpet to herald the imminence of a materialist heaven upon Earth.

To Loren Eiseley this mythology was an arid delusion:

> ... modern man is being swept along in a stream of things, giving rise to other things, at such a pace that no substantial ethic, no inward stability, has been achieved.... Progress secularized, progress which pursues only the next invention, progress which pulls thought out of the mind and replaces it with idle slogans, is not progress at all. It is a beckoning mirage in a desert over which stagger the generations of men.[3]

Through the Looking Glass

Classical science and the idea of progress are failing myths, but from the debris produced by their collapse can be salvaged fine material for building anew. Quantum theory is indeed, as Niels Bohr once said, "a philosophical treasure chamber,"[4] and the new sciences in general are studded with gems of wisdom.

Bohr, Danish Nobel laureate in physics, also pointed the direction to other treasure chambers: the traditions of non-Western civilizations. In his search in the late 1920s for a way to express the paradox of the quantum interconnectedness of wave and particle, he coined the term *complementarity.* As he struggled to escape the prevailing dualistic mind-set of classical physics and win acceptance for his concept of the pairing and interdependency of opposites, he was aided by his discovery that this is a fundamental principle of classical Chinese thought. Significantly, Bohr chose the Taoist *t'ai-chi,* the dynamic circle that embraces the opposing energies of *yin and yang,* as the central symbol of his coat of arms late in life, when Denmark's highest royal honor was bestowed upon him.

The problem Bohr faced is a reminder of how difficult it is to shake loose from cultural preconceptions to penetrate to new understandings. Either/or thinking is so fundamental to our conceptual system that it is as hard for us, as it was for him, to imagine opposites combining to form a whole. How can matter be paired with anti-matter? Existence contain nonexistence? Creation involve destruction? Death include life? The unknown increase with the growth of knowledge? The far away be close at hand? Time encompass the timeless? The past also be the future? Hate embrace love? How can good include evil?

It is supremely difficult for us to turn our gaze inward upon the perceptions that shape our construction of reality. "The aspects of things that are most important for us are hidden because of their simplicity and familiarity," Ludwig Wittgenstein wrote.[5] We stand, as it were, in a hall of mirrors formed of our cultural preconceptions, and to our searching gaze the mirrors all around us reflect back these cultural images.

Bohr found that the philosophy of another civilization could help him slip through the looking glass, and we can use the same magic to follow him. Significantly, a number of the most innovative scientific minds of this century have received conceptual inspiration from non-Western cultures. A short list includes Albert Schweitzer, Teilhard de Chardin, Alfred North Whitehead, Carl Jung, Albert Einstein, Werner Heisenberg, Erwin Schroedinger, Arthur Eddington, John Eccles, John Archibald Wheeler, Loren Eiseley, Gregory Bateson, David Bohm, George Wald, Ilya Prigogine, Barbara McClintock, R. D. Laing, Stanislav Grof, Karl Pribram, Roger Sperry, Ralph Abraham, Francesco Varela, Fritjof Capra, and Rupert Sheldrake.

A G. K. Chesterton novel tells of a village boy in the west of

England who lives on a hillside carved with one of the great prehistoric horses. He feels an irresistible longing to leave home and search the world for a mystic symbol to give meaning to his life, but he has not gone far when, looking behind, he realizes that the cottage in which he grew up, along with the horse, are parts of just such a huge symbol. He needed distance to see the larger pattern.

Analagously, experience of other cultures can give us altered perspectives with which we can look back and see our culture of origin with new eyes.

The Web of Life

"No single culture or ideology can bring salvation to the earth," declares Raimundo Pannikar.[6] There are still many in the West who would dispute this, and fundamentalism in religion and science is their response to a growing apprehension of civilizational crisis. Fortunately, there are many others in the Americas, Europe, and Australasia whose response to the same sense of crisis is an increased awareness of and sensitivity to cultural diversity and a recognition of the resources available to humanity from this varied pool of experience.

The growing willingness to explore other ways of knowing is reflected in several forms:

- A cautious but steady move by many Christian and Jewish sects from doctrinal to practical ecumenism, and the opening of dialogue with other faiths.
- A growing familiarity of Westerners with the classical religions of Asia, and the establishment of meditative, devotional communities in most countries in the West.
- A revival of interest in mystical traditions within the great religions, and the growing influence of the teachings from Christianity of St. John of the Cross, St. Teresa, Hildegard of Bingen, and Meister Eckhart; from Judaism of the Kabbalah and Martin Buber; from Islam of the Sufi Rumi; from Hinduism of the *bhakta* poet Kabir; from Buddhism of *The Tibetan Book of the Dead;* and from Taoism of Lao-tzu.

- An acknowledgment of ancient goddess worship and the power of the feminine, and an associated revival of the study and practice of the nature-spirit traditions.

This occurs at a time of reassertion of non-Western traditions long suppressed by European imperialism and obscured in more recent decades in the shadow of Western technoscience. Colonized peoples such as the Native Americans, Siberians, Polynesians, and Aboriginal Australians are reviving suppressed shamanic and similar spiritual practices, teaching this lore to the new generation, and in some instances instructing outsiders as well.

In entering into their understanding of reality—their medicine—we are being offered, along with spiritual learning, an opportunity for healing that is needed in many areas. One is between us and these native peoples, on whom our ancestors, during the European expansion, attempted genocide or at least ethnocide, the extermination of cultures. A second is our own collective psyche, where we bear the suppressed wound of the guilt of this ancestral, racial crime.

A third is between ourselves and nature, which we of the modern West similarly have attempted to dominate and exploit. In place of our objectified, materialist view of the Earth, the way of the shaman offers a spirit connection with all animate and inanimate forms. It teaches us to preserve "the Song of the Land, the Spirit and Flesh of the Ancestors," as Aboriginal Australians know it. It teaches us to honor the souls of the great winds and the waters. It teaches us to walk softly with respect among our green relatives, the trees, and to listen to the feathered friends, the four-, six-, and eight-footed, and all the other companions who crawl and swim.

The words of Sealth, Chief of the Duwamish, are heard again:

> Every part of this earth is sacred to my people. Every shining pine needle, every sandy shore, every mist in the dark woods, every clearing and humming insect is holy in the memory and experience of my people. . . . the beast, the tree, the man, they all share the same breath.
>
> Man does not weave the web of life, he is merely a strand in it. Whatever he does to the web, he does to himself.[7]

56

Here we are given an agenda: to enter into a way of knowing that weaves together matter, mind, and spirit to the benefit of all created forms—a truly *holistic science*.

We do not have to start from scratch, for many among our contemporaries on this globe are already living such a science. Their example gives me courage to attempt a daunting task: an outline of a reconstituted science for the twenty-first century. In this endeavor I will be guided by Blaise Pascal's seventeenth-century caution, sadly disregarded in the formulation of classical science: "There are two equally dangerous extremes, to shut reason out, and to let nothing else in."[8]

Holistic Science

A New Understanding of Time
The first element of our holistic science should be a multidimensional and varied time. Time is a cultural construct, and the concept with which we have been working in the modern West—metrically even, one dimensional, unidirectional time—is too limiting.

The previous two chapters began the discussion of this topic, which is of such importance that all of chapter 6 will be devoted to it.

Respect for Diversity
We must cherish and nurture variety in landforms, life forms, cultures, ways of knowing, and styles of expression. As Charles Darwin revealed long ago, organic diversity protects life by providing flexibility for evolutionary adaptation in perpetually changing environments. Cultural variety is equally indispensable as a pool of alternative codes of human existence.

Diversity has intrinsic beauty and is the source of creativity. "Wherever there is life, there is twist and mess," writes Annie Dillard.

> The texture of the world, its filigree and scrollwork, means that there is the possibility for beauty here, a beauty inexhaustible in its complexity, which opens to my knock, which answers in me a call I do not remember calling, and which trains me to the wild extravagant nature of the spirit I seek.[9]

As a stimulus to new ways of understanding, diversity is an antidote to the closed, smug mind and a healthy reminder that no one has a corner on truth. "Tolerance," wrote Mahatma Gandhi, "implies a gratuitous assumption of the inferiority of other faiths to one's own, whereas *ahimsa* [nonviolent protection of life] teaches us to entertain for the faiths of others the same respect as we accord our own, thus admitting the imperfections of the latter."[10]

The intolerance of classical science for other ways of knowing can be understood in part as its reluctance to admit any imperfection in its worldview, while its more general assault on the diversity of environments, species, and human cultures reflects its drive to dominate. The new sciences, Ilya Prigogine and Isabelle Stengers tell us, have

> rid themselves of a conception of objective reality that implied that novelty and diversity had to be denied in the name of immutable universal laws. They have rid themselves of a fascination with a rationality taken as closed and a knowledge seen as nearly achieved. They are now open to the unexpected, which they no longer define as the result of imperfect knowledge or insufficient control.[11]

Our holistic science thus will be less controlling and more humble in its claims to wisdom, recognizing that today's knowledge all too often becomes tomorrow's absurdity.

Reempowerment of the Feminine

One form of diversity to be cherished is that of gender. Male and female construct and experience the world differently, and in balance, these differences complement and strengthen each other. In classical science, as in most other areas of modern Western civilization, there has been a serious imbalance toward the masculine to the detriment of life on this planet.

Our holistic science must reempower women and the feminine aspect of being. And there is no mystery about where to begin to redress the balance: All scientific activities should involve women in at least equal numbers to men. In order for women's concerns to receive attention, women should set the new scientific agenda. Fortunately, the work of the women's movement and feminist scholarship give us a head start on the necessary reordering of scientific priorities and realignment of power. This has included studies of prepatriarchal societies and both the study and the revival of the practice of ancient goddess traditions.

In her book *Dreaming the Dark,* the American psychotherapist and witch Starhawk draws on these sources in pointing a direction for the realignment of power:

> a power based on a principle very different from power-over, from domination. . . . the power we sense in a seed, in the growth of a child, the power we feel writing, weaving, working, creating, making choices. . . . It is the power that comes from within. . . . If we are to survive the question becomes: how do we overthrow, not those presently in power, but the principle of power-over? How do we shape a society on the principle of power-from-within?[12]

Impermanence and Unpredictability

"An ordered world is not the world order," Martin Buber told us.[13] This is not a fixed-law universe. Stability and resultant predictability were central to the vision of classical science, but the new sciences portray a natural reality in which tiny fluctuations, sudden and unpredictable, can produce enormous structural changes.

As the subatomic physicists, evolutionary cosmologists, morphogenic biologists and chaos theorists are showing, reality is remade every instant, and the existing world exercises only an indeterminate influence on this new creation. What endures—appearances to the contrary—is not material substance. The mystics have always told us that what connects present to future is not a continuity of objects but a continuity of potential and expectation, the dream of what may be.

> *Clouds are hills in vapour,*
> *hills are clouds in stone,*
> *a phantasy in time's dream.*[14]
>
> Rabindranath Tagore

Our holistic scientists must be prepared for the insecurity of working without immutable, universal natural laws. Their experience (to adapt James Gleick) will be like walking through a maze whose walls rearrange themselves with each step taken.[15]

Engagement in Co-creation

The walls of the maze rearrange themselves with our every step because they are not separate from us. Remember John Wheeler's words: "May the universe in some strange sense be 'brought into being' by the participation of those who participate? . . . The vital act is the act of participation." All of manifest reality exists through relationship. It is like the rainbow, created by the interplay of water vapor, light waves, and our sight. The rainbow is brought into being in a unique form and position by each participant observer.

As Martin Buber says, "We live our lives . . . within the streaming mutual life of the universe. Inscrutably involved, we live in the currents of universal reciprocity."[16]

Inscrutably but actively involved. Take as an example infectious disease. Like all other life forms on this planet, the microorganisms responsible for disease live in interdependence and must adapt themselves to the behavior of their hosts, just as we must adapt ourselves to them as our houseguests. Over the millenia as the human species has increased in number, clustering closer and closer together in ever larger groupings along with our domestic animals and attendant scavengers, the bacteria and viruses have also multiplied and flourished. Moving from host to host has become as easy for them as hitching a ride in a friendly town. No longer are there weary miles of empty highway to travel. The microorganisms must be careful, however, to restrain their virulence lest they find too many houses empty. Thus, it is to their advantage that we develop partial immunity and in other ways modify our lifestyles to keep the relationship balanced. Across the generations, both they and we change our physical forms in response to one another.

Our health is a function of reciprocity, first within the ecosystem we call our body (not overlooking the crucial role played by a calm and centered mind in its well-being), and then within the wider ecosystem of family and community. "Basic to the evolution of the brain is our early attachment and dependency on other people," write Robert Ornstein and David Sobel. "Our social nature links us fundamentally to others throughout our lives. When these links are strained or ruptured, the health consequences are profound."[17]

In our awe at the grandeur and immensity of the universe, we sometimes forget that it is made little bit by little bit, through myriads of seemingly insignificant interactions—and in no other way. This is what the Hindus call *leela,* the never-ending divine play, in which all of us—star, microbe, leaf, mountain, seahorse, human, region of space, forget-me-not—are both dancers and the dance. "Everything here is alive thanks to the living of everything else. All the forms of life are connected," writes Lewis Thomas.[18]

Our holistic scientists will be humbly aware that they co-create the universe with each simple act.

Recognition of Unity

A science that understands the world to be one of universal relationship will have limited use for objectifying, reductionist, and dualistic concepts.

"The language of objects captures only one corner of actual life," wrote Martin Buber.[19] Our focus now should be on interconnectedness rather than separate objects—things. We seem to have been mesmerized by our passion for naming and categorizing into forgetting that these are no more than handy pigeonholes and labels. The fact that our ancestors and our contemporaries in other cultures have other categories with different names should serve as a reminder that all divisions are fictions. Lao-tzu, two and a half millenia ago, warned that naming is a mixed blessing:

> The unnamable is the eternally real
> Naming is the origin
> of all particular things.[20]
>
> Tao Te Ching

An emphasis on parts rather than the whole has been encouraged by the reductionism of classical science. "Even as a melody is not composed of tones, nor a verse of words, nor a statue of lines," said Martin Buber, "one must pull and tear to turn a unity into a multiplicity."[21]

Our holistic science, recognizing that the whole is more than the simple sum of its parts, should hold as central the principle of synergy, the creative force generated in a natural system through its functioning as a whole. This force radiates throughout the system, communicating energy, purpose, and direction. Contrary to reductionist thinking, it is not the parts but the whole that sets the primary agenda for the organism, ecosystem, and planet. It is also synergy that explains why systems, as their scale increases, exhibit new phenomena and changes in some of their behaviors, including enhanced abilities.

Out goes the idea that in order to know the whole it is sufficient to look at some of the parts. Out with it goes another reductionist tool: "Occam's razor," the precept that the simplest explanation is the best. Because of this preference, monocausal theories have prevailed all too often in classical science. Our holistic scientists, recognizing that the net of existence is woven from all sides with intertwining strands, will know that simplistic answers are insufficient and neat and tidy ones few and far between.

If objectification and reductionism have taken a beating from the new sciences, so too has dualism. Bohr's complementarity is now more than sixty years old, and within the past twenty years chaos theory has provided two remarkable examples of the unity of opposites.

The first example concerns scale. As noted above in the discussion of synergy, changes of scale in systems can produce new phenomena and altered behavior—but only in some instances. In others, there is a persistence of the same patterns at every level, rendering the dualistic distinction between "big" and "small" irrelevant. "Self-similarity in symmetry across scale"[22] is the revelation of the new nonlinear mathematics of fractal geometry—a revelation that has given science a healthy push back toward holism.

The second example involves the distinction between "simple" and "complex," a dualism prevalent in classical science and one of its major analytical tools. The work of the chaos theorists suggests that these two are not so easy to tell apart, for each contains features of the other. Things may in one dimension get simpler and simultaneously, in another, more complex. Gleick writes, "Simple systems give rise to complex behavior. Complex systems give rise to simple behavior. And most important, the laws of complexity hold universally, caring not at all for the details of a system's constituent atoms."[23]

An illustration from marine biology reveals what a tricky business this really is. The nanomia, a jellyfish-like creature related to the Portugese man-of-war, poses the intriguing question: complex organism, or collection of simple organisms?

At the top is an individual modified into a gas-filled float. Below it are organisms that act like little bellows, squirting out jets of water which propel the colony; by altering the shape of their openings they are able to alter the direction of the jets. Through their coordinated action the *nanomia* colony is able to dart about vigorously, moving at any angle and in any plane, even executing loop-the-loop curves. Lower on the stem there are other organisms which are specialized for the ingestion and digestion of nutrients for the rest of the colony. Long branched tentacles arise from them and are used to capture prey. There are also bracts, consisting of inert, scalelike organisms that fit over the stem and help protect it from physical damage. Finally, there are sexual organisms, which produce gametes which through fertilization can give rise to new colonies.[24]

Concluding with the observation that some of the individuals are even coordinated through connected nerves, Rupert Sheldrake comments that biologists cannot decide whether this is a unitary organism or a colony.

A Universe of Interconnected Meanings

This apparent biological conundrum is no conundrum at all if we understand the universe to be one of interconnected meanings rather than one of interacting objects. Objects in and of themselves do not have meaning; this they gain in context, in relationship. It is what flows between—the exchange of information—that makes sense of things. Communications spin the web of reality. "All of nature," says physicist David Bohm, "is organized according to the activity of significance."[25]

The nanomia, whether single organism or colony, is a unified communications system. This gives it meaning. It is a whole, defined by its shared sense of purpose. In this it is the rule rather than the exception. All life forms are both organism and colony. The human body, for instance, is swarming with companionable microbes, without which it could not function. Equally, we live in colonies of fellow humans, and our actual physical form is developed out of the communications network we call culture. Recall Ornstein's and Sobel's comment: "Basic to the evolution of the brain is our early attachment and dependency on other people." None of us can be born, grow, or exist in isolation. The perception that we are separate entities is, as the Hindus say, *maya*, illusion.

We accept that mammals and other "higher" vertebrates have fairly sophisticated systems of communication, and the word *language* is now being used to apply to sea mammals as well as our fellow primates. A few bold ornithologists are extending it to birds. At the other end of the scale, molecular biologists, although operating determinedly within the reductionist, mechanistic paradigm, routinely use the concept of information in describing the function of DNA in all life forms. Even so, is it an overstatement to say that communications spin the web of natural reality? I believe not.

It was late August of the year my wife, Jo, and I spent living in the Himalaya when I wrote the first draft of this chapter, and we were witnessing lively communication in our surroundings. I noted in my journal:

> The monkeys are responding to information they are receiving from the orchards on our hillside. The reddening apples call them down from the jungle each afternoon for a rambunctious feast, while they in turn signal to the village dogs with their chatter that there is fun to be had in the chase. Soon the monkeys will be joined on the higher terraces by brown bears, summoned out from their mountain lairs by golden tassles on the ripening corn. Meanwhile, the foot-long lizards, who hunt insects and their own smaller relatives along the field margins, are changing their skin coloring to match the tawny hues of autumn.

As I write this final draft, I am being given another lesson in communication. Every so often I have to leave my computer to respond to urgent banging on the cat door at the rear of the house. It is a weka parent requesting a food handout for its voracious brood. I should explain that we now live in a remote part of New Zealand surrounded by native forest—bush, as it's called here. Our most numerous companions are weka: flightless birds the size of domestic hens with glossy cinnamon-colored feathers, orange beaks and legs, and bright red button eyes.

In Maori tradition, weka are our older and wiser relatives, procreated by the goddess Haere-awaawa and the forest god Tane before he fathered humans. They are feisty, companionable, and very intelligent. In our eighteen months here they have revealed to us a rich language, and we are now able to distinguish from their vocabulary which birds are on their own territory and which are on another's, which are adults and which are young, which are fighting and which are copulating, which are single and which are couples, which are feeding babies in the nest and which are feeding older offspring on the move.

As we learn about them, they are learning about us—and it goes beyond knowing how to cadge food. Most remarkably, they have shown a desire to be helpful. I am slowly clearing out bits of junk such as plastic cartons and milk containers thrown into the bush by former property owners. The weka have caught on to what I'm doing, and on occasion they have assisted my search by pecking loudly on concealed items to lead me to them. Most touching of all was the gift of a plastic bottle stopper dropped at my feet by a weka as I was chopping wood one day.

I grew up on stories of the mind-reading ability of an animal. Freckles, the family dog in my infancy, had an uncanny knowledge of when Mum or Dad was heading for home. Apparently he could judge precisely when to leave the house and race miles down our country road to meet the car at a particular corner. Recent studies initiated by Rupert Sheldrake are producing worldwide observations of ESP linkage of this kind between pets and their "owners."

In *The Presence of the Past*, Sheldrake presents remarkable evidence of the intricate coordination of purposeful activities in groups of animals, birds, fish, insects, and invertebrates—coordination extremely difficult to explain if they do not possess systems of communication, a collective consciousness, or both.

An example familiar to most of us: a flock of birds feeding on the ground that suddenly rises into the air as one. Naturalist Edmund Selous, who studied this phenomenon over a period of 30 years, observed that often the birds fly up together without any external provocation. He became convinced that no normal sensory explanation could be found for this instantaneous, unified movement.

Another apparent example of group mind is provided by African fungus-growing termites, which live in colonies of two million or more. The termites build a mound up to ten feet high over an underground nest with a system of columns and air ducts so intricate that it appears to have been constructed to a blueprint. Armies of workers begin separate columns, with each column built to arch inward at the top to meet another column exactly. The work often takes several termite generations to complete, but every laborer knows where to place the next pellet. By the way, the termites are blind!

An impressive body of evidence also has been accumulating over the past forty years of the sensitivity of plants to signals from their environment and their ability to communicate in return. An early work published in 1973, *The Secret Life of Plants,* had such revolutionary implications for plant biology that the scientific community generally dismissed its evidence as implausible. Its authors, Peter Tompkins and Christopher Bird, were ridiculed for their assertion that plants possess consciousness and even emotions. To an open mind, however, what they and others subsequently have reported is stunning. Here are a few examples.

At Kimberton Hills Research Farm, west of Philadelphia, measurements of sap flow in plants reveal they prepare systematically for severe weather changes. They rush sap to their roots in anticipation of a coming storm, a process that enables them to send sugar up to leaves and boughs when the weather has quieted and so repair any damage. How they know the storm is coming is beyond human comprehension.[26]

In experiments conducted in the 1950s at the Institute of Agrophysics in Leningrad, bean plants linked with sensors to light and watering devices proved capable of switching the machines on and off to give themselves the right amounts of "daylight" and water for healthy growth.[27]

And what should we make of the following tree story? A red oak attacked by gypsy moth caterpillars will increase the amount of inedible tannin in its leaves, varying the levels throughout the tree in an asymmetrical pattern. This forces the caterpillars to explore for edible leaves, thus exposing them to birds. At the same time, *untouched* red oak trees in the vicinity also increase their tannin levels![28]

Numerous experiments with electrodes fitted to trees and other plants have measured their responses to events around them. Not only do plants react to damage inflicted on other plants and to physical threats to themselves, but they also react to the *thoughts* of experimenters. Plants, it seems, are mind readers![29]

Perhaps all this should not surprise us when we recall the quantum effects discussed in the previous chapter. A suggestive parallel to the ability of animals and plants to communicate with their human companions is offered by Bell's theorem, with its demonstration of the ability of separated twin particles to "communicate" changed states to one another instantaneously.

Another discovery from quantum physics, the interplay between subatomic particles and experimenter, may help to explain a different and even more mysterious kind of "interspecies" communication—that between humans and machines. This has been revealed by studies in the School of Engineering and Applied Science at Princeton University.

To answer a fundamental but straightforward question—can human consciousness affect matter?—two straightforward techniques have been employed at Princeton. One is a kind of electronic flip of the coin, the other a kind of electronic pinball machine. In experiments with both devices, operators have tried to skew outcomes simply by an exercise of will. Since 1979 these tests have been repeated hundreds of thousands of times under the strictest research protocols to see whether a statistically significant deviation from random chance would result. It has, and the Princeton researchers conclude that human thought can affect the functioning of sensitive microelectronic devices.[30]

Startling, yes. But Albert Einstein from his grave might retort: "What's so surprising? I told you ninety years ago it's communications that count." Einstein did more than anyone else in the twentieth century to disturb our civilization's settled vision of the shape of physical reality. He based his theories of the relativity of time on the argument that what has significance is not events in and of themselves but rather the receipt of information about events. The revolutionary shift in perception he effected was from a universe of objects to a universe of signals.

Communications do indeed spin the web of reality. What flows between creates a unity. In Japanese there is no literal equivalent of the English "I love you," for with the bond of love the separation between "I" and "you" is dissolved.

With their attention directed to patterns of communication, to the intangibles that create unities, our holistic scientists will understand that they are contributing meanings to an interconnected universe.

It is the material that provides the means.
It is the immaterial that gives meaning.

Chinese proverb

Consciousness As the Ground

Consciousness is the foundation of being. Although denied in the modern West under the influence of the mechanistic materialism of classical science, this was the belief of our forebears in almost every culture.

For three hundred years since the Spanish invasion, a Colombian mountain people, the Kogi, have lived in isolation to preserve an ancient wisdom. In the beginning, they say, there was only the Mother. She was *aluna*, the mind. She was memory and potential. Everything that ever was or ever will be had to be conceived in *aluna*, in consciousness, before creation could begin.[31]

Nature is the incarnation of a thought,
and turns to thought again. . . .
The world is thought precipitated.

Ralph Waldo Emerson

In this, the Kogi, Emerson, and the Aboriginal Australians are of one mind. In the Aboriginal Dreamtime the totemic beings, the Ancestors, wandered the continent, singing out the names of everything that crossed their path—animals, birds, plants, waterholes, rocks—thus singing the world into existence. They were poets in the original Greek sense of *poesis*, which means creation. Every Aboriginal since the Beginning has been the guardian of the Song of his or her totemic Ancestor and through it of a section of the land crossed by that Songline. Their obligation is to keep the land the way it was. To do this they periodically must "go walkabout": a ritual journey treading in the footprints of the Ancestors and singing the Ancestors' Songs, without changing a word or note. Thus they recreate the creation. The land exists first in the mind. In order to be born, it then must be sung. To be reborn or maintained, it must be sung again and again.[32]

"To put the conclusion crudely—the stuff of the world is mind-stuff."[33] The speaker is the British cosmologist Arthur Eddington, a contemporary of Einstein and a major exponent of relativity theory. As we have seen, it was the surprises produced by subatomic phenomena that evoked doubts among the early quantum theorists about the validity of the classical dictum that mind and matter are distinct. The challenge to answer the questions they raised was met by a theoretical physicist of the next generation, David Bohm. With his overarching hypothesis of undivided wholeness in flowing movement, he has pointed science back to a recognition of consciousness as inherent in the material universe.

Bohm's argument, in a nutshell, is that we exist in a seamless reality, which is in constant flux. In this flow, this holomovement, things can be seen to form and dissolve—to *unfold* into manifest existence, the *explicate order,* and then *enfold* back into the *implicate* order. "If you've ever seen a whirlpool," he says, "you've seen how the water gushes up from the center, then falls out and down and around to come up again through the center over and over, the movement in the whole being both simultaneously outward and inward."[34]

Bohm uses the phrase "things can be *seen* to form and dissolve" because he believes that our minds play an active role in constructing what is perceived in the explicate order. We will be mistaken, he says, if we think these "things" have a separate existence, for "whatever part, element, or aspect we may abstract in thought, this still enfolds the whole and is therefore intrinsically related to the totality from which it has been abstracted."[35]

He is able to explain the quantum paradoxes in these terms. The so-called particles, although appearing to have an independent existence because of our habit of fragmentary thought, are simply aspects of an underlying whole, as are the experimenter and the instrument of measurement as well. "Both observer and observed are merging and interpenetrating aspects of one whole reality, which is indivisible and unanalysable."[36]

This also resolves the mystery of nonlocality: the ability of separated twin particles to respond instantaneously to each other's altered motion. The "particles have to be taken literally as projections of a higher-dimension reality which cannot be accounted for in terms of any force of interaction between them."[37]

Consciousness resides in this higher-dimension reality, the implicate order, and is manifest along with matter in the explicate order: "Mind and matter are not separate substances. Rather, they are different aspects of one whole and unbroken movement."[38] All matter has the potential for consciousness and life, Bohm believes, for the implicate order is "life implicit," flowing as it does from (and with) a great intelligence: " . . . people had insight in the past about a form of intelligence that had organized the universe and they personalized it and called it God. A similar insight can prevail today without personalizing it and without calling it a personal God."[39]

"The world is the everchanging foam that floats on the surface of a sea of silence," wrote the Bengali poet Rabindranath Tagore. Throughout Bohm's work there are echoes of Hindu philosophy, particularly Advaita Vedanta, which can be explained in large part by his friendship and two decades of dialogue with the Indian philosopher and spiritual teacher Jidda Krishnamurti.

Similar influences can be seen in the thought of English biologist Rupert Sheldrake, resulting from his recurrent periods of residence in India and study of both Hinduism and Buddhism. Bohm's and Sheldrake's theories, emerging from different areas of the natural sciences, complement and reinforce each other. When Bohm says "deep down the consciousness of mankind is one,"[40] he is giving expression to a central tenet of Sheldrake's hypothesis of formative causation.

Just as Bohm developed his theories in response to a major problem in physics, so Sheldrake was prompted by a long-standing perplexity in biology: the development of form. How do organisms know what shape to take?

An early and appealing explanation, to which the development of high-powered microscopes was the nemesis, was that each seed or sperm contained a tiny but complete version of the full-grown organism. The current orthodoxy is that the necessary information is programmed in the chemical genetic material, DNA. Sheldrake finds this an unsatisfactory answer. Although DNA provides the physical raw material, no indication has been found therein of any blueprint of form. Among several problems with the genetic explanation to which Sheldrake points is the fact that cells in different parts of an organism, e.g., human arms and legs, are genetically identical. How then can it be said that the genes carry the coded information necessary for arms to develop differently from legs?

In place of the mechanistic, molecular answer, Sheldrake offers the hypothesis that each organic species exists in a field of consciousness, a *morphic field,* with *resonances* that carry information from the accumulated experience of that species. This field supplies guidance for *morphogenesis:* the development of appropriate form in each individual in the species. The morphic field also gives direction for regeneration and the repair of damage in individuals of species that have that capacity, as also for the complex, cooperative behaviors (noted earlier in this chapter) in which many organisms engage without apparent need for learning.

The idea of an invisible field shaping matter within it and exercising influence on things outside may seem a bit fanciful until we recall that this idea is commonplace in physics. Magnetic fields and gravity are familiar examples. Sheldrake's innovation is to extend field theory to biology.

He believes that formative causation is universal in nature, embracing inorganic as well as organic systems. He also suggests that a morphic field can outlast the matter around which it forms.

> When any particular organized system ceases to exist, as when an atom splits, a snowflake melts, an animal dies, its organizing field disappears from that place. But in another sense, morphic fields do not disappear; they are potential organizing patterns of influence, and can appear again physically in other times and places, wherever and whenever the physical conditions are appropriate. When they do so they contain within themselves a memory of their previous physical existences.[41]

"Memory is inherent in nature," Sheldrake argues, and it is "habit" that explains the close similarity of form and behavior through time and across generations. Habits, although powerful in their constraint, can be changed; hence evolution: the emergence of new behaviors and new forms. Given that a morphic field embraces an entire species or inorganic system, the resonances of an innovation potentially affect every individual in the field. All humans, for instance, "draw upon a collective memory, to which all in turn contribute."[42]

Sheldrake acknowledges his debt to the early-twentieth-century French biologist Henri Bergson and to vitalism in general, with its emphasis on purposefulness in nature. Convinced that creative consciousness is the ground of being, he is of the school that believes the rules of the cosmic game themselves are evolving.

Sheldrake describes the universe as "essentially thought-like,"[43] and Bohm, as we saw, speculates that "a form of intelligence . . . organized the universe." The same conclusion is reached by the American neurophysiologist and brain surgeon Karl Pribram: "Mental properties are the pervasive organizing principles of the universe."[44]

Like Sheldrake and Bohm, Pribram was led to the development of a new general theory, with implications extending far beyond his own discipline, by an intractable problem in his field of research. Repeated studies of humans and animals had revealed that major injury to one or another portion of the brain does not result in loss of a particular memory or set of memories. Where then is memory "stored"? Pribram had decided that it must, in some way, be distributed widely in the brain rather than be stored in particular localities, but he lacked a conceptual model.

The development of holography gave him the insight he was seeking. Holography is a technique of lensless photography that records on a photographic plate the hologram, an interference pattern created by the wave field of light scattered by an object. Although the hologram appears to contain only meaningless swirls, when exposed to a laser beam it projects a three-dimensional image of the original object, apparently suspended in space. Most remarkable is the fact that any piece of the hologram will reconstruct the entire image. Pribram writes:

> It seemed immediately plausible that the distributed memory store of the brain might resemble this holographic record. I developed a precisely formulated theory based on known neuroanatomy

and known neurophysiology that could account for the brain's distributed memory store in holographic terms.[45]

Pribram then faced another question: Who is looking at the hologram? The old answer of "the little person in the head" did not appeal to him. Prompted by the absence of a lens in holography, a radically different conclusion suddenly suggested itself: There need be no intermediary between "real world" and "mind"—no separation between "outside" and "inside." In the words of Saint Francis of Assisi: "What we are looking for is what is looking."

The brain, Pribram decided, directly records interference patterns from a hologram: the manifest world. In David Bohm's terms (Pribram had just discovered Bohm's writing), the brain and the perceived object both belong to the *explicate order,* which is a hologram of the underlying *implicate order.* This is "a holographic universe," Pribram declared; ". . . each organism represents in some manner the universe, and each portion of the universe represents in some manner the organisms within it."[46]

> In the heaven of Indra there is said to be a network of
> pearls so arranged that if you look at one you see all the
> others reflected in it. In the same way, each object in the
> world is not merely itself but involves every other object,
> and in fact is every other object.
>
> Buddhist sutra

> To see a world in a grain of sand
> And a heaven in a wild flower,
> Hold infinity in the palm of your hand
> And eternity in an hour.
>
> William Blake

Pribram, like Bohm before him, was struck by the consistency with which mystics of every tradition have described a holographic universe in which all separations—space and time included—are maya. "How did these ideas arise for millenia before we had the mathematics to understand them?" Pribram asks. "Maybe in the holographic state—in the frequency domain—4,000 years ago is tomorrow."[47]

Or, in the words of an Australian Aboriginal elder: "Many men afterwards become country, in that place, Ancestors." By spending a whole life walking and singing the Ancestor's Songline, a person becomes the track, the Ancestor and the Song.[48]

Development of Empathy

The acknowledgment that consciousness is the ground of being inevitably must impress our holistic scientists with their awesome responsibilities and their joyous opportunities. They cannot, like classical scientists, strike the pose of pure spectators of nature. The world is not "out there," and knowledge is not confined to the individual mind. "Consciousness is a singular of which the plural is unknown," wrote the quantum physicist and philosopher of science Erwin Shroedinger.[49] The ever-shifting interconnections that create and recreate this universe are affected and effected by perception, feeling, thought, and purpose.

> Is it the flag that moves or the wind that
> moves? No, it is the mind that moves.

And mind is a powerful and mysterious instrument to be used with more circumspection than has been our wont in recent decades. In lamenting the casualness with which many contemporary Christians mouth the words of their faith, Annie Dillard could have included classical scientists (or, for that matter, historians) with equal justice:

> On the whole, I do not find Christians, outside of the catacombs, sufficiently sensible of conditions. Does anyone have the foggiest idea what sort of power we so blithely invoke? Or, as I suspect, does no one believe a word of it? The churches are playing on the floor with their chemistry sets, mixing up a batch of TNT to kill a Sunday morning.[50]

In a participatory universe, consciousness is dynamite! In these circumstances, our participatory scientists will be well advised to heed the ancient Buddhist precept of mindfulness. As a first task, they should be mindful of the "lenses" through which perception of the manifest world is filtered.

In writing of the holonomic brain function, Karl Pribram observes ruefully that our normal state of awareness is not "in the frequency domain," for we generally see the world through "a cruder form of a lens."[51] As he points out, the eye (literally a lens), along with the "brain's mathematics," are subject to a wide range of conditioning, which affects what they register as real. There are many examples of this, the effects of hypnosis and variance in pictorial perception from culture to culture being among the more familiar.

If we are vulnerable to such external conditioning, what can be meant by mindfulness? Rupert Sheldrake gives us a clue with his emphasis on the importance of habit in shaping and sustaining fields of consciousness. We should be mindful constantly of the habits of thought of our culture. Moreover, we can feel empowered by the knowledge that even one individual's break with those habits changes the resonances in the morphic field, leading rapidly in some cases to the creation of an entire new field of consciousness in consonance with the principle, observed by the chaos theorists, of sensitive dependence on initial conditions.

Indeed, one of the habits we should change is the perception that conditioning is "external" to ourselves. "What is needed," writes David Bohm, "is for man to give attention to his habit of fragmentary thought, to be aware of it, and thus bring it to an end. Man's approach to reality may then be whole, and so the response will be whole."[52]

I am not suggesting that this is a simple process. Mindfulness is developed only over time with dedicated discipline. "Patience is the reward of patience," Saint Augustine is reputed to have observed with an irony worthy of a Zen master. Equally, it can be said that mindfulness is the product of mindfulness. And remember: This is not an "either/or" world. To some degree we will remain subject to conditioning—which is as it should be.

Inner awareness is the second task in mindfulness. In order to be whole people, our holistic scientists must become familiar and comfortable with their own bodies, feelings, sexual urges, emotions, sensitivities, sense of beauty, ethical biases, and the personal history in which these are rooted. In a world without separations, the inner and the outer scientist must be in harmony. Fortunately, as Prigogine and Stengers point out, "the coming together of our insights about the world around us and the world inside us is a satisfying feature of the recent evolution in science."[53]

The development of humanistic and transpersonal psychology, with the attendant studies of consciousness, has provided effective tools for heightening self-awareness. It also has revealed the depth of resources in other ways of knowing available to each of us to supplement and enrich the rational intellect, as well as to serve as buffers against its inveterate tendency to believe that it has all the answers. Later I will examine more fully these inner sources of intuitive wisdom and will consider their source.

Mindfulness of the welfare of what we study is the third task. In touch with their own feelings and moved by the heart as much as by the intellect, our holistic scientists will identify with their research subjects, animate and inanimate. Empathy and compassion replace detachment and objectivity in the new participatory science.

What then becomes of scientific rigor? To repeat the answer I gave in the first chapter in arguing for an engaged history: Each intellectual craft has its well-tested rules of good conduct to direct disciplined, self-critical research, and these can apply as well to an empathetic and compassionate science as to an objectifying one. The stonemason does not betray the rigorous discipline of her craft just because she is deeply moved by spiritual passion and impish humor as she carves angels and gargoyles on the cathedral architrave. "Feeling and longing," wrote Albert Einstein, "are the motive force behind all human endeavor and human creation, in however exalted a guise the latter may present themselves to us."[54]

An empathetic science is a better science for it allows the scales of skepticism to fall from our eyes. As Saint Augustine told us: "A thing is recognized only to the extent it is loved." If we open our hearts to the beings and processes we desire to understand, they open their hearts to us and reveal themselves. I will write of my own experience of this in the next chapter, but for now let me simply state that classical science has been hamstrung by its adamant denial that belief affects what can be seen. Many things will reveal themselves only to those who believe.

This effect, which is consistent with Rupert Sheldrake's morphic field hypothesis, is most strikingly evident on the "frontiers" of scientific research, particularly in those areas dependent on subtle effects, such as the investigation of paranormal psychic phenomena and the development of homeopathic medical treatments. Where powerful skepticism is brought to bear, experimental results in these fields often are unable to be replicated.

Empathy opens the way for communion with our research subjects. In a world of universal consciousness, we must be mindful of what we can be taught by our fellow travelers, animate and inanimate, on this amazing, whirling journey among the stars. Biologist Barbara McClintock, American Nobel laureate, attributes her success in unraveling some of the mysteries of "jumping genes" to her companionship with Indian corn:

> I found the more I worked with them, the bigger and bigger the chromosomes got and when I was really working with them I wasn't outside. I was part of the [system]. . . . it surprised me because I actually felt as if I was right down there and these were my friends. . . . As you look at these things they become a part of you.[55]

Significantly, McClintock has practiced Tibetan Buddhist meditation, and equally significantly, she is a woman. We may reasonably hope for the empathetic trend in science to be hastened by the increase in the proportion of women among scientists.

In a world without separations, caring for the welfare of our research subjects is caring for our own welfare. Appalling as it is to think of the effects on the consciousness of the laboratory animals who suffer from heartless experiments, it is worse still to contemplate the effects on the collective consciousness of a civilization that will tolerate the torment of fellow creatures in the name of the acquisition of knowledge.

In a deeply moving article entitled "Science and the Sense of the Holy" written not long before his death, Loren Eiseley reminded us that "the degradation of animals in experiments of little, or vile, meaning was easily turned to the experimental human torture practiced at Dachau and Buchenwald by men dignified with medical degrees. . . . Without the sense of the holy, without compassion," he continued, *Homo sapiens* "can become a gray stalking horror—the creature who devised Belsen. . . . One can only assert in science, as in religion, that when one has destroyed human wonder and compassion, one has killed man, even if the man in question continues to go about his laboratory tasks."[56]

Eiseley observed that "science must sooner or later devise for itself [an ethic] if mankind is to survive," and he suggested that his fellow scientists turn to our hunting ancestors for guidance about what that ethic should be.

Around the world among the peoples who live by hunting, there is a universal and invariable rule: The hunter must never dishonor the prey. The hunted animal gives its body to sustain the life of the hunters, and as their part of the bargain, the hunters must ensure that the animal's spirit flies free. "All the rituals," Eiseley writes, "suggest even toward hunted animals a respect and sympathy leading to ceremonial treatment of hunted souls." For hunters to diminish an animal's spirit is to diminish their own. The welfare of the animal's soul and their own is one and the same.

Our holistic scientists will say, with Loren Eiseley, "we are in a mystic sense one single diffuse animal, subject to joy and suffering beyond what we endure as individuals."[57]

Attunement to the Silent Center

> We join spokes together in a wheel,
> but it is the center hole
> that makes the wagon move.
>
> We shape clay into a pot,
> but it is the emptiness inside
> that holds whatever we want.
>
> We hammer wood for a house,
> but it is the inner space
> that makes it livable.
>
> We work with being,
> but non-being is what we use.
>
> Tao Te Ching

"The point is that the raw material doesn't really have to come from anywhere. . . . the universe can start off with zero energy and still create matter."[58] When Stephen Hawking, who dismisses mysticism as "a cop-out,"[59] declares as he does here that everything can be created from nothing, we realize how dramatic is the shift in twentieth-century science away from pure materialism, and how far it has traveled toward the perennial wisdom, whether or not individual scientists are aware of the fact. A central concept in all mystical traditions is the potential existent in nothingness, the dynamic fullness of the void: *sunyata*, as it is known in Hinduism and Buddhism. A firm bridge has been built for our holistic science to both mysticism and the new psychologies, a bridge linking matter, mind, and spirit.

From mystical traditions and transpersonal psychology alike comes the insistent counsel: For wisdom deeper than intellectual knowledge, look within; go to the still, silent center. As we have seen, scientists offer similar advice: David Bohm, Rupert Sheldrake, Karl Pribram, Barbara McClintock, and, before them, Albert Einstein, Werner Heisenberg, Erwin Schroedinger, Wolfgang Pauli, and Arthur Eddington, to name but a few. The language of the different traditions varies, but all bring a single message:

> You must go beyond all your imagery, beyond your thoughts, into the divine darkness. That's where you meet God. . . . And really the journey towards God is a journey into the unconscious. . . . You know, in a Hindu temple the inner sanctuary is always dark. You go through the courts of the temple, which are filled with light, the figures of the gods, but when you come to the inner sanctuary you come to the heart, the inner center of your own being, and you encounter God in the darkness. God without form.[60]

The words are those of the British Benedictine monk Bede Griffiths, whose ashram in South India was a meeting ground of the mystical traditions of East and West. His advice on how to come to the inner sanctuary? "Meditation is the secret."[61]

A variety of disciplined techniques, tried and tested around the world through the millenia, allow us to reach what Huston Smith calls "the sacred unconscious," a state that unites us with a higher and deeper wisdom. I use the composite "higher/deeper" because this state is a paradoxical one. In it you go deeper into yourself and yet are lifted out into unity with the transcendent. This should not surprise us if we remember both that consciousness is universal and that our substance has been in existence, in one form or another, since creation. In our individual bodies and spirits there exists the wisdom of humanity and the universe at large—but we must pause and listen.

> Free from desire, you realize the mystery.
> Caught in desire, you see only the manifestations.
>
> Yet mystery and manifestations
> arise from the same source.
> This source is called darkness.
>
> Darkness within darkness.
> The gateway to all understanding.
>
> Tao Te Ching

A second paradox is that in this silent, wordless darkness the forms, words, and tasks of everyday life are illuminated. It is a creative state in which intuition and imagery are enhanced. Even those who do not meditate may have had the comparable experience of an answer to a vexing problem suddenly coming to them "from nowhere" while they were "thinking of nothing in particular," or insights coming equally "unbidden" in dreams or daydreams.

The history of science provides many famous examples of this kind. Albert Einstein describes being given the basic principles of his theory of relativity through kinesthetic sensations in his limbs while riding on a streetcar. Nikola Tesla constructed the electric generator after its complete design and a fully functioning prototype appeared to him in a vision. Werner Heisenberg found the mathematical solution for the uncertainty principle while in an altered state of consciousness induced by severe hay fever. The design for the crucial experiment leading to the Nobel Prize–winning discovery of the chemical transmission of neuronal impulses occurred to the psychologist Otto Loewi during sleep. Similarly, while sleeping, Flemish chemist Friedrich August von Kekule was given the answer to a problem of molecular structure with which he had been wrestling. The benzene rings revealed to him in his

1865 dream were seen by others only in 1988, with the aid of newly developed scanning tunnel microscopes.

It is significant that the form in which von Kekule saw the rings was the ancient Greek symbol of the Uroboros, a snake swallowing its own tail. In psychologist Carl Jung's terminology, this is an archetypical symbol carrying condensed information from the collective unconscious. The existence of these universal archetypes, which surface frequently in dreams, meditations, and altered states of consciousness, explains the emotive power, transcending cultural boundaries, of myths and fairy tales, poetry, music, dance, sculpture, painting.

It was for this reason early in the chapter that I said we live in myth and symbol and cautioned that we be mindful of our imagery. Whether we label what we do "science" or "art," the symbolic representations of our codes will have power reaching far beyond their rational content. "Words run gently into the unsayable," as the German poet Rainer Maria Rilke told us.

The Jungian theory of the power of archetypes in the human psyche is reinforced and extended by Sheldrake's understanding that fields of consciousness embrace all manifest systems to sustain habitual form, and by the revelation from the chaos theorists that "over and over again, the world displays a regular irregularity." They call it "the power of self-similarity."[62]

We may speculate that it is the reflection of these physical archetypal forms, resonating with the patterning in our own cellular structure, that lends such psychic force to the geometrical designs of mandalas—ancient objects of meditation for Hindus and Tibetan Buddhists that were adapted for contemplation in medieval Christianity. Other ancient expressions of universal patterning are the elaborate interlaced designs on Celtic crosses, a pre-Christian survival, and the representations of radiating fields of inner energy that characterize Aboriginal Australian art.

> *The centre is still and silent in the heart of*
> *an eternal dance of circles.*
>
> Rabindranath Tagore

To understand the dance of circles, our holistic scientists must go in silence to the still center.

An Intentional but Mysterious Universe

There is good news from the life sciences. Contrary to the Darwinian representation of nature as driven by competitive aggression, there is mounting evidence that the biosphere is a symbiotic, altruistic, self-sustaining system. Our holistic scientists can affirm with Martin Buber that "love is a cosmic force." This is a purposeful, intentional universe dedicated to the generation and nurturance of life.

For more than a hundred years the major stumbling block to this claim of intentionality has been Darwin's hypothesis of random natural selection as the governing mechanism of evolution. The theory, which has been the reigning orthodoxy, holds that useful organic variations appear by chance, not design, and predominate only if they pass the acid test of competitive reproductive advantage. This is a good thesis to explain some developments, but it is insufficient to serve as the exclusive explanation of evolution, or so accumulated evidence now suggests to many working in diverse areas of biology and paleontology. Lewis Thomas muses:

> It makes an interesting problem: how do mechanisms that seem to be governed entirely by chance and randomness bring into existence new species which fit so neatly and precisely, and usefully, as though they were the cells of an organism?[63]

What's more, chaos theory points up a flaw in the logic on which the Darwinian hypothesis rests: The existence of random data ("chance" organic variations) cannot be held to prove that the underlying process (evolution) is random.

This is an intentional universe, but it is also mysterious—a universe that runs on paradox. Its purpose is life; its mechanism is death. We all live in order to serve as prey for each other. Everything passes away, but nothing is lost. It is a universe of purpose, but its ends are not determined and its intentions do not bind us. As again Martin Buber explains, the old dilemma of "fate" or "freedom" is an illusory dualism.

> Fate and freedom are promised to each other. Fate is encountered only by him that actualizes freedom. . . . this free human encounters fate as the counter-image of his freedom. . . . He believes in destiny and also that it needs him. It does not lead him, it waits for him. He must go forth with his whole being: that he knows. It

will not turn out the way his resolve intended it; but what he wants to come will come only if he resolves to do that which he can will.[64]

A scientific equivalent? Chaos theory: "The system is deterministic, but you can't say what it's going to do next." The words are those of American physicist Doyne Farmer. "On a philosophical level, it struck me as an operational way to define free will, in a way that allowed you to reconcile free will with determinism."[65]

An artistic equivalent? My wife, Jo, is a fabric artist. She began a mandala, embroidering in silk around the perimeter of the circle and working her way inward with complex, multicolored stiching. She had no distinct design in mind. "I knew it would mirror my inner state, and I wanted it to shape itself." What emerged unbidden was a beautiful rose at the center of a tightly integrated figure. Did she draw the pattern, or did the pattern draw her toward it? Did she create it, or was it already existent in consciousness?

Similarly, California artist Susan Seddon Boulet tells us that many of her exquisite and powerful shamanic images were painted before she studied shamanism and fully understood their significance. "My learning came after the images."

"The fairest thing we can experience is the mysterious. It is the fundamental emotion which stands at the cradle of true art and true science," said Albert Einstein.[66] Being truly creative, our holistic scientists will honor the unknowable, recognize the permanence and sacredness of mystery, and allow themselves to be guided by its intention.

The Tao is always at ease.

It overcomes without competing,

answers without speaking a word,

arrives without being summoned,

accomplishes without a plan.

Its net covers the whole universe.

And though its meshes are wide,

it doesn't let a thing slip through.

Tao Te Ching

Spirit in All Things

This section and the next will be brief, for like the first, "A New Understanding of Time," they will have a chapter all to themselves.

> The eternal dancer dances
> in the flower of spring,
> in the harvest in autumn,
> in thy limbs my child,
> in thy thoughts and dreams.
>
> Rabindranath Tagore

Every thing—and the void as well—is imbued with spirit. We live in a sacred universe in which divine power infuses space, earth, water, air, all creatures, and our own being. The breath that gives life is the breath of spirit.

In a sacred universe there must be sacred limits. In this I observe a fundamental, and potentially fatal, difference between classical science and other metaphysical systems. However powerful those systems may be, all have sacred areas that are off limits to humans. For instance, an Aboriginal Australian must never kill his or her totemic animal, nor show to the uninitiated the *Tjuringa,* the sacred plaque recording the Ancestor's Songline. In Nepal, before the advent of the foreign climbing expeditions, the Sherpas and other high mountain peoples would never go to the great summits, for these are the abodes of the gods and goddesses. To preserve at least a fragment of this sacred space, the government of Nepal has declared the exquisite pinnacle of 24,000-foot Machapuchare forever off limits to mountaineers.

By contrast, nothing has been sacrosanct for classical science; there has been no stopping place, no limit. Many readers will be familiar with the story of Enrico Fermi's team of physicists experimenting with nuclear fission under the University of Chicago stadium in 1942. Though uncertain that their first sustained neutron chain reaction would stop, they felt compelled to proceed, willy-nilly, in the interests of scientific knowledge. If things had not gone as they did, the planet might not be here now. Albert Einstein's admonition seems apt: "All means prove but a blunt instrument if they have not behind them a living spirit."[67]

Our holistic science will lay aside the driven symbol of the straight line and adopt once more the ancient symbol of the circle. It represents harmony, moderation, balance—optimization rather than maximization.

> *We are a circle within a circle, with no beginning and never ending.*
>
> Wiccan chant

Restoring Harmony with Nature

A central task of our holistic science is to restore a more modest sense of the relative place in nature of the human species. Humans are no more and no less important than any other life form or inorganic system. All are filled with consciousness and spirit.

For centuries the "high civilizations" have manufactured religions, philosophies, and sciences that inflate the importance of the human—or, more strictly speaking, of men. Here I reluctantly part company with many whose ideas otherwise have my sympathy—thinkers such as Sri Aurobindo, Teilhard de Chardin, and Ken Wilber, who argue that the human species has a superior role in evolution. I agree rather with Stephen Jay Gould that "humans are just a little twig on a gigantic bush of evolution . . . not a terminal direction."[68] It is my belief that our role is unique but not superior.

In 1980, when I was in Canberra, Australia, an Aboriginal leader visiting from Arnhem Land in the tropical northern bush stood on the back porch of a friend's tract house and looked sadly out at the clapboard garages, paling fences, and telephone poles. "This land has lost its Song," he said. In a similar vein, Annie Dillard observes that "nature's silence is its one remark," and this she attributes to the fact that "we as a people have moved from pantheism to pan-atheism."

> God used to rage at the Israelites for frequenting sacred groves. I wish I could find one. . . . We have drained the light from the boughs in the sacred grove and snuffed it in the high places and along the banks of sacred streams. . . . Silence is not our heritage but our destiny; we live where we want to live. . . . It is difficult to undo our own damage, and to recall to our presence that which we

have asked to leave. It is hard to desecrate a grove and change your mind.[69]

Acknowledging the error of our claim to superiority, in all humility we should now ask our spirit companions of nature to return and assist us, in the light of day, to restore the mighty legend of the green Earth.

Listen.

This living flowing land
is all there is, forever

We are it
it sings through us—[70]

Gary Snyder

4

ALL THAT EXISTS LIVES

All that exists lives. The lamp walks around.
The walls of the house have voices of their own.

Chukchi shaman, Siberia, 1900

The Assault on the Trees

It is an irony that classical science, which had as its original purpose the enhancement of human knowledge of nature, became alienated from the living world. From its beginnings it turned its back on the ancient understanding of the cosmos as organism, preferring a human creation, the machine, as its conceptual model.

Therein lies the tragedy: In the modern West we have had the hubris to declare that humans, uniquely possessed of reflective awareness, are superior beings and that mechanistic nature exists for our benefit. Thus, the objective of the "natural sciences" became the domination of natural *objects,* or as that great Victorian admirer of technoscience, Karl Marx, put it, "the subjection of Nature's forces to man."[1]

My father, born at the other end of the Victorian era from Marx and on the opposite side of the globe, recalled that when he was growing up in New Zealand early in this century "the bush was the enemy." "Clearing" the native forest with axe and fire was synonymous with progress.

The assault on the trees continues. In the year and a half before Jo and I left our California home for India, we steadfastly resisted attempts to hack down trees along the road frontage of our property. Our house was on a steep hillside in the Marin outer suburb of Fairfax, especially dear to us for its heavily wooded terrain. Trees, however, are a bane to the linesmen of Pacific Gas and Electric Company, and periodically PG&E contracts with "tree maintenance" companies to go street by street cutting them back or, in some cases, removing them entirely. Fortunately, they require permission of property owners before laying chain saw to limb.

We declined to give this permission for many months until we could arrange a day on which we could be present to supervise the surgery. We talked with the trees to explain, as best we could, what was happening and why and then negotiated with the chain saw men, branch by painful branch, to ensure that the bare minimum was removed.

One of our joys in leaving for our lengthy sabbatical in India was the knowledge we would be among forested mountains, and that joy was realized when we moved into our house in the village of Naggar, amid cherry and fir trees on the lower edge of a vast conifer forest stretching five thousand feet to the snow line. We immediately made a vow to our green relatives that we would direct our energies so they might prosper during our stay. We asked them in return to protect us and help us learn.

A few evenings after our arrival, Gangadhar Sharma, our new-found friend from the village, was drinking tea with us on our verandah and extolling the virtues of his forested Kullu Valley. For him the dry, bare lands of Lahul and Spiti, over the high passes on the Tibetan plateau to the north, lack the beauty only trees can give. We had read of the growing onslaught on the Himalayan forests as population pressure in India and Nepal drastically reduces fuel supplies, and we had already observed pack ponies filing off the mountain slopes at daybreak, laden with freshly cut, green wood. So we asked him with concern: "Aren't these precious forests being depleted?" "They were," he said, "but now they are protected." Trees all along the edge of the forest with lower limbs roughly hacked off seemed to say otherwise.

The next morning before breakfast, a neighbor and her two sons climbed the fence with sickles and set about cutting down two of the smaller trees along our path. Jo and I rushed out to protest. There was a considerable language barrier (our Kullu Deshi being as meager as their English) and an equally considerable conceptual barrier. In return for their "tidying up" the yard, the property manager had offered them the leaves as cattle feed and the limbs as firewood. They could not understand why we would say "no" to such a mutually advantageous deal. We could not explain that we love trees and personally experience pain when they are slashed, nor that we felt we were failing in our trust to protect and nurture them and the critters they harbor during our guardianship of the property. We stuck to our guns: Not one stick more was to be cut. They went away grumbling about irrational foreigners, and Jo spent the rest of the morning meditating among the trees, talking with them about our sadness.

As we became more familiar with the area we realized there was only one nearby tree, apart from those in the orchards, that was unscathed. It was a tall pine beneath which nestled a tiny wooden and stone shrine to Mata Devi, the Mother Goddess. This was sacred ground. The Mother gave protection to the tree, and the pine for its part opened its arms to an array of birds more varied and numerous than came to any of the other trees. The Earth needs more such sacred ground for all its living things.

This parable points to both our problem and its solution.

Four Assumptions and Two Precepts

Before proceeding, I want to spell out my working assumptions for this chapter, all of them flowing directly from the material already discussed in the book.

> The widespread perception of an ecological crisis is well founded.

Although the crisis is of global proportions, as the parable of the trees suggests, we in the West, as the progenitors of the mechanistic world view and disproportionate consumers of the Earth's "natural resources," are under a particular imperative to change our ways. Whether we like it or not, we cannot go on as we are. As Thomas Berry states bluntly:

"The industrial order at this scale of magnitude can be done once; it cannot be maintained; it can never be done again."[2]

Science cannot give all the answers.

Like every other explanatory system, science is partially mistaken. To put it another way, science gives only a partial view. Faced with a crisis that has its roots in science, we must open ourselves to other ways of knowing.

Through other ways of knowing we can reconnect with an older human wisdom.

For our ancestors and a majority of our non-Western contemporaries, this is a unified, spirit-filled cosmos in which, as Bruce Chatwin says of Aboriginal Australia, "the structures of kinship reach out to all living men, to all his fellow creatures, and to the rivers, the rocks and the trees."[3] It is a "self-contained, self-organizing organism," as Joseph Needham described the classical Chinese universe. "The harmonious cooperation of all beings arose . . . from the fact that they were all parts in a hierarchy of wholes forming a cosmic pattern, and what they obeyed were the internal dictates of their own natures."[4] This indivisible cosmos stands revealed again in the new sciences.

By acknowledging the living consciousness of the Earth we open ourselves to learning from our companions in nature.

There is deep wisdom in the rhythms of the Earth, and millions upon millions of years of varied experience of being is stored by our fellow creatures. By attuning ourselves again to their voices, we can become aware of the harmonious resonances that flow in our own bodies. We can know unity.

The earth and myself are of one mind. The measure of the land and the measure of our bodies are the same.

Chief Joseph of the Nez Perce

And where is the start to this mystical path? In the dirt, my friends. We must become like Tolkien's Farmer Maggot: "There's earth under his old feet, and clay on his fingers; wisdom in his bones, and both his eyes are open."[5]

There you have the four assumptions. Now for the two precepts.

First, we must, as best we can, unlearn the dualistic teaching of our European languages that sets "man" apart from "nature"—an inside (the human) separated from an outside (the "environment").

We should be aware that many cultures, ancient and modern, do not make this distinction. In Maori the word for the Earth and for the placenta are one and the same: *whenua*. After birth, as before, it is *whenua* that cradles and nourishes each living being. There is no separation: We are nature. Everything flows into everything else. Thoreau understood this principle: "Shall I not have intelligence with the earth? Am I not partly leaves and vegetable mould myself?"

Experiencing nature as myself, I become far more protective of it/myself. In *Arctic Dreams* Barry Lopez writes:

> For some people, what they are is not finished at the skin, but continues with the reach of the senses out into the land. If the land is summarily disfigured or reorganized, it causes them psychological pain. Again, such people are attached to the land as if by luminous fibers; and they live in a kind of time that is not of the moment but, in concert with memory, extensive, measured by a lifetime. To cut these fibers causes not only pain but a sense of dislocation.[6]

A hauntingly beautiful and sad National Geographic documentary film, *Australia's Twilight of the Dreamtime,* chronicles the threatened way of life of a Northern Territory Aboriginal people, the Gagudju of Kakadu. It concludes with an epitaph:

> During their long history, the Gagudju have built no great monuments, but they have lived for more than forty thousand years in total harmony with their environment. They have not destroyed any land nor diminished its spirit. That is their monument, and, in the long term, that may be the most important of all.[7]

Let this serve for us as a challenge to do as well.

Which brings us to the second precept: Everything we are given by the Earth must be held sacred. We enter this life under an implicit covenant: We will be provided for, body and soul, on condition that we nurture the body of our Mother Earth and honor the spirits of our brother and sister creatures. We must walk among them with love and deference.

The Gagudju have an elder, Nipper Kapirigi, whose task it is to patrol the waterholes along the Kakadu escarpment in order to sustain their Song. As he walks barefoot, spear in hand, he cries out to the spirits at each bend in the stream, announcing his approach and asking their permission to proceed.

Soon after daybreak one morning during our year in the Kullu Valley, I was hiking in the jungle about a mile from our house. Descending a steep, winding path, a man from the next village above ours passed me with a greeting and a short way ahead stopped at a giant sal tree. Giving *namaste* before this forest goddess, he bent and touched his head to the moss-covered ground at her roots. Then he continued down the mountain.

The Parable of the Otter

In his book *Strangers Devour the Land,* Boyce Richardson gives a dramatic account of an experience with spirit in nature in a radically different environment. The locale is subarctic northern Quebec, and the people involved are two of Richardson's friends, Cree hunters Isaiah Awashish and his seventeen-year-old son Willie. Isaiah, in his late fifties, has a hunting territory of a thousand square miles, with which he has an intimate familiarity born of a lifetime of survival from his skill in hunting its animals.

The winter freeze was imminent, and the two men, traveling in an outboard-motor–powered canoe, were checking traps far from their bush camp. Crossing a river above two sets of rapids, they had just stepped ashore on a small island when a rare miscommunication resulted in their losing hold of the canoe, which was swept away to the far bank. "They were stripped of all their equipment," writes Richardson. "They could not swim off the island because the waters in this part of the world are always too cold for swimming. No prudent man would plunge into a northern river in October."[8]

They did have knives and one bit of good luck. The island on which they were stranded had been burned over, leaving dry, solid trees. They set about building a raft, which took them all morning. When the job was finished, Isaiah told Willie he would go alone. They stood at the head of the rapids, the water racing past them. The father walked up to his son, shook his hand and began to sing. Willie later recounted what happened:

> I knew from this water that even if there were two of us in the canoe, paddling for all we were worth, we would be carried down almost to the next rapids. But the logs in our raft were really long: the current would have ten times as strong a grip on them as it would have on a canoe. And yet here was my father intending to go into the rapids alone, on this raft. He came up to me and he sang this song about the otter . . . .[9]

Isaiah was drawing on his *metew*, his powerful relationship with the hunting spirit forged through a lifetime of attunement to the animals. He gave the otter a promise he would not kill so many of its kind that year if it would help him out of the jam.

> He had just a small piece of stick, that's all he used for a paddle ... and he went straight across the river on the raft. The current didn't bother him at all, he went straight across the rapids. I should have had the sense to know that my father would know what to do to get out of that situation.[10]

Isaiah would talk little about this incident or others like it. He made it clear there were awesome powers to be respected. "If you are in a dangerous situation," he said, "you cannot just demand of the otter or some other animal that he get you out of it. You have to give something back. . . . You are offering . . . a piece of your hunting spirit."[11]

Nature's Silence or Nature's Voice?

Nature's silence is its one remark.

Annie Dillard

Humans talking with animals and nature spirits? Surely this is the stuff of fairy tale and legend? For the great majority of people, whose experimentation ended with disappointingly one-sided childhood conversations with a household pet, Annie Dillard's observation would seem to be both accurate and conclusive: Nature addressed does not reply.

Still, we are left with a puzzle. Stories of humans talking with animals and nature spirits are found in the mythology of every civilization. The anthropological record of contemporary indigenous cultures also abounds in accounts of communication with the natural world. Now we hear of people in our own society reporting dialogues with nature. Whatever has possessed all these people—our ancestors over hundreds of generations, as well as our contemporaries in cultures both exotic and familiar—to make such claims?

Given that the belief in the possibility of interspecies and spirit communication appears to have persisted throughout human history, it might be wise for us to consider the range of possible explanations. Here is my attempt at a list:

1. These people are lying.
2. They are deluded.
3. They are kidding.
4. They are dramatizing events or speaking symbolically.
5. They are in an altered state of consciousness, drug-induced or otherwise.
6. They are possessed of supernatural abilities.
7. They have learned the necessary skills.
8. They have this ability because their culture supports the belief in interspecies communication.
9. They are in a different relationship with animals and spirits, which encourages these beings "to get in touch."
10. In their construction of reality, they draw the lines of demarcation differently from ours. For example, perhaps

their category "human" incorporates or overlaps with the categories "animal" and "spirit" as we know them.

If this list were to be the basis of an opinion poll on the subject in present-day America, I would guess that explanations one through three would be heavily favored. Numbers four and five might do fairly well with college graduates, and six might gain a modicum of support if specific mention were made of Saint Francis of Assisi.

My own vote would be different. I would favor explanations four through ten. Although each of the first three items is useful in explaining some instances in the vast range of reported incidents of humans talking with other beings in nature, they do not necessarily provide a sufficient explanation of the phenomenon. Certainly every culture and generation have their share of the dishonest, deranged, stupid, and clownish. On the other hand, an extensive reading of history and anthropology, as well as many years of living in cultures radically different from the one in which I was born and raised, have persuaded me that humanity has long been possessed of great wisdom and that no one culture or civilization has ever had a corner on the truth.

When numerous people state in all sincerity that they have experienced something profound, I think it wise to listen. Willis Harman has a word of wisdom on the subject:

> Instead of starting with a limiting bias and having to defend against the anomalous, let us start with the assumption that any class of inner experiences that have been reported, or of phenomena that have been observed, down through the ages and across cultures, apparently in some sense exist and have a face validity that cannot be denied. The need then is for a science to accommodate all that exists.[12]

Guided by Willis' sage advice, let us explore these latter possibilities. I believe we have much to learn from these other ways of knowing.

Speaking Symbolically

In the oral traditions, literature, music, dance, visual arts, and religious ritual of every known culture—including the secularized West of the present day—humans engage in conversation and other forms of communication with animals and spirits. This is a timeless motif that speaks of a deep longing in the human soul for unity with the natural world from which we spring. Is this fantasy, or is it possibly the case that proves Joachim-Ernst Berendt's point that "language knows more than we know, and we can learn if we listen to it"?[13]

Fiction or otherwise, our sense of bonding with our fellow creatures is the affirmation of life itself. In the forlorn and recently emptied children's bunkhouse of a Nazi extermination camp at the end of the Second World War, Elisabeth Kubler-Ross found drawings of butterflies scratched by small fingers into the woodwork.

To the Iroquois, the other side of the world is inhabited by prophetic spirits who long ago taught humans the techniques of hunting, fishing, and farming. The people have obligations to these spirits. During the midwinter festival, for example, the Life God's power, weakened by the Winter God, must be renewed. Wearing braided husk masks, members of the Corn Husk Society perform rituals to bring back the Three Sisters: corn, beans, and squash.

Symbolic statement, dramatization, and ritual can serve as a powerful first step for those of us who have grown up in secularized urban cultures, far removed from any sense of sacred nature. Joanna Macy, my friend and former faculty colleague at the California Institute of Integral Studies, periodically convenes a "Council of All Beings" in a park or in the countryside. Following guided meditation and rituals, each of the people present asks a particular animal, other organism, or feature of the natural landscape for permission to enter into its consciousness. Through the "eyes" of this chosen being, each person contemplates what is happening on Earth and, in turn, speaks of the insights gained, advising humans in particular on what must happen to bring healing to this living planet.

The illumination and transformation of understanding that can come from such an empathetic engagement with a form in nature is described by Martin Buber in his early book *Daniel:*

> I walked on the road one dim morning, saw a piece of mica lying there, picked it up and looked at it for a long time. The day was no longer dim: so much light was caught by the stone. And suddenly,

as I looked away, I realized that while looking at it I had known nothing of "object" and "subject"; as I looked, the piece of mica and "I" had been one; as I looked, I had tasted unity. . . . Then something flamed up inside of me as if I was about to create. I closed my eyes, I concentrated my strength, I entered into an association with my object, I raised the piece of mica into the realm of that which has being.[14]

Buber is describing an altered state, an experience familiar to many members of the psychedelic generation. Later in this chapter I shall discuss shamanic and other techniques for inducing altered states of consciousness that can provide this powerfully transformative sense of oneness.

The Totem

"To stand within the presence of the earth," as the philosopher William Barrett puts it,[15] was the common condition of humans for all but the last few generations. They did not require an altered state to experience the kinship of all nature. Recall the last three items in the list of possibilities given earlier:

They have this ability because their culture supports the belief in interspecies communication.

They are in a different relationship with animals and spirits which encourages these beings "to get in touch."

In their construction of reality they draw the lines of demarcation differently from ours, e.g., perhaps their category "human" incorporates or overlaps with the categories "animal" and "spirit," as we know them.

These three belong together because they are all found in cultures that have a unitive construction of reality, i.e., that do not separate humans from nature.

In the Beginning, New Zealand Maori tell us, the Mother, Papa, and the Father, Rangi, lay together in each other's arms shutting out all light. Bored with this dull situation, their children pushed them apart, and since that time Rangi and Papa, Sky and Earth, have lived in separation.

Then their three sons started to squabble. The angriest was Tawhirimatea, the elements, who remained loyal to Father Sky. To this day he periodically assails both his powerful brother, Tane, the forest, and his less powerful brother, Tangaroa, who took refuge from the conflict as the ocean. The two sons of Mother Earth have children of their own: Tangaroa, the fish, marine mammals, and *taniwha* (sea dragons), and Tane, the land creatures, including Tu, humans. The birds also are said to be children of Tane, but their role is enigmatic, for it is they who are the spirit messengers between ancestral Sky and Earth.

Everything, animate and inanimate, thus has a common ancestry, and the *whakapapa*, the genealogy that traces this universal kinship, explains how each form in nature acquired its *tikanga*, its particular and characteristic behavior. This includes human behavior, both human nature and human custom, which are seen simply as pieces in the all-embracing, interlocking pattern of existence.

The *whakapapa* also recounts the great voyages from the ancient homeland, *Hawaiiki*, of the canoes that brought humans, animals, and some of the reptiles, birds, and plants to *Aotearoa* (New Zealand). It maps the landforms into which the boats and voyaging heroes and heroines were transformed. These in turn mark out the ancestral lands of the tribes descended from each canoe, as well as providing points of reference for departure by spirits of the dead on the long journey home to *Hawaiiki*.

It will be observed there is no separation between human history and natural history. Although there is a word in Maori for ritual and incantation, *karakia*, the language has no need to distinguish "religion" from "science." As in other totemic cultures, Maori cosmology weaves all of existence, human and nonhuman, past and present, life and afterlife, into one story that has tangible form, being embodied in the very ground, water, and air. Naturally, these are recognized as *tapu*, sacred.

New Zealand ecologist Geoff Park writes:

> Before contact with the missionaries of the nineteenth century, Maori believed their physical health and wellbeing were achieved in two principal ways. One was by maintaining the mauri of their

places—the life force by which their natural elements cohere. The other was by lifelong observance of the laws of tapu. Rites and rituals broke down the barriers between people and other species, allowed people to flow spiritually into nature and for nature's rhythms to permeate their own being. A host of daily tasks depended on conscious connection, both to benefit nature and limit human excesses.[16]

In totemic cultures the power to work magic is derived from subtle attunement to the spiritual essence of natural forms. Each people has a rich lore prescribing the means by which the strengths of different forms—animals, birds, insects, trees, crabs, tides, winds, moon, etc.—can be invoked to assist humans. Thus *karakia*—Maori incantation—traditionally was accompanied by the use of charms composed of such things as leaves, feathers, bone, abalone shell, *pounamu* (New Zealand jade), or carved wood.

You may recall the discussion in the introduction of guardian spirits in the form of sea creatures summoned by the Polynesians in times of peril on the great ocean voyages, just as the Cree hunter Isaiah Awashish, stranded on the river in northern Quebec, called on the otter for aid. As Awashish emphasized, these are no casual requests. To be heard, the supplicant has to have a deep and long-established spiritual relationship with the totem, and in return for help there must be a reciprocal gift. For everything asked and taken on this Earth, something must be given back. "We live," as Martin Buber said, "in the currents of universal reciprocity."

The wild animal or other nature spirit is an equal partner in establishing the process, and there are times when animals will call on humans to render aid. Jim Nollman in his book *Animal Dreaming* gives accounts of several such contemporary incidents on the coast of British Columbia involving orcas (the so-called killer whales).

He recounts an old Makah Indian story about fishermen who were out in their longboats one day when a strange orca with two dorsal fins appeared in their midst. Hurling a ballast stone, one of them wounded the animal over its blowhole. The orca swam to shore, where it beached itself, but when the fishermen paddled in to examine it more closely, instead of an orca they met a man who implored them to repair his damaged boat. This they did. The stranger, thanking them, launched his boat, but as the fishermen watched him paddle out, the boat entered a large wave and vanished, to be replaced by two large dorsal fins. The orca blew and was gone. Nollman comments:

> This story depicts a situation that is common to American Indian mythology: that animals possess a power to control the way that humans perceive them. The orca had metamorphosed into a man with a broken boat, because that was the only way a fisherman would be able to recognize a being in distress.[17]

I have a parallel story of insects seeking assistance, which also involves "shape shifting," in this case from enemy to friend. One summer during the California drought of the mid-eighties, Jo and I were camped high on Mt. Shasta. Every time we prepared a meal, yellow jackets would buzz agitatedly around us. Jo, who had been stung on two separate occasions the previous autumn, was determined to overcome her fear of these wasps, so she tried to tune in to what they wanted. She realized they were in dire need of liquid, as everything on the mountain was parched. As soon as she set out a shallow pan of water, the yellow jackets calmed down and drank thirstily. Sugar added to the water was a big hit. For the rest of our time in camp, we had a steady parade of contented drinkers.

On returning home, Jo committed herself to continued support for the wasps. The sugar-water station she set up on our verandah attracted hundreds of daily drinkers, and Jo was a sight to behold when she replenished supplies. She was the center of a buzzing cloud, her hands and bare arms covered with appreciative "yellow friends," as she now called them. Over-eager imbibers would occasionally fall into the sugar mix, and Jo or I would pluck them out with a finger and settle them carefully on the railing to dry their wings. Never once were we stung.

After a while we noticed that messengers were coming to Jo to tell her when the sugar water had run out. If she was in the house, the messenger would buzz outside the window nearest to her. If she was in the yard, it would fly persistently just in front of her nose. It was to Jo they came, not to me. Sometimes on walks through the nearby woods she would be accosted by a "yellow friend" telling her fresh supplies were needed. This could be a mile or more from home, but whenever it happened, the pan was indeed empty. Such rapport was established that it felt as though Jo and the wasps had a shared consciousness. It was as though she had entered their morphic field—taken on "yellow-jacketness," as she describes it.

Again we are reminded that awareness exists throughout nature, and that humans, though endowed with special abilities, are not superior in power of mind to their living companions. Recognition of this fact makes people in totemic cultures ever alert to the messengers sent by the Great Spirit: the owl that hoots three times at dusk, the lizard on the doorstep, the rainbow over the sacred mountain. Dreams are of special portent, and humans must pay them heed. Sometimes they are ominous, for although this is a balanced and harmonious cosmos, it is not entirely benign. Even doomful warnings can be empowering, as Isaiah Awashish explains: "If you dream that you will be sick, you can prepare for that, you can prepare by offering something to the sickness. . . . If you do not dream about it, and you get sick, then that is the end of you."[18]

The life of the great Maori leader Te Puea Herangi offers many examples of the power of dreams, none more dramatic than the one that saved her life in 1936. Te Puea, then in her early fifties, was seriously ill with heart disease and TB. X-rays revealed enormous cavities in one lung and infection in the other. Doctors and friends believed she was dying, and Te Puea herself began preparing her own *tangi* (funeral ritual). On the night of July 26 she fell into an apparent coma from which her doctor could not wake her. She suddenly came to after four hours, and the doctor was astounded to find her heart and lungs immensely improved. Within a week her strength was restored, and subsequent x-rays showed that the TB was completely dormant.

Te Puea was in no doubt about the cause of her miraculous recovery. As she slept, her dead mother and uncle, the former Maori King Mahuta, had come to tell her she was not ready to die. They had shared their spiritual strength with her so she could resume her efforts to restore the economic well-being and *mana* (spiritual power and prestige) of her people. Te Puea lived another sixteen years and achieved many of her visionary goals.[19]

One claim often advanced for the superiority of scientific culture is that our rational understanding of natural laws has liberated us from the fearful superstitions of our "primitive" ancestors. Theirs, it is sometimes said, was a world of mysterious and malign forces beyond human comprehension and control, with demons great and small waiting around every bend in the forest path.

Certainly we should not romanticize the life of indigenous peoples, who often suffer great hardships and have their full share of fears about the forces of nature. But equally we should not underestimate the sense of security provided by the presence of ancestral and other guardian spirits, nor the empowerment derived from a spiritual communion with nature. "No one is ever alone, unseen, or unheard."[20] This, reports Richard Nelson, is the teaching of the Koyukon hunters of Alaska. He continues:

> A covenant of mutual regard and responsibility binds me together with the forest. We share in a common nurturing. Each of us serves as an amulet to protect the other from inordinate harm. I am never alone in this wild forest, this forest of elders, this forest of eyes.[21]

The Paths of Return

Is there a way back to a place where we can again hear nature's voices? There are many such paths.

The first is silence. Perhaps "stillness" is the better word. The clamor of an overstimulated urban consciousness too often gets in our way in the wilderness. Animals and other nature spirits choose their own time and form in which to reveal themselves to us, and our eager intent to contact them can be a barrier.

"Learning to stalk muskrats took me several years," writes Annie Dillard in *Pilgrim at Tinker Creek*. The trick, she found, is to lose self-awareness, to become one with stream, earth, and air. "I am the skin of water the wind plays over; I am petal, feather, stone." Of one particularly close and prolonged encounter she writes that the muskrat "never knew I was there."

I never knew I was there, either. For that forty minutes last night I was as purely sensitive and mute as a photographic plate; I received impressions, but I did not print out captions. My own self-awareness had disappeared. . . . I have often noticed that even a few minutes of this self-forgetfulness is tremendously invigorating. I wonder if we do not waste most of our energy just by spending every waking minute saying hello to ourselves. Martin Buber quotes an old Hasid master who said: "When you walk across the fields with your mind pure and holy, then from all the stones, and all growing things, and all animals, the sparks of their soul come out and cling to you, and then they are purified and become a holy fire in you."[22]

One year, Jo and I camped for ten days beside a small lake well off the beaten track in Mt. Lassen Volcanic National Park. In the first few days, we were disappointed by the absence of animals, despite tracks indicating that the lake was normally a source of drinking water. As we became more settled, we realized how "hyper" our energy had been when we arrived from the city—"the tense hum of consciousness," Annie Dillard calls it. It was the animals and birds who let us know when we had become calmer. By midweek the place was swarming with smaller critters—chickarees, golden-mantled ground squirrels, chipmunks, and gophers. The chipmunks were soon rummaging through our tent and packs in search of nuts and cereal, and the gophers grew so chummy that they were burrowing out at our feet to beg food, taking it from our fingers.

The larger animals returned to drink at the lake: deer throughout the day, racoons and foxes under cover of dark. Also at night we were serenaded by a pack of coyotes. Increasing numbers of birds visited our campsite, and the appearance of a Cooper's hawk gave us a lesson in the squirrels' alarm system, their high-pitched signals emptying the neighborhood in no time flat. We were also visited by an owl, reminding us of a miraculous gift we had received a few summers earlier while camping high in the Colorado Rockies: As the sun rose on two successive mornings, the great horned owl Bubo had flown to a perch above our campsite to spend the daylight hours with us.

The Lassen expedition also had its special gift. Shortly before leaving on the trip I had been reading a biography of Saint Francis of Assisi, whose author to my surprise had dismissed as unscientific nonsense the celebrated story of birds settling on Francis at the end of his week-long mountain vigil and fast. Certain that this was possible, I asked in meditation that I might have a comparable experience.

One morning as we sat by the lake, something I first thought was a large insect landed on one of my red socks. With delight I realized it was a hummingbird. This tiny, rainbow-hued creature flew onto my knee and sat looking up at me for a moment before going to Jo. It pulled at her hair, sat on the bridge of her glasses, and finally settled in her lap on the palm of her hand, looking directly into her eyes. How long it stayed, we have no idea. The time was so precious that we lost all sense of duration. We felt we had been kissed by the Great Spirit.

With stillness comes the power to see. This is beautifully described by William Barrett:

> Rocks and trees. I have grown to know them particularly this winter; they have accompanied me on my walks, or rather I have learned to enter into their company. . . . Oak, maple, ash, chestnut, beech—these are now without their telltale leaves, and I have had to learn to read them by their barks, each as individual as fingerprints. With some I have come to know the particular curves and twists of their branches like the individual features of friends.
>
> The rocks are no less individuals. Whoever thinks matter is mere inert stuff has not looked long at rocks. They do not lie inert, they thrust forward, or crouch back in quiet self-gathered power. Like a cat sitting so still that his tail has ceased twitching. . . . In the gray light of winter they come alive in their color too— smoke-gray or blue-gray, molded and subtle in their shading that shifts as the gray light shifts. The living rock! More than an idle phrase. Out of the living rock the waters of spirit.[23]

Barrett is quoted at length because he has a special message for urban folk. As he explains, his intense experience of nature is "in no remote wilderness," just a strip of woods along the Hudson River where he can walk alone.

> Usually it takes a mile to begin to be free. The important thing is to find freedom in the movement of your body first, let the mind

be what it will. By the second mile I am set free in the body, the havoc of the mind and the idiocy of its ideas recede. I am no longer homeless. I am there. . . .

I can understand why earlier mankind could worship trees. Perhaps I already do so myself. My ancestors were Druids, after all, and perhaps I am only rounding out the cycle by returning to their fold . . . . Nature worship! Mysticism! . . . Here among my rocks and trees I have passed beyond the need of such labels. . . . We forget that what we call mysticism was once a natural condition of mankind, and could be again if we let ourselves enter it. The mysticism that matters is one that has no need of the word.[24]

Silence and the gift of sight. The gift of hearing too. Satish Kumar writes of a foot pilgrimage through Britain:

The first sound of Scotland was the sweet song of the cuckoo, captivating and engaging. . . . Every day, over and over again, we heard the cuckoo serenading us. As we went along and focused on its tune we could distinguish the differing voices of individual cuckoos. It was a surprise to me as I had thought that all cuckoos sing with the same voice but then perhaps cuckoos think the same of human beings.[25]

Music is another path of return. It is significant that we commonly use the phrase "attunement to nature," but few of us, I imagine, give even a passing thought to the implications. "Attune: bring into musical accord," says the *Oxford English Dictionary*. If we recall that according to Sheldrake's hypothesis of formative causation, morphic fields are vibrational with resonances carrying the information that shapes organic and other natural forms, it should not surprise us that rhythm is universally used by shamanic peoples to contact the nature spirits.

In *Songlines*, Bruce Chatwin records the following comment from central Australia by an Aboriginal land-rights worker:

Sometimes, I'll be driving my "old men" through the desert, and we'll come to a ridge of sandhills, and suddenly they'll all start singing. "What are you mob singing?" I'll ask, and they'll say, "Singing up the country, boss. Makes the country come up quicker." Aboriginals could not believe the country existed until they could see and sing it—just as in the Dreamtime, the country had not existed until the Ancestor sang it. . . . In Aboriginal belief, an unsung land is a dead land: since, if the songs are forgotten, the land itself will die.[26]

In Maori oral tradition are preserved chants used by the ancestors hundreds of years ago to summon guardian spirits during the voyages to New Zealand from *Hawaiiki,* and instruction in similar sacred chants is still given to aspiring navigators in other parts of Polynesia and Micronesia. It was in song, we may recall, that Isaiah Awashish called upon the otter in his hour of need. In less perilous times he has his drum. "The hunter talks to his drum," says Isaiah, "and the drum decides what is possible and what is right. The drum is like a person, you can talk to it and it will reply. . . . The hunter secures his relationship with the land through his drum.[27]

When Jo and I lived in our Himalayan village, the most ancient of the temples, the shrine to the Mother Goddess, was being rebuilt because of a cracked foundation. Each daybreak and dusk, the goddess was saluted with drumming, and every stage of construction was marked with ritual music on drums and long, ornamented mountain horns that sounded like stags roaring across the ridges.

In the autumn for the festival week of Dussehra, the goddess herself is carried twenty miles to Kullu town, famed throughout India for its dances honoring the assembled gods and goddesses of the valley. They are a reminder that dance is one of the most powerful and ancient means of reconnection with the sacred rhythms of the cosmos. In the paintings of upper paleolithic European caves of 16,000 B.C.E., and the even older cave art of Aboriginal Arnhem Land alike, can be found the image of the dancing sorcerer. Spirit dances abound in the ritual traditions of Native Americans, just as the dancing forms of Krishna, Shiva, the elephant god Ganesha, and Shakti, the Mother Goddess appear in the folk cults of Hinduism. In the south Indian language Tamil, the word for *shaman* is *camiyati,* "God-dancer."

In some cultures, dance is essential to the maintenance of the Earth's fecundity. In traditional Hawaii the New Year was sacred to the god Lono, returning to renew the fertility of the land. This was the season for hula, intended to arouse sexually this deity of cosmic reproduction. The eroticism that made hula so offensive to Christian missionaries was considered by Hawaiians to be the very essence of the dance's spiritual power.

Music and dance are used by individuals and groups in several countries of the contemporary Western world in an effort to reconnect with nature. In music, the work of Paul Winter with wolves and sea mammals is perhaps best known. Another American musician working in this field, Jim Nollman, gives accounts of remarkable "jam sessions" with orcas and other sea and land animals.

In one instance, for three successive evenings he played an electric guitar through an underwater sound system, which also picked up the vocalizing of orcas attracted by the music. The first night's session lasted three hours, with the whales vocalizing constantly but not coordinating with Jim's harmonies and rhythms. On the second night one orca "sang" along with the guitar, while the rest of the pod "chose to stay in the background, jibber-jabbering among themselves in a quieter tone." On the third night the orcas as a group sang Jim's chords back to him with ornamentation. "Once," he writes, "I made an error in my repetition of one of the orca's phrases. The whale repeated the phrase back again— but this time at half the speed!" After breaking a guitar string, Jim had to change the key. The orcas followed suit. After an hour he began playing more complicated rhythms, with frequent shifts of key, and the orcas went right along with him. It was interspecies jazz.[28]

The Wiccans and other self-described modern pagans use songs, chants, and dances in their rituals that honor and draw strength from the natural elements. They point us to yet another path: attunement to the recurrent rhythms of the Earth.

Living as most of us do in the inflexible routines of the mechanized city, we have to make a conscious effort even to be aware of the solar and lunar cycles that are the immediate controlling forces in nature: the alternation of night and day, equinox and solstice, the waxing and waning of the moon, the ebb and flow of tides, menstruation, freeze and thaw, animal migration and hibernation, and the seasonal patterns of plant death and regeneration, with their changing palette of colors painting and repainting the landscape.

This in turn is a reminder of the visual arts as paths to reconnection:

painting, fabric art, sculpture, carving, pottery, basket weaving, etc. Through the eye and hand of the artist we feel the pulsing heartbeat of nature.

One of our artist friends, Leah Klapperich, gathers objects from the land—thistles, mica, driftwood, Spanish moss, seaweed, shells, lichen, acorns—and sculpts them into nature spirit masks so evocative that one shudders to find oneself transported back to the realm of the "little people." They remind me of a puckish face peering out from a wreath of leaves that Jo and I once discovered in the back corner of an old parish church in Kent, England. A notice explained that it was an ancient wooden boss found in the last century during a reconstruction of the church rafters—a relic of pre-Christian pantheism and a reminder of the primordial sacredness of the ground upon which the church was raised.

The celebration and invocation of spirit in nature is the universal motif of the art of primal peoples. To put it another way, what we identify as their "art" is a visual expression of their reverence for and spiritual kinship with the nature companions.

The Tlingit of the southeast Alaskan coast wear the tales of their totemic ancestors—bear, salmon, seal, whale, and bird—worked into the fabric of their brilliantly colored woolen ceremonial garments. The primacy of Grandfather Raven is acknowledged by the pride of place he is given on many of their hats. It was he who brought light into the world, and his continuing gift is *tlogwe*, connection with *Hashageinyaa*, the Great Spirit. As his grandchildren, the Tlingit repay the gift by insuring his immortality through their art, song, dance, and ritual. Thus he can sing, as they also sing to their grandchildren: "You are my inspiration and my encouragement to speak. You are my power to dream."[29]

Talking with the Devas

What are "nature's voices," and who can hear them?

Everyone, is my answer to the second question. If we will only be still, listen, and trust, we will hear. There are messages for every one of us, and as in other areas of our lives, their form and content vary from person to person. Our natural aptitudes in this field are as diverse as they are in music, mathematics, or foreign languages, but as in those other fields we are all capable with work of improving our skills.

What we first hear are the signals back and forth between the forms in nature themselves—the calls of the animals, birds, and insects; the varying patterns of movement; and the shifting colors and textures— about which Martin Buber, William Barrett, Satish Kumar, Annie Dillard, and others have been telling us. Attentiveness to this rich and complex web reveals the mind in nature, and as we attune to that mind we are ourselves subtly transformed in our way of being.

Then we are able to receive more direct messages. Recently a friend remarked: "I usually meditate and worship in my garden because when I'm inside, I hear the plants and trees calling to me." For many of us the messages from the nature spirits will come silently in ideas or images, which seem to form in our minds during our times of reverie and meditation in the outdoors. The more we open ourselves to these ideas and images, the stronger they become, particularly when we ask for answers to the questions they evoke. Speak to the nature spirits, and they will reply. They may surprise you by speaking out loud.

The West African shaman Malidoma Somé tells of his first encounter, while a very young child, with a spirit who spoke. He was out in the bush chasing a rabbit while his mother gathered firewood. Suddenly there was a tiny old man sitting between him and the rabbit. The old man asked Malidoma why he wanted to hurt his little brother, who had done him no harm. Malidoma was at a loss for words, and his bewilderment increased as the spirit stood up, told him to be friendly to rabbits in the future, and disappeared into a crack that opened in the Earth.[30]

The Australian farmer Michael Roads was equally amazed when he first heard nature's voices. He was an adult, and the spirit messages were answers to questions in his own mind. Although the voices were silent and disembodied, they were powerfully clear, and he was left in no doubt as to which river, tree, or animal was speaking to him.[31]

Every religious tradition has accounts of spirit voices heard by humans giving reassurance, warning, and guidance. Despite the fact that our own contemporary culture severely discourages any acknowledgement of disembodied voices, many people do hear them, as they will attest to any sympathetic inquirer. For some people the voices are a regular source of counsel, and there are those who have been thus guided into new ways of life.

One of the best-known modern examples of such guidance is the foundation of the Findhorn Community in northern Scotland. In 1963, Peter and Eileen Caddy and Dorothy Maclean, acting on the guidance Eileen received from what she called "the God within," towed a camping trailer onto a sandy plot next to a rubbish dump and began to grow vegetables to supplement their unemployment benefits. Their initial focus was on learning to cooperate with nature spirits, and the result was a garden so spectacular that it remains the attraction for which Findhorn is famous, despite its subsequent development into a spiritual community of three hundred members running educational programs for thousands of participants each year.

In developing the garden, the three Findhorn founders were guided by messages given to Dorothy Maclean by nature entities she identifies as angels or devas, the architects of the physical composition of organisms. In a manner consistent with Sheldrake's later hypothesis of formative causation, she discovered that each organic level—for example soil, plant, whole garden—has specialized nature spirits directed by a deva.

The devas were eager to contact and advise Dorothy. Their messages included practical directions on all aspects of gardening, from composting the soil, planting suitable crops at the right time and place, thinning, and pruning, to harvesting. In addition, they spoke with her about the nature of life itself, including the cocreative role of human consciousness. An example:

> We see life in terms of the inner force while you see only the outer form and cannot see the continual process taking place. We should like you to try to think in our terms, because it will make things easier for both of us—you will be closer to reality and will also be able to understand us better. . . .
>
> When you look at plants, know that what you see has an inner counterpart simply pulsating with the life you see and much more. As your mind becomes more familiar with this concept and you think of the plants as glowing and moving with life, you will in fact add to that life. By thought, you add to their force and at the same

time you draw upon the Source of all life, generating more and more power and more and more life.[32]

Similar experiences of receiving direct instruction from nature entities, at both the philosophical and practical levels, are reported by Machaelle Wright in developing Perelandra, a nature research center in Virginia. Wright's book *Behaving As If the God in All Life Mattered* recounts in detail how she was taught by devas to create an exceptional garden without the use of pesticides or herbicides.

Michael Roads also learned that he could protect his crops without violence against pests by striking bargains with them. In *Talking with Nature* he recounts how he dealt with wallabies (a species of small kangaroo) who were eating so much of the feed on one section of his farm that it would not economically support cattle. He had tried shooting and poisoning the animals, but this had proved both ineffective and deeply painful for him. In frustration he stood one evening in the middle of the affected land and shouted to the wallabies in the bush that they could have the first twenty yards of grass if they would leave the rest for the cattle. The deal was accepted: The wallabies restricted their eating to the edge of the fields, and he was able to increase his herd from thirty to ninety head. Sadly, when he later sold the farm, the new owners resumed shooting, and wallabies again overran the land.[33]

From Michael Roads and Machaelle Wright we get the same advice we were given by Cree hunter Isaiah Awashish: In calling for aid from our nature companions, we must be prepared to offer something in return for what we are given. It is for this reason, among others, that some land should be left untouched for use by the nature spirits. This includes small areas adjacent to our gardens that humans do not enter, such as are to be found at Findhorn and Perelandra, as well as much larger wilderness preserves. We should recall Emerson's words: "In wildness is the preservation of the world."

In communicating with nature spirits there are skills to be learned, as Jo and I discovered during our Himalayan year. We did have a good experience with a small swarm of wasps that were starting to build a hive on the ceiling of the little verandah of our village house. They were beautiful large orange and red wasps, gentle creatures with whom we had become familiar during our months in Naggar, but the prospect of having a hundred of them sharing our tiny sitting area made us uncomfortable. So we both meditated and, expressing our love for them, asked their deva if they would kindly move out under the eaves, a little way along the front of the house. Within twelve hours they had moved there to begin building a neat conical hive from which in ones and twos they visited us on the verandah.

I am embarrassed to admit that I took the added precaution against the swarm's return of smearing insect repellent on the vacated verandah ceiling! Doubts about my ability to communicate lingered, as things had not always gone as smoothly for us.

There is a spiritual adage about being careful what you ask for because you may get it. When we moved to Naggar, we put out a general welcome to the critters to join us. Our hope was that we would see gentle furry and feathered friends flocking from the wild to our wooded yard, which we intended to be a nature haven. What we learned (and had we paid closer attention to Machaelle Wright's advice we would not have had to learn it the hard way) was that when issuing an invitation, you should be specific about who is included. Along with some of the creatures we had hoped would come arrived most of the village's large pack of stray dogs, one of whom later presented us with a litter, and indoors an amazingly active menagerie of mice, rats, big spiders, centipedes, and a scorpion or two. Perhaps the intention was to give us practice in deva negotiation. Mostly through Jo's good work, a livable balance was ultimately restored, though not before the rats, in one amazing midnight rampage, chewed up a hundred pages of my book notes to build nests for their young!

I can add a more reassuring family story. Back in California, Jo became a student of the Basque teacher Angeles Arrien. During a weekend vision quest led by Angeles, Jo was looking for a campsite near the property boundary of a rancher about whose ill temper Angeles had cautioned the group. Uncertain exactly where the property line ran, Jo prayed for a sign. She reports the result in her journal:

> Instantaneously—and I do mean instantaneously—a raven, one of the four totem animals of our collective quest, landed about 100 yards farther on where the track curved up. It walked across the track four times, back and forth, back and forth, and then flew off. I thought, "That's where the property line is." And it was!

Nature spirits will also give practical help with routine chores. As we develop our New Zealand property as a nature reserve, one of my tasks is cutting hiking trails through the dense undergrowth of the rain forest. I have found that clearing the vines, scrub, and ferns is infinitely easier if I first explain to the plants what I am doing and ask for their cooperation. If I neglect to do this, it is far harder to remove the brush, and I get scratched much more often. Similarly, if I have a heavy rock to lift, I ask its help. I am amazed by how much lighter boulders can become when they are acknowledged as sentient beings.

To return to the question of the manner in which spirit in nature reveals itself: As will now be apparent, the forms are diverse, ranging from the subtlest of indications embedded in the natural processes around us to audible messages and visible appearances. Different people are approached in different ways, depending on their capabilities and their various understandings of spirit.

For some of us, it seems, lessons have to be delivered bluntly. Barry Lopez has an engaging story from a remote Alaskan village of a man hunting a wolverine from a snowmobile. Following the animal's tracks for miles, he finally saw it in the distance. Each time he crested a rise, there it was, just out of range on the next ridge, looking back at him.

> The hunter topped one more rise and met the wolverine bounding toward him. Before he could pull his rifle from its scabbard the wolverine flew across the engine cowl, hitting him square in the chest. The hunter scrambled his arms wildly, trying to get the wolverine out of his lap, and fell over as he did so. The wolverine jumped clear as the snow machine rolled over, and fixed the man with a stare. He had not bitten or even scratched the man. Then the wolverine walked away. The man thought of reaching for his gun, but no, he did not.[34]

Psychotherapist Jack Zimmerman tells a very different tooth and claw story. His kitten, Shadow, contracted feline leukemia, for which the veterinary prognosis is certain death. Jack, however, knows the power of love, and he and a friend cradled Shadow in their arms around the clock for forty-eight hours until she was healed. Shadow understood that she should repay this gift. Before her illness she had had no patience for being indoors, particularly when there were visitors in the house. Now she is attentive to her human companions, and without fail, when any of Jack's clients are distressed, she comes to the therapy room to sit with them and give them comfort.

A parallel case of love repaid is reported by Larry Dossey in *Healing Words*. A boy named Hugh Brady befriended an injured pigeon, nursed it back to health, and tagged it with the number 167 before setting it free. The next winter, Hugh was rushed for an emergency operation to a hospital two hundred miles from home. While in recovery, he heard a tapping at the window on a bitter snowy night. He asked a nurse to open the window, and in flew pigeon 167 to land right on his chest. How this winged spirit could have found his young friend in need is a complete mystery.[35]

Throughout the book I have been emphasizing that the external reality we perceive is not independent of our mental constructs. In this dynamic universe of interconnections, our concepts open channels for the flow of some messages and block the flow of others. In contacting us, the nature spirits use the wavelengths we make available to them. In other words, they can approach us only in ways we can comprehend.

Machaelle Wright says that nature spirits manifest to her as "swirling spheres of light energy" because she tends to see reality "in terms of energy rather than form." Not having read fairy tales in childhood, she is uncomfortable with the traditional concept of "the 'little people' of the woods." Nature spirits tell her, however, that they do sometimes appear to people as elves, fairies, gnomes, and the like because many of us have highly stylized mental pictures of the fairy world drawn from a long European tradition.[36]

From this perspective, we can understand why spirit manifests in different ways in different cultures and consequently why it is often difficult for one people to credit another people's reports of sightings. Immersion in another culture, however, sometimes allows us to tap into that field of consciousness, with the result that exotic images may appear to us.

Why do so few individuals in contemporary Western cultures hear or see nature spirits? An answer is suggested by Marion Zimmer Bradley in *The Mists of Avalon*, an imaginative retelling of the Arthurian legend. With the spread of Christianity in Britain, leading to neglect of the practice of nature worship and to the desecration of

Celtic sacred groves and springs, the mists shrouding Avalon thickened. This prevented all but the most stalwart believers from reaching this holy island where the sacred rites of the old faith were maintained. Lost in the mists of unbelief, Avalon became unreal, a figment of myth.

Thus, for most of us "the little people," so familiar to our ancestors, have become unreal, shut out behind our veil of unbelief. Our stylized thought forms, shaped by scientific rationalism, are such that nature spirits cannot reach us. Recall Annie Dillard's words:

> We have drained the light from the boughs in the sacred grove and snuffed it in the high places and along the banks of sacred streams. We as a people have moved from pantheism to pan-atheism. . . . It is difficult to undo our own damage, and to recall to our presence that which we have asked to leave. It is hard to desecrate a grove and change your mind.[37]

Hard but not impossible. We can open our minds and hearts again to spirit in nature. Remember: We are not alone. We can communicate with the consciousness of all the other life forms in this universe. Vision and reality are not separate. We can make the world we want. Dream back the bison. Sing back the swan.

The Rambler's Guarantee

I have a guide to the hiking trails of Marin, the hilly California county where we lived for a number of years. In one corner is printed this message:

> The publisher offers the following guarantee. If you're lost out in the woods somewhere, please note that my phone number is on the map. Just call me up. Good rambling! *Jerry Olmstead*

To those of us who are trying to find our way back to the woods, another offer of assistance is made by the nature spirits. They are waiting for our call, and there is no need for a telephone. If their guarantee seems to you as dubious as Jerry's, I urge you before yielding completely to skepticism to look for yourself at the testimony of Michael Roads,

Machaelle Wright, and the Findhorn people. I urge you also to explore the literature of the mystical traditions, which offers many accounts of spiritually enlightened men and women being visited while in meditation by animals, other nature entities, and spirit guides. Francis of Assisi has his counterparts in every religion and every period of human history.

One concern that legitimately might arise is the usefulness of a sage as a role model for the average person. Is it helpful to know that Cuthbert, a seventh-century saint of Lindisfarne, was escorted ashore by otters after his nightly meditations in the breakers; that Ramana Maharshi, the twentieth-century Indian sadhu, arbitrated disputes between bands of wild monkeys and was visited frequently by snakes and mongooses in his meditation cave; or that his Hindu contemporary, the female ascetic Anandamayi Ma, was called to the rescue by pomegranate plants crushed beneath a pile of bricks during repairs to a Benares temple? Number six in the earlier list of possibilities spoke of people possessed of supernatural abilities. Perhaps these are they? Undoubtedly these men and women were exceptionally spiritually evolved, but they were mere mortals. Even assuming superior natural aptitude, there is no reason to assume that the skills they perfected cannot in some measure be learned by all of us.

Every indigenous tradition recognizes the value of training in attunement to spirit in nature. Advanced instruction is reserved for those who are judged to be especially adept, but the capacity of everyone to learn how to hear and see the voices and other signals from nature is acknowledged in the education in these skills given to all children.

Closer to home, scientific research in a parallel field appears to offer supporting evidence. Over the past twenty years, researchers at SRI International and the Mobius Society in California, and at the Princeton Engineering Anomalies Research Laboratory (to cite just three places among several worldwide), have conducted carefully controlled experiments in distant viewing and extrasensory perception. The findings reveal that while certain people are more talented than others, all of us have the ability to visualize distant places and events and to read minds. The findings also show that practice enhances such abilities.

The personal experience of increasing numbers of Americans and Europeans with firewalking suggests that a shift of consciousness can bring the "supernatural" within the bounds of the normal. We are fortunate to live at a time when opportunities are becoming more readily available in Western countries to experience altered states of consciousness under the careful guidance of experienced group leaders. Good examples are the work of psychotherapists Stan and Christina Grof and of the anthropologist and neoshaman Michael Harner.

Building on Stan's earlier path-breaking research with psychedelic drugs, the Grofs have developed a technique they call holotropic breathing to induce powerful altered states. During their guided sessions, people commonly transcend the normal limits of time and space to gain visions of past or future and to enter into the consciousness of other beings, including animals, plants, natural elements, and the planet as a whole. The experience is almost invariably one of complete merging with another entity. Stan writes:

> The experiential identification with various animals can be extremely authentic and convincing. It includes the body image, specific physiological sensations, instinctual drives, unique perception of the environment and emotional reactions to it. These phenomena have certain unusual characteristics that distinguish them clearly from the ordinary human experience. Their nature and specific features often transcend the scope of human fantasy and imagination.[38]

He comments that experiences of plant consciousness

> often lead to profound new understanding of the [life] processes involved and are associated with fascinating philosophical and spiritual insights. The most common of these insights is the awareness of the special quality and purity of the existence of plants that make them important examples for human spiritual life. . . . They seem to represent pure being in the here and now in full contact with the immediate environment, which is the ideal of many mystical schools. . . . Sequences of this kind leave no doubt in the experiencer that the phenomena of life cannot be explained by mechanistic science, and that they prove the existence of creative cosmic intelligence.[39]

The Shaman

Some of the most powerful experiences recorded by the Grofs involve encounters with animal spirits, "perceived not only as divine in nature, but as teachers and friends offering help and spiritual guidance."[40] Those who have such meetings reveal a deep understanding of the function of sacred and totemic animals and their role as spirit helpers to shamans.

Shamanism, which is found worldwide, is the oldest known religion and healing system. There is archaelogical evidence of its practice twenty thousand years ago. The shaman is the healer of the whole person—body and soul—and of whole communities. He or she is a bridge for humans to the worlds of nature and spirit and as such is commonly held in awe and apprehension. Entry to the "profession" frequently involves a traumatic experience of death and rebirth—typically a near-fatal illness or (in the terminology of Western psychology) a psychotic break—as well as years of study with an older shaman.

Jeanne Achterberg, whose research is revealing the effectiveness of imagery as a healing tool to supplement biomedical practice, writes:

> The shamans' treasure trove of information is approached and applied in a special state, or "place," that permits interactions among the living and not living, the animals, and literally all the particles of the universe. Amazing cross-cultural agreement exists for this point, enough to shame our Western souls for not earlier attempting to glean information from this medical school of the millenia.[41]

The shaman has the ability to enter at will into an altered state of consciousness and to invoke the assistance of spirit helpers, most frequently in the form of animals. Shamans "journey" in the visionary realm—the Dreaming of Aboriginal Australians. One of my shamanic teachers, Sandra Ingerman, explains:

> When shamans enter nonordinary reality, the rules of the outer world are suspended. Horses fly, plants talk, fairies and leprechauns abound. Time as we know it is suspended. Shamans may, in ordinary time, spend half an hour journeying, but during that

journey they may watch the sun rise and set. Outer rules of space are equally voided in these nonordinary worlds. With the aid of a spirit helper, great distances can be crossed in a moment or two of outer time.[42]

To work their healing, shamans have techniques to take other individuals and groups of people with them on these "magical flights," where the unity and harmony of all things in Earth and sky can be directly experienced.

Both Achterberg and Ingerman acknowledge a debt to Michael Harner, through whose gentle and good-humored teaching they have gained direct experience of the shamanic journey. I have described Harner as a neoshaman because, for all his profound anthropological knowledge and experience of ancient lore, he has found ways to accommodate shamanism to contemporary Western cultural forms. By so doing, he has led many of us to a way of knowing that was lost to many generations of our European ancestors.

In Harner's workshops, rhythmic drumming induces an altered state in which a participant, lying in silence with eyes covered, can experience a vision of flying or entering into the Earth. In this vision, the participant will ask an animal or guardian spirit to reveal itself and lead her on a "journey" of discovery to give her the answer to a question about her own life or the life of someone who has requested help in healing.

Recently I read a description by Richard Nelson of flying as a bald eagle, which beautifully captures my own experience of shamanic trance. In his case the vision was induced not by drumming but by an intense period of standing in the wild, fixed eye to eye with a perched eagle.

> As I watch the eagle rise steeply above the bay, I let myself drift out beyond an edge, as though I were moving across the edge of sleep. I feel his quickened heartbeat in my temples, stare up through his eyes at the easy invitation of the sky, turn and look back at the figure of myself, cringed against the leaning snag below. I am filled with the same disdainful surge that releases him from his perch, feel the strain of air trapped in the hollows of his wings.
>
> Fixed within the eagle, I see the bay slowly dilating below. . . . At three thousand feet . . . I can feel the lash of gusts as the eagle planes above the mountain, gaze through his eyes at the fissured,

snow-laden peak, and share the craving that draws him more deeply into the island's loneliness. . . .

I am lost in a dream of eagles, balanced on the precipice of sky. . . . I have the eagle's eyes and the eagle has mine.[43]

Frog and Eagle

These meetings across the boundaries of nature and spirit can profoundly transform our understanding of the place of humans in the cosmic order. They also can open permanent channels for personal communications from nature spirits. I offer two examples from my own experience.

The first, to which I was witness, involved two of Michael Harner's students: Jo and a friend, Zaida Nuñez, who has worked as well with shamans in her native Venezuela. When Jo's father was dying some years ago, she prayed he would communicate with her after death, which he did unmistakably, if rather whimsically, in the form of a frog. Eighteen months later she was missing him, and she asked in meditation that he visit her again. She remarked to me that at least she would always know he was with her when she saw a frog.

That same evening there was a meeting of our couples group at the Nuñezes' house, part of which, as always, was spent in meditation. As we were preparing to leave at the end of the evening, Zaida (who knew nothing of Jo's comment to me earlier in the day about her father) said, "I don't know what this means, Jo, but all through the evening I have seen a frog sitting on your shoulder."

The second story concerns a series of powerful synchronicities, flowing from a shamanic journey, that led Jo and me to the house in Naggar in which we spent our Indian sabbatical.

In June 1984, I participated with about thirty others in a shamanic journey to seek guidance in finding a new campus for the California Institute of Integral Studies, the San Francisco graduate school of which I was then president. While almost everyone else had visions of locations around San Francisco Bay (many startlingly accurate, as it was to prove), my personal journey took me to a high Himalayan valley. I recognized it as Kullu, which I had visited two summers earlier. I thought

I should be in California, not continents away in India, but my animal guide, a bear, told me I was in the right place. The bear led me far up into the forests, from where an eagle took me soaring out over the valley. Below I saw a building on a terrace high above the left bank of the Beas, the mother river of the Kullu Valley.

Four years later when my leave was due, Jo agreed we should spend it in relative isolation in the Himalaya. No doubt she was persuaded by my glowing descriptions of Kullu's alpine beauty, and she was particularly drawn by a guidebook photo I showed her, captioned: "The Kullu Valley from the Naggar Castle."

As the time of our departure for India approached, we repeatedly were asked by friends whether we had arranged for somewhere to live. We told them we would first go to a place where I had stayed on my former visit—a guest lodge in Manali, a small resort town at the head of the valley—but that we would soon move to a rented house which "would be there waiting for us." Even a letter from the guest-lodge proprietor warning us that most of the houses with Western-style amenities in Manali had recently been converted to hotels did not reduce our confidence, because we have come to trust that we are divinely led.

Our arrival in India was delayed by a missed flight connection en route, but despite the inconvenience, we were sure a fellow traveler was right when she commented, "There is always a purpose in these things." Because of our late arrival, lunch with an Indian friend in New Delhi was postponed a day, and then, at the last minute, he moved the location. Just as we finished the meal, an American woman he knew walked into the room. She said she was leaving that evening for the U.S. and inquired about our plans. To our surprise and delight, she told us she had just returned from a month in the Kullu Valley and proceeded to draw a sketch map to guide us to a house that might be available for rent in Naggar, the valley's ancient princely and spiritual center, now a relatively small village about twenty miles downriver from Manali. "It is a blue and white house standing quite on its own," she said.

As we drove up the valley at the end of a fifteen-hour overnight journey from New Delhi, we were excited that we could indeed make out the house far above us across the river. We were even more excited and rather awed, as our taxi wound its way up the steep road to Naggar two days later, to realize that the village is on a small plateau two thousand feet above the left bank of the Beas, just as I had been shown in the shamanic journey five years earlier.

Nila Garh, the Blue House, stands on its own small terrace, midway between the ancient temple of the presiding deity of Naggar, the goddess Tripura Sundari Devi, to the south, and, to the north, the former home of the Russian mystics Nicholas and Helena Roerich, now a museum housing a collection of Nicholas Roerich's luminous paintings of his spiritual explorations in Tibet and Mongolia.

Ten days later Nila Garh was ours. Sitting on the tiny verandah looking out on a spectacular vista of valley, river, and towering mountains, we happened to compare the view with the guidebook photo that had so attracted us before leaving the U.S. To our astonishment, we realized it was shot from right above the house, not—as the caption claimed—from the castle a half mile away in the village.

And what of the miraculous meeting with the good angel in Delhi who pointed us to a house we might never otherwise have found? There is no systematized rental market in this remote Himalayan valley; word of mouth must suffice. Consider the wonderful twists and turns of time and place—delay, postponement, changed location—necessary for there to have been that "chance" meeting. I am quite certain we could not have planned it so perfectly.

What are we to make of these happenings? Were they merely bizarre coincidences, or are they evidence of guidance from the spirit world? There can be no proof one way or the other, so to opt, as I do, for the second interpretation is an act of faith.

Michael Roads has a word of advice for those of us confronting situations of this kind—advice given him by a tree:

> Proof has become mankind's obsession. It is an intellectual attachment which, rather than expanding your horizons, is rapidly becoming a restriction. Proof can easily become a denial of that which "IS," and the seeds of tragedy are contained in this. Those who feel these words resonate in their hearts will need no proof, while those who do not could accept none.[44]

There is a postscript to the story of the Blue House. It was Eagle who had guided us to that place, and it was Eagle who came to us again at the end of our six months in Naggar.

Our last days there proved traumatic. In the midst of farewells from village friends as we packed to leave, we received the totally unexpected news that we had been fired by the California Institute of Integral Studies. We felt betrayed and deserted by our colleagues at home. What happened in our final hour in Naggar, therefore, was powerful and propitious.

Just as we locked the Blue House and carried the last of our belongings up the steep mountain path, a magnificent imperial eagle, with an eight-foot wingspan, landed in a tree directly above our waiting taxi. This was astounding, as previously we had had only one distant glimpse of this rare bird. We were moved to tears, and we felt profoundly reassured. A spirit messenger had come with good tidings:

A watchful Eye is over thee.
Eagles soar aloft as messengers.
And turtles bring their gifts for shields.

In the mist thou shalt find the way,
for I am with thee.

In forests look for My Precepts.
Amidst mountains listen for My Call.
In the rippling of the stream be aware of My Whisper.[45]

Nicholas and Helena Roerich

The Open Temple

There is a sacred mountain in Japan ascended by a path that leads from one Shinto temple to the next. The temples at the foot of the mountain are large and ornate, but as the path climbs higher they become ever smaller and simpler. The last is a plain shelter open on all four sides. Through this the path leads into the forest.

On such a path we must now walk, away from our elaborate human constructions and out again into our natural home.

5

OUR MEDICINE,
THEIR MEDICINE

We are at a moment in history when we face both a fearful crisis and a profound opportunity. The crisis stems from the recognition that our world is increasingly unhealthy for humans and other life forms, despite the brilliance and power of medical science. Fortunately, this is also a time of spiritual revival, when people are reawakening to the age-old understanding that mind and spirit can heal. From the ancient wisdom of the healing traditions of our own and other civilizations, we are learning again that health and harmonious balance are one and the same.

Loss of Confidence

People in the West have lost confidence in biomedicine. They are no longer certain it promotes health.

The most obvious explanation is the emergence of terrifying new plagues, such as cancer and AIDS, in the face of which medical practice appears impotent. To make matters worse, doctors seem to regard the life-threatening existence of lethal technologies and a poisoned natural environment as beyond the scope of their responsibility. Their professional credibility has been damaged by the number of new drugs and therapeutic devices that in recent years have been revealed to have injurious side effects, particularly for women and children.

Things are not improved in the eyes of the general public by skyrocketing costs for medical treatment, hospitalization, and health insurance while doctors' incomes float, like hot-air balloons, higher and higher above the general average. Then there are the disturbingly frequent reports of clinical mistakes that result in the maiming or death of patients, and the widely publicized stories of the macabre "living dead," sustained as grotesque mummies by high-tech clinical gadgetry. "The main requirement of a hospital is that it should do the sick no harm," said Florence Nightingale. In America, certainly, there is little confidence today that this requirement is being met.

The seriousness of these doubts signals a dramatic change in public opinion. Less than a generation ago, doctors were held in the highest esteem, and their word was gospel. They were the experts in an acclaimed field of endeavor. Throughout the first three-quarters of the twentieth century, biomedicine was revered as the science progressively delivering humankind from the scourge of disease. It was the epitome of modern Western progress, the supreme proof of the power of science to benefit humanity. Its dethronement has negative implications for classical science as a whole.

The loss of confidence in biomedicine has also opened the door to a sympathetic consideration of non-Western medical systems and to the resurrection of alternative health therapies, formerly popular in the West. This is perhaps the most startling development of all, given the disrepute into which medical practices other than allopathy (biomedicine) had sunk. Under the assault of scientific medicine, they had been relegated earlier in the century to the garbage-heap of quackery and superstition, with many of their practitioners outlawed.

What's Wrong?

Something is fundamentally wrong with Western medicine. The problems just identified—those that have shaken public confidence—are the surface manifestations of a deeper pathology. What is it?

Succinctly stated, it is the mistake of treating living things, our own bodies included, as though they were mere machines. With biomedicine we are reaping the whirlwind of a science that has attempted to dominate nature, which it represents as a collection of manipulable material objects. Devoid of spirit and lacking consciousness, the natural world can be treated as alien and inferior, fair game for reorganization and improvement.

Century's end brings the ultimate expression of mechanistic materialism: biotechnology, the reengineering of genetic chemical codings to fix inherited defects and to improve the general physical constitution of humans, animals, and plants. With recombinant DNA, the biochemists claim to have given humans the power to control natural evolution. Mastery of the great machine is within our grasp, they tell us.

Nature is "the other"—separate and apart—and this dualism extends to the human body. The mind has consciousness; the body is simply matter in motion, a machine directed by the brain. Health is defined as the smooth functioning of this physical machine. We should note that another separation is slipped tacitly in here: that of the individual from the community. Health is understood as an individual, not a group, phenomenon.

The separations go further. As a machine, the body must have separately identifiable parts, which can be kept in working order for a reasonable length of time with proper maintenance. It is an assembly, a collection of segments. Modern physiology gives us a visual representation of the lines that divide it into compartments. Just think back to the anatomical models and diagrams in the health textbooks in grade school. The body's outer coating is shown as layers of skin. The arteries, capillaries, veins, nerves, and intestines are pictured as linear pathways in the body. Tissue is portrayed as lining organs and passages. But as a living organism, the body must be a single, indivisible whole. It is a continuum, with flesh merging, and substances and energies flowing throughout. Yet we are accustomed to perceive it as a system of interacting parts.

This segmentary view has shaped and been shaped by medical practice. Diseases are said to attack the body, and each disease has a specific cause: genetic, microorganic, or a combination of both. Each disease also has a specific "seat" in the body. This concept of localism makes possible the specialization of medical practice, defined by either a body part or a disease category. It also makes possible specific therapy localized in the body, most commonly chemical or surgical intervention.

The concept of "body as machine" lends itself to the use of human-made machines to replace its defective or worn "parts," to sustain its functions, and to diagnose its illnesses. Being amenable to calibration, these machines produce numerical data and are therefore considered to give more accurate, i.e., scientifically exact, indications of the body's condition than either the patient or doctor, technologically unaided, is capable of doing. The machine readouts become the arbiters of the dividing line between health and ill health.

Hospitals are the focus of medical practice because of the specialization and division of roles of health professionals; the emphasis on asepsis and anesthesia, both requiring controlled use of chemicals; and, most importantly, the reliance on machines. Because machines are used for diagnosis as well as treatment, the healthy go to the hospital along with the sick. We are born there, and we die there. In the womb we have already become patients, and such we remain: lifelong wards of our medical guardians.

And what is it they guard us against? Death and its agent, disease. If health is defined as the smooth functioning of the physical machine, death is the moment at which the machine stops and cannot be restarted. It is not loss of consciousness nor the departure of the soul that defines death in the modern West, but simply the instant when the pump stops.

Death in our materialist culture has an awful finality to it. Unlike so many other civilizations where death is a doorway to new life, for us it is the end because it terminates physical existence. Its prevention is therefore the chief objective of the doctor, and biomedicine's proudest claim is that it has delayed death, i.e., lengthened average life expectancy.

"The war against death is fought on the battlefield of disease." Military metaphors of this kind are so commonplace in the discussion of biomedicine that it is easy for us to overlook their significance. They suggest that humans are locked in a struggle for survival against hostile forces of nature. Diseases, we are told, are external entities lurking in wait to attack our bodies should we drop our guard. They are the modern hobgoblins.

The maintenance of health is the doctor's acknowledged task. But it is the treatment of the sick—curative rather than preventive medicine—to which most attention is given. This is the ground for heroic battles against death. I remember a surgeon explaining on National Public Radio why relatively few medical school graduates opt for preventive specialties like pediatrics: "Who wants to be up at 2 a.m. telling a mother to boil the milk, when you could be saving lives—dramatically saving lives?"

Turf Wars

Doctors generally have claimed credit for the overall improvement in health that occurred in Western societies in the century from the mid-1800s. This, they have asserted, was the result of the progressive conquest of disease through the advance of medical science, with its increasingly sophisticated technology and organization. The claim was historically important for the biomedical profession because it provided its major justification for a systematic campaign to exclude everyone but allopaths from the practice of medicine.

When they formed their professional associations in the nineteenth century (British Medical Association, 1832; American Medical Association, 1847; German Aerzteverein, 1872), the "regulars" (as they were then known) were just one among many medical sects. At that time they competed with homeopaths, herbalists, chemists, eclectics, hydropaths, midwives and a host of faith healers. In the Americas and other lands across the globe that Europeans had invaded, indigenous systems of healing survived and even flourished in some places.

The picture was very different by the 1920s. In Europe and North America, governmental regulations enacted at the behest of the biomedical associations, combined with strict controls on medical school admissions and curricula, had cleared the field of alternative health practitioners, or (as in the case of midwives) subordinated them to allopathic doctors. Branded as purveyors of witchcraft, indigenous "medicine men" and other spirit healers had been outlawed. As far as possible, the same was done in European and American colonial territories.

The effects were dramatic. For example, in the U.S. there was a precipitous decline in the number of healthcare givers available to the public. Even the size of graduating classes from American medical schools was reduced drastically. In 1904, there were 5,747 graduates; by 1922, the total had dropped to 2,529. Allopathic doctors reaped large financial benefits. Before 1900, the majority could barely scrape together a respectable living. By the 1920s, U.S. physicians' average incomes had climbed to four times that of all gainfully employed.

Another dramatic effect was to transform a predominantly female occupation into an almost exclusively male preserve, and a white one at that. In launching its campaign, the American Medical Association had made no secret of its objective: to improve the financial condition of its members by eliminating competition and raising the social status of doctors. To this end, they targeted nonwhites and women, whose participation as independent health practitioners (in their view) lowered the profession's public standing.[1]

The rationale given for the takeover was that allopathy, by contrast to other health practices, is medical *science*. In the prevailing climate of adulation for science in the first half of the century, this argument was swallowed hook, line, and sinker—and along with it, the "body as machine" approach.

As I noted earlier, the allopaths claimed credit for nineteenth- and twentieth-century declines in European and American mortality rates and the concurrent improvement in general health. Certainly they had increased patients' chances for survival following surgery and other clinical procedures by taking seriously the observations of bacteriologists, such as Louis Pasteur and Robert Koch, and applying the products of the new chemical industries to the control of germs and the reduction of pain. Hospitals after 1900 were less lethal places.

Significant overall declines in death rates, however, had begun as early as the first quarter of the nineteenth century, before a scientific basis for the germ theory of disease had been established. The most important factors appear to have been improved nutrition, environmental sanitation, personal hygiene, public health education, and prenatal and postnatal care for mothers and babies. Later, immunization may have been an added factor, though this is debatable.

The doctors were on shaky ground in attributing the positive health trends to medical intervention. Thomas McKeown, Birmingham's professor of social medicine, explains:

> It is only in the past few decades that it has become evident that this interpretation is quite inaccurate, that the health of man is determined essentially by his behavior, his food and the nature of the world around him, and is only marginally influenced by personal medical care. Intuitively we believe that *we are ill and are made well;* it is nearer the truth to say that *we are well and are made ill.*[2]

He concludes that the practical consequences have been negative:

> Misinterpretation of the major influences, particularly personal medical care, on past and future improvements in health has led to misuse of resources and distortion of the role of medicine.[3]

The medical profession's exaggerated claims for its role in human health leaves it vulnerable to criticism at a time when the statistics are not looking so good. Again, at century's close, injurious personal and group behaviors, combined with a poisoned environment, are taking a lethal toll, and a profession that has generally discouraged commitment of resources to public health and preventive medicine is losing favor.

Origin Myths

There is another wrinkle to this tale. In constructing their claim for inclusion in the scientific fold, the nineteenth-century allopaths traced their professional lineage back to ancient Greece. Hippocrates was declared the "father of medicine," a man who took the "important and radical step in human thought" that ultimately led to biomedicine. As we are informed by a standard medical history text:

> Ancient Greek medicine is incomparably closer to modern medicine than any other historical form. This is hardly surprising, since modern medicine could not exist without the Greek precedent.... Disease was no longer regarded as a supernatural phenomenon; it was approached from a rational, naturalistic, and scientific point of view.[4]

It is classic to attribute the origins of rationalism to the Greeks. This is a myth that has worked for the physical sciences. Why should it not serve equally well for medicine? The trouble is that if we examine Hippocrates and his contemporaries, we find that their beliefs and practices bear virtually no relationship to modern Western medicine.

Health and ill health were understood by them to be the result of balance or imbalance in the "humors" of the body: blood, phlegm, yellow bile, and black bile. These four humors originated in the heart, brain, liver, and spleen, respectively, and corresponded to the fundamental elements of the universe: air, water, fire, and earth.

Nature (Greek: *physis*) was believed to have a strong healing tendency of its own. The physician's task was merely to assist nature to restore the harmonic balance of the humors. It was by manipulating the four qualities—hot, cold, wet, and dry—that equilibrium in the body could be restored. A disease of the yellow bile, for instance, which was hot and dry, could be treated by cold and wet remedies.

Though the Hippocratic physicians sometimes resorted to surgery and the prescription of herbs and minerals, regulation of diet and of the patient's daily routine were their main concerns. They laid great emphasis on the influences on the patient's health of the sun and moon, planets and stars, climate and locality, community and family.

The detailed beliefs and practices of the Greek physicians of old are not things most of us will want to commit to memory. The significance lies in how many of the core elements of this system were common throughout the ancient world. They survive to the present day in traditional Arabic, Indian, and Chinese medical systems.

These are holistic systems: They rest on an understanding that health and harmonious balance are one and the same. There must be balance within the person—a harmony of body, mind, and spirit. The body's constituent patterns are influenced by the pulsing energies that flow through all of nature, affected by the passage of the heavenly bodies, the cadence of the seasons, fluctuations in climate and crops, and the "tides in the affairs of man." Human health is understood to be a cultural phenomenon. Sick societies make for sick people, and vice versa.

Health care is concerned not with isolates but with "the pattern which connects." Nature is recognized as benign, and health is assumed to be the normal state. Respect for the sacred forces of the universe is essential, and the healer's task is to find corresponding balances in rituals and physical treatments. In these traditions, healing is a sacred profession, and doctors are philosopher guides or gurus rather than repairmen. Their prime concern is not disease but the maintenance or restoration of equilibrium in individual and community. The emphasis is on relationship and connectedness.

In seeking an improved alternative to the current biomedical model, these classical health systems of Eurasia appear to have much to teach us. But did they work? There is a widespread belief in the contemporary West (and, for that matter, among urban elites in most other parts of the world) that people were sickly in the old days. "Thank God for modern medicine," it's often said.

Frankly, I think this is mistaken. As far as I can judge from the evidence of physical anthropology and premodern history, the health of ancient peoples overall was no worse than ours, and some probably had lower rates of disease than we do. There were certainly times when large numbers of people sickened and died, but the great plagues were aberrations and were noted as such by contemporaries. When there was enough food and the water was pure, when the society was stable and the culture self-confident, when the future seemed predictable—in such times humans by and large have been healthy.

Patchwork Medicine

We need a healthy system of medical care. The ancient systems suggest valuable elements, but I doubt that any one of them fits the needs of our contemporary cultures and environmental situations. I am not willing to adopt them wholesale, nor am I willing to throw all of biomedicine into the trash can. It, too, has good things to offer. As Andrew Weil, M.D., a holistic health advocate, observes:

> Allopathic medicine is very good at managing trauma, acute bacterial infections, medical and surgical emergencies, and other crises. It is very bad at managing viral infections, chronic degenerative diseases, allergy and autoimmunity, many of the serious kinds of cancer, mental illness, "functional" illness (disturbances of

function in the absence of major physical and chemical changes), and all those conditions in which the mind plays an active role in creating susceptibility to disease. It is not wise to go to an allopathic doctor with a disease that allopathic medicine cannot treat. It is also not wise to go to other sorts of practitioners with diseases that allopathic medicine can treat very well.[5]

New healing systems may well be patched together from the varieties of human medical experience. I speak of healing systems in the plural because these are cultural products. Different societies will develop variations that are most effective for their circumstances. In fact, this is the case already.

Looking around the contemporary medical world, we can find excellent "patchwork" examples to serve as inspiration for further eclecticism. In China's western province of Szechwan, the Chengdu College of Medicine has had access for centuries to a superb garden of medicinal plants maintained by a local Buddhist monastery. The college pharmacy and library have a wealth of information on traditional healing applications of herbs and other plants, animal extracts, and minerals. In recent years, chemical analysis of traditional medicines along with comparative study of allopathic drugs has facilitated the combination of Western biomedicine with Chinese classical medicine in patient care offered by the school's clinic. Of the five years required of students to graduate from the college, one-third is now devoted to the study of allopathy.

The Arigner Anna Government Hospital of Indian Medicine in Madras, with a fine library of ancient and modern medical texts, is a comparable center of research, teaching, and clinical practice. While its wards may be supervised by senior nurses with allopathic training, its clinicians are drawn from the three classical Indian medical systems: Unani, Ayurveda, and its southern variant, Siddha. A patient typically receives a combination of therapies: massage with medicated oils to relieve pain and stimulate healing flows in the body, oral dosage with mineral emetics to purge toxins, the regulation of diet and exercise to restore harmonic balances, and herbal medicines to treat specific ailments. Practice of these classical medical systems is considered a sacred art, with doctors responsible as much for the spiritual as for the physical welfare of those in their care. Doctors, nurses, and patients alike offer *puja* (prayer and worship) before any procedure.

Boston's Lemuel Shattuck Hospital provides an American example of eclecticism with its Chronic Pain Unit. Approximately twenty clinicians under a director trained in Chinese classical medicine offer an array of therapies drawn from various healing systems. They include allopathic drug therapy, massage, individual and group psychotherapy, yoga, dietary instruction, meditation, biofeedback, t'ai chi, physiotherapy, and acupuncture. The only patients admitted are those for whom other more traditional treatment programs have failed. During eighteen weeks they see four practitioners at each visit. Not only do the patients gather weekly for support meetings, but the practitioners also meet regularly to discuss how each patient is doing under the diverse regimen. A patient who is tensing up during massage, for example, may be found to need more counseling to explore deep-seated issues or a changed course of acupuncture treatment.

In the coastal village of Mapua in New Zealand's South Island, Dr. Tim Ewer specializes in the treatment of cancer, allergies, and CFS (chronic fatigue syndrome). His biomedical qualifications are distinguished, including membership in the Royal College of Physicians, London, but in dealing with these intractable diseases his approach is holistic. In obtaining a patient's medical history, Dr. Ewer gives careful attention to environmental, nutritional, and psychospiritual factors, and as a diagnostic tool he uses "the person's own body as a biofeedback device" through a bioenergetic system of muscle testing. Treatment integrates what he describes as "a variety of therapeutic approaches in order to help the person balance his or her physical, mental, emotional, and spiritual self." He continues:

> The types of remedies used include physical aspects (such as dental amalgam removal, bowel detoxification, appropriate exercise); nutritional changes; vitamin, mineral, trace element, and enzyme supplementation; Western and Oriental herbs; simple and complex homeopathics; a large range of flower remedies; acupuncture; other energetic interventions; and discussion on emotional and spiritual aspects. I also consider referral to other therapists where appropriate, e.g., physical manipulation. In the end these are all part of a spectrum of possibilities which aim to help people heal themselves.[6]

Interdependency

A good starting place in the search for healthy medicine is a recognition that we are part of a great community of organisms. "Everything here is alive thanks to the living of everything else. All the forms of life are connected," microbiologist Lewis Thomas reminds us.[7] Nature is not "the other," out there, separate from us. It is in us and we are of it. Each of us is an ecosystem, swarming with microorganisms who depend on us and on whom we are dependent for our existence. Germs cohabit with us, as companionable as the family dog and cat and far less dispensable. Some, admittedly, seem almost unrelievedly malevolent, but most—even the unfriendly ones—in manageable doses provide us with immunities.

"We swim in germs," I used to say to my graduate students leaving on research trips to India. I urged them to enter the pool at the shallow end, to ease themselves gently into this new culture of organisms, eating and drinking with some restraint at first but equally not trying to avoid local dishes. I told them they should welcome minor ailments as opportunities to become acclimatized, and I encouraged them steadily to become more adventurous. Most importantly, I urged them not to go in fear and trembling of illness. Self-confidence is healthy.

I have spent considerable portions of the past thirty-five years in Calcutta and have witnessed there the damaging effects of the belief that germs are waiting to get you in every morsel of food and every human and animal encounter. Many fearful foreigners, petrified by the city's noxious reputation, arrive grimly determined to create a sterile cocoon in which they can be safe from the alien germs clawing their way relentlessly out of the Hooghly River. When, as invariably happens, a family member gets dysentery or a viral infection, anguished hours are devoted to a postmortem on where the defenses had cracked. The tendency then is to throw heavyweight medicinal armaments at the infection and reinforce the defensive perimeter. In my unscientific observation, these are the folks who most often become seriously ill and leave for home, hating India and Indians.

Thomas McKeown's emphasis on the interdependency of life forms suggests we should be more cautious than we have been in declaring total war on disease:

For an understanding of the infections it is unsatisfactory to consider separately an organism and its host. They are living things which interact and adapt to each other by natural selection. The virulence of an organism is not, therefore, a distinct character like its size or shape: it is the expression of an interaction between a particular organism and a particular host.[8]

As classical Greeks, Arabs, Hindus, and Chinese, along with the West's own homeopaths, herbalists, and folk healers, would tell us, health comes not from the domination of nature but from finding a right balance for ourselves within it.

Pour on the DDT, and the celebrated carnage among the malarial mosquitoes is followed by infestations of other pests whose natural predators have incidentally been done away with. And then with horror we find DDT in our own bodies, carried back to us by the organisms that feed us. The ultimate irony is that while the corrosive effects of this lethal poison continue their damage to humans and other animals, later generations of mosquitoes have developed genetic resistance to the insecticide.

A similar thing has happened with antibiotics. The development of sulfa drugs in the 1930s, followed by penicillin and related antibiotics, seemed to have handed medical science a stunning victory over bacterial infections. The prescription of heavy dosages of these drugs became routine, even for viral infections against which they are ineffective. Now some bacteria have developed resistance to antibiotics, which for their part appear to have wreaked havoc on many individuals' immune systems at a time when viruses have become more virulent.

Again it is a question of degree. Antibiotics are a godsend when used with discretion for the treatment of severe infections, but they are not needed for less critical ailments. In dealing with these, we will be much kinder to the body if we forget fancy pharmaceuticals and turn back to tried-and-true home remedies. Every culture has a fund of traditional knowledge of curative agents that are readily available, easy to use, usually less expensive, and good for general health.

Here are some that have worked well for me. For a cold or sore throat: a heated mixture of lemon juice and honey, or, alternatively, hot chicken broth. For motion sickness: a slice of fresh ginger, chewed. To relieve the sting of nettles: sorrel leaf, rubbed on the skin. For a burn on my hand: mud from a thermal pool on California's Mt. Lassen (a Native American remedy that was highly effective). For cuts and scrapes: a poultice of leaves of the New Zealand shrub kawakawa (a Maori practice). For the heart and circulatory system: woodear mushrooms (also known as tree ears and favored by the Chinese), hawthorn berries (an old English remedy) or garlic (used in folk medicine throughout the world). For sinus congestion, including hay fever: the combined extracts of horseradish, garlic, fenugreek, marshmallow, and ascorbic acid; or the vapor of eucalyptus leaves steeped in boiling water, and inhaled (an Aboriginal Australian remedy). For arthritis: extracts of beche-de-mer, celery seed, white willow, and devil's claw, with glucose. For tonsillitis: an Ayurvedic mixture of herbs marketed in India as Septelin. For intestinal parasites: another remedy from India—fig extract.

Total war on disease is unwise; it is also unnecessary. In this regard the heroic myths of modern medical history obscure an organic truth: most (perhaps all) diseases are self-limiting. The principle that Charles Darwin outlined, natural selection, is at work to ensure that the decimation of one or more generations of any population of organisms (humans included) will be followed by the birth of increasing numbers of individuals who are genetically less susceptible. They are the offspring of those who are best adapted to survive the initial onslaught.

Optimization, not maximization, is the principle of nature. To survive and prosper, bacteria and viruses need to strike a balance between virulence and ineffectiveness. If they are to continue to munch on us and with us, they must not be too successful in killing us or each other.

Inadvertently, this principle was demonstrated in Australia in the 1960s and 1970s when myxomatosis was introduced in an effort to wipe out rabbits, a scourge of the pastoral industry. This virus is transmitted by mosquitoes from the pustules of animals that have contracted the disease. Initially, the microbiologists made the error of using a form of myxomatosis so virulent that too few infected rabbits survived long enough to form the pustules necessary for transmission. Their rapid deaths protected their fellows. Not until an optimum level of virulence was achieved could the virus sustain itself and effect a dramatic change in the Australian countryside. Victory was declared. But the rabbits had the last laugh (or, at least, the next laugh). Just in time, they developed extensive immunity.

Like all other life forms on this planet, the microbes responsible for disease live in interdependence and must adapt themselves to the behavior of their hosts, just as we must adapt ourselves to them as our houseguests. Thus it is to their advantage that we develop partial immunity and in other ways modify our lifestyles to keep the relationship balanced. Across the generations both they and we alter our physical forms in response to one another.

The Illusory Crusade

"As our knowledge changes, the world changes," I wrote in a previous chapter. No matter how deeply ingrained is the belief in progress, the fact is that science cannot reduce the extent of the unknown. When we gain "more" knowledge, i.e., conceptualize differently, we alter the interactions between ourselves and other life forms. The pattern that connects is changed, and our knowledge becomes passé.

The fallacy of the idea of medical progress is the fallacy of the fixed-law universe. Those who celebrate battle honors in "man's conquest of disease" talk as though a set list had been drawn up at creation, with medical science given the task simply of crossing off the diseases one by one until the list is exhausted. Such people did not give heed to John Wheeler: The cosmic game of "Twenty Questions" is played without a word chosen in advance. They have failed to understand the meaning of the cancer and AIDS epidemics, namely that the very cells of our bodies, along with the microorganisms with which they are interlaced, are changing in response to the "progress" of our science.

Had we comprehended the fact our bodies are not immutable, we might have responded with less alacrity to the nuclear industry's blandishments to place our anatomy before their radiation devices. Also, we might have been less eager to gulp down such copious quantities of the chemical industry's synthetic compounds. Forebodings were expressed by such groups as vegetarian societies, organic gardening and farming clubs, and natural health associations, but these were people with little scientific or political clout. Besides, their argument seemed so unprogressive. They argued that Earth's living systems were well adapted to the organic and inorganic chemicals and levels of radiation found in nature, but there was no telling what would be the systemic effects of the new chemicals and increased radiation. Now we see that their warnings should have been taken more seriously. Which makes me, for one, nervous as molecular biologists and their venture capitalists contemptuously dismiss similar expressions of concern and plunge headlong into genetic engineering.

Humans are not the only organisms capable of learning. Here again we bump up against that presumptuous modern fallacy that of all the intricate, interconnected living things, only we are possessed of conscious purpose. There are so many players in this game of life that they can never be numbered, and we are deluded if we think that the initiatives lie only with humans.

We stand a good chance of putting an end to the game itself if we persist in thinking that there are only two sides and that we must wipe out all those whom we label as opponents. On the threshold of a new millenium, we contemplate with horror what has been wrought by two centuries of onslaught on the nonhuman. With all the advances of medical science, can we talk of an improvement in health when the ecosystem that supports life on the planet may be fatally wounded by our science-based technologies? Does the extension of the human life span have spiritual value when it is accompanied by an exponential increase in the destruction of other species?

Our science needs to lay aside the driven symbol of the straight line and adopt once more the ancient symbol of the circle, which represents harmony, moderation, and balance—optimization rather than maximization. Our own bodies give us a teaching in this area. They present the paradox that substances and processes essential to our survival also can kill us. Consider coagulation of the blood. By stopping bleeding it enables wounds to heal, but it also can produce fatal clots in the heart, lungs, and brain. Organisms work like that—on trade-offs: What's good for one thing is not particularly good for something else. Advantages come with disadvantages. Or, if you like, everything contains its opposite.

Material existence in its entirety is a trade-off. We get to live only because we die. For every gift received something must be given; so we are taught by the native traditions. It is an exchange: Each part of nature draws energy from some other part, and death is the coin of exchange.

"Everything here is alive thanks to the living of everything else," but equally everything here is alive thanks to the dying of everything else.

The heroic ambitions of modern medicine have done us a disservice by creating the mirage of a crusade against death, as though some ultimate victory were possible over this oldest of our companions. The doctors themselves are the ones who are most oppressed by the illusion because all too often the patient's death is perceived as their defeat. In the words of that old curmudgeon George Bernard Shaw: "Don't plan to live forever. You are bound to be disappointed."

The Body's Consciousness

While we are speaking of paradoxes, let's consider the perplexing question of how most of us stay healthy most of the time, even though we all harbor potentially pathogenic microbes. When the annual flu epidemic hits, why do some succumb and others not? And why do we ourselves get ill one season and not another? How can there be people who test HIV-positive for many years yet do not develop the typical symptoms of immune deficiency? How are we to understand people like my mother who defy medical prognosis with spontaneous remission from incurable conditions—in her case, leukemia?

Allopathy prides itself on its knowledge of the causes of illness, but unlike some other systems of health care, it has little to say about the causes of wellness. Its concentration on the etiology of disease and the pathology of the body provides only fragmentary answers to how we stay healthy. Again, understanding in this area may come from "the pattern which connects": body with mind and spirit, mind and spirit with culture, individual with community, humans with nature.

One of my hatha yoga teachers used to say, "Put your consciousness in the soles of your feet." She was encouraging us to be aware that mind is not confined to the brain but infuses every cell of the body. One of the keys to good health is to "get out of our heads" and tune in to this diffused consciousness. Our body will let us know what it needs if we learn to be sensitive to it. There is great wisdom in our bodies.

I emphasize the word learn because this is a capacity that can be developed with a little effort. For those whose daily occupation does not involve sustained physical activity, the place to start is with moderate exercise, such as gardening; regular walking, swimming, or dancing; or a conscious body/mind/spirit discipline like t'ai chi, aikido, or yoga. With exercise we attune to the rhythm of our body.

Along with active physical awareness we should develop inactive awareness. We need to meditate regularly and in the silence invite ourselves into self-knowledge. A daily period of silent meditation is healing in and of itself. It also provides the space in which we can sense bodily *dis-ease* and intuit ways to restore balance.

In the past thirty years there has been a remarkable amount of research on the beneficial physiological effects of meditation. Early studies of TM (Transcendental Meditation) by Herbert Benson and R. Keith Wallace used electrodes during meditation and blood samples drawn before and after. The results showed decreases in heart and breathing rates and a lowering of blood pressure, along with reduced oxygen consumption. This physiological calm occurred within minutes, indicating the value of meditation as an antidote to the health-eroding stress of modern life.[9]

Subsequently, other researchers demonstrated the health benefits of a wide range of contemplative and meditative techniques from the world's spiritual traditions. Jon Kabat-Zinn is director of the Stress Reduction Clinic at the University of Massachusetts Medical Center in Worcester. In its first thirteen years, more than six thousand medical patients went through the clinic's eight-week program of mindfulness meditation, an ancient Buddhist practice. Kabat-Zinn comments on the results: "We do have good evidence that mindfulness helps the people we see deal more effectively with their life situations, including the diseases that bring them to our clinic." He cites a sharp drop over the eight weeks in the number of medical symptoms patients report, as well as in psychological problems such as anxiety, depression, and hostility. Follow-up studies have shown that improvements are maintained by a great majority of patients for years after their participation in the program. "There is nothing magical or mystical about meditation," Kabat-Zinn writes. "Basically, it is about paying attention, purposely, in the only time you have to live, namely this present moment."[10]

Some unlearning also may be needed. If we carry work loads that are physically and emotionally punishing, or if we engage in sports that

damage our bodies (the two often seem to go together), it will be difficult for us to sense our body's subtle points of balance. It becomes impossible if we mask the body's messages (pain, for example) with drugs,
whether pharmaceutical or recreational. We need this unlearning because all of us in Western societies have been bombarbed since birth
with cultural messages encouraging workaholism, violent sports, and
drug use. We also have been taught to distrust our own capacity to
know whether or not we are well. We are told that we must rely on
medical experts and their diagnostic technologies to make the judgment for us.

Take back the responsibility for your own wellness. Self-empowerment is healthy.

In a commentary on a long-distance swimming event at the Barce-
lona Olympics, a Russian former world-record holder described what
he did to combat exhaustion during his races: "I would feel the rhythm
of my body and see every little cell."

In sports, visualization has become an accepted technique to enhance
achievement. The high jumper is trained to make her jump again and
again in her mind's eye, each time rolling clear over the bar. The diver
and the gymnast run movies of their routines in their heads until they
are imprinted perfectly. The weight-lifter visualizes the flawless press.

All of us can use visualization to enhance our well-being. "The image
is the world's oldest and greatest healing resource," writes psychologist
Jeanne Achterberg. Like all thoughts, images are "electrochemical
events, which are intricately woven into the fabric of the brain and the
body." Research has demonstrated the negative physiological effects of
worry, anger, and other mental stress, but "what has not been proposed
often in modern times is that the reverse must also be true. . . . if we can
become ill through our misbehaviors, even die from hexes and broken
hearts, then we must also be able to make ourselves well."[11]

In her book *Imagery in Healing*, Achterberg looks at the extensive research on the effects of images on immunity:

> Even though the immune system is violently assaulted by many
> types of behaviors and thoughts, there is information that it can
> also be enhanced and programmed through conscious acts. Ac-
> cording to new research, a variety of techniques—specific images,

positive feelings, suggestions, learning to respond to stressors in a relaxed way—all have the potential for increasing the ability of the immune system to counter disease.[12]

Each of us can develop the capacity "to see every little cell" in our body. In North America and Europe there are now teachers and support groups to help with training in guided imagery, hypnosis, biofeedback, and the like. People who have employed visualization for self-healing tell remarkable stories.

Here's one from the prestigious journal *Archives of Internal Medicine.* Under the scrutiny of doctors at the University of Arkansas College of Medicine, a thirty-nine-year-old woman was able, at will, to change her skin test for chicken pox virus from positive to negative and back again. She repeated this shift in her immune system on request several times over a period of months. How did she do it? By imagining the redness and swelling surrounding the skin test getting smaller and smaller, while sending healing energy to the area.[13]

I'll give you a story of my own. From my late twenties I have had troublesome varicose veins in my left leg. Swelling and discoloration increased steadily through my thirties and forties, becoming so bad that the lower leg was swollen at the end of each day to about twice the circumference of my right leg. The skin temperature of the two legs was also radically different, the left feeling as though it were on fire. Doctors and family members urged me to consider surgery or an injection, but I did not act on their advice. I had seen both my mother and a colleague at the University of Michigan suffer severe pain after surgery for similar conditions, and they reported unsatisfactory long-term results. Their experience reinforced my ingrained aversion to letting the doctors loose on my body.

Ten years ago the condition had become so serious that my acupuncturist expressed concern about the danger that the clots would cause a coronary or cerebral thrombosis. Despite his reservations about many allopathic procedures, he urged me to see a vascular surgeon without further delay. I was deeply concerned and thought I should follow his recommendation. I sat one morning in meditation, seeking inner guidance for a decision. The answer came slowly but clearly: I could heal my leg. I determined to do just that, without surgery.

I recalled advice given me ten years earlier by another of my Ann Arbor yoga teachers, Ron Chalfant, a chiropractor and Ayurvedic practitioner. He had suggested that I hold in my mind an image of my leg swathed in cooling blue-green light. I now used this as the starting place for twice-daily meditations in which I visualized my leg as slim and restored to full function. Over and over I ran my fingertips lightly up the leg, in my mind's eye repairing the damaged valves in the veins and reopening the flow of blood. I concentrated intensely on one tiny segment after another, encouraging each to heal.

Shortly after I had begun this process, Jo and I spent a weekend at Shenoa, a retreat center in northern California founded by former Findhorn community members. One of the founders, Catherine Christensen, saw me limping and offered to do a healing on my leg. She asked me to sit on a chair and Jo to sit beside me. She then had us visualize the healing as she passed her hands up and down, close to but not touching the leg.

Within six months of my decision to take matters into my own mind, my leg was so improved that it was barely distinguishable from its mate. Its good health has been sustained, though the leg does serve these days as a barometer of stress, warning me with moderate swelling when I have lost my calm center. I now pay attention and restore the balance.

I have no question that this healing was the result of my clear intention and visualization. We *can* heal ourselves.

> *We are bees,*
> *and our body is a honeycomb.*
> *We made*
> *the body, cell by cell we made it.*[14]
>
> Rumi

Community and Health

We can heal ourselves. We can also assist others in their healing, as Catherine and Jo did for me. Our ancestors prayed for each other's welfare. Most people still pray for one another. And prayer works; you have my word for it. Into the bargain, you have the word of every religion that ever was—the book religions of the great civilizations and the folk religions that predate them.

If you find science more persuasive, remember the evidence cited in the previous chapter from the School of Engineering and Applied Science at Princeton on the effects of conscious intention on matter. Also take a look at the research on healing powers catalogued by Michael Murphy in *The Future of the Body*. He cites a wide range of cases involving plants, animals, and humans. I'll give two examples.

In the 1950s and 1960s, Bernard Grad conducted experiments at Montreal's McGill University with the spiritual healer Oskar Estebany, who demonstrated that he could restrain disease and hasten the healing of injuries in animals. Working with two carefully matched groups of mice, none of which he touched, Estebany directed his healing energies toward one group and disregarded the other. The mice that had his blessing healed much more rapidly than those that did not.

To test the effect of prayer on human health, Dr. Randolph Byrd in the 1980s randomly divided 393 patients in a coronary care unit at San Francisco General Hospital into two groups of approximately equal size. Those in one group would be the target of prayers for their rapid recovery, with three to seven people praying daily for each of them. Neither patients, staff, nor doctors knew who were targeted, and each person who prayed was given simply the subject's first name, diagnosis, and general condition. Byrd collected health information on all patients without knowing which were the prayer recipients. Congestive heart failure, cardiopulmonary arrest, and pneumonia occurred less frequently in the group receiving prayer than in the control group, and statistically the recovery from disease of the former was significantly better.[15]

Please don't get me wrong. When I say that prayer works, I am not asserting it is 100 percent effective in every instance. The same caveat applies to my statement that we can heal ourselves. There is no such thing as the infallible healing technique. Any doctor from any medical tradition will tell you that, and we should not feel inadequate, self-blaming, or guilty when our intercessions fail. The human body is a complex organism enmeshed in a vast web of material and spiritual energies, and our intention is but one of many forces working upon it. What we should hold in our heart is the knowledge that prayer for ourselves and others is beneficial remarkably often.

You may ask, how did I get from imagery to prayer? Because in the contemporary West, prayer is the most familiar form of conscious visualization on behalf of others' health and welfare. Perhaps it has always been the most familiar form everywhere. Significantly, prayer acknowledges the sacred and recognizes that divine help is available. It is no accident that the roles of priestess/priest and doctor are unified in most cultures.

> Almighty God, who hast given us grace at this time with one accord to make our common supplications unto thee; and dost promise, that when two or three are gathered together in thy Name thou wilt grant their requests . . .

This Anglican version of a very early Christian prayer reminds us that group intercession has special power. Jeanne Achterberg clothes this in the language of science:

> The theme that weaves through all the behavioral and social scientists' work on illness is that much of illness is caused by disharmony—disharmony with nature, with self, and especially with the community. When the entire community becomes a healing network, when time is devoted to focusing acutely on the problem, and when the patient's support system becomes active and obvious, healing of many ailments becomes possible.[16]

Dr. Dean Ornish, an American cardiologist most famous for his successful diets and exercise programs, discovered to his surprise that nothing in his treatment of people with severe heart disease was more important than support groups. Although his patients are all different, Ornish says, they seem to share a sense of isolation: "From parts of themselves and their own feelings; from other people and a sense of community; and from something spiritual, a sense of being part of something larger than oneself." He has found that the connectedness gained in support groups is healing "in ways that go far beyond just unclogging arteries. Hearts begin to open in other ways."[17]

Psychiatrist Dr. David Spiegel saw the health benefits of social support in a study he and his colleagues conducted at Stanford University. Women with severe breast cancer who attended weekly ninety-minute support-group sessions lived an average of eighteen months longer than women with comparable cancers who did not, even though all received similar medical treatment. Spiegel comments:

> The added survival time was longer than any medication or other known medical treatment could be expected to provide for women with breast cancer so far advanced. Something about the intense social support the women experienced in these sessions appeared to influence the way their bodies coped with the illness. Living better also seemed to mean living longer.[18]

Caring community sustains wellness. Strongly bonded families and stable, culturally assured societies give nurturance. Loving companionship and fulfilling relationships are a source of healing. Nothing does a person more good than to have fun with a lover or friends—to swap stories, play games, laugh, sing, and dance; to share happiness and sadness; to drink and eat good food with others; to touch and be touched.

Love yourself. Love other people and be loved. Love fellow creatures and the Earth that nurtures all. Love life. These things are healthy.

Wellness is a group phenomenon. Here again there is need for unlearning. We have been misled by biomedicine's emphasis on the isolated individual into undervaluing the importance of social bonds to health.

In practical terms this has resulted in the U.S., and to a lesser degree in other Western nations, in a misappropriation of resources. General wellness would be improved vastly if public health, instead of receiving a meager 5 percent of the medical dollar, were given a large chunk of the 90 percent that goes to the treatment of individual patients, especially to the treatment of affluent elderly people. Nutrition and health education, family health care, community and environmental health, mental health counseling, and conflict resolution have been short-changed. It should be no surprise that national health is deteriorating in the U.S. and many other countries in the West.

Self-Confidence and Health

The folly is compounded by the worldwide promotion of this dysfunctional medical model as the hallmark of progress. When we consider the lamentable state of third-world health, we must not forget that for a century and a half from the early 1800s, there was a sustained assault on traditional healing systems by European and American colonial authorities. There is tragic irony in the fact that while the West was congratulating itself that its gift of biomedicine was lifting the non-Western world from a swamp of medical incompetence, its political, economic, and cultural invasions were undermining the cultural stability and self-confidence of these peoples.

Health depends, in Ivan Illich's words, on "the dynamic stability of a culture."[19] At the core of health is a people's collective confidence in the validity of their beliefs about the world around them, confidence in the efficacy of their social institutions and technologies in dealing with that world, and the reasonable assurance of a future that this provides. The wellness and illness of individuals are affected by conscious understandings shaped by the definitions of health and ill health prevailing in the culture.

Given the critical influence of imagery on health, it is not hard to understand how devastating it is for a people to be persuaded that their understandings of life, death, and the sacred are at best benighted and at worst demonic. That their systems of healing are worthless and their revered doctor-priests no more than quacks and witches.

Why did colonized peoples accept such negative images? Because they had suffered humiliating conquest and in many places witnessed the death of thousands upon thousands of their compatriots, stricken by the invaders' diseases from which they had no natural immunity in the first generation of contact.

Contemporary lessons can be learned from this tragedy. For one thing, disempowerment is sickening. Whether for a whole culture or for an individual, it is not healthy to be made to feel inferior and ineffectual. For a generation, feminists have been asking us to acknowledge this fact in relation to the disempowerment of women. They are right. We need to go further and recognize the damaging consequences for society as a whole of a medical system that declares all lay people incompetent of self-care, that says the doctor knows best. As Illich comments: "Instead of mobilizing the patient's self-healing powers, modern medical magic turns the patient into a limp and mystified voyeur."[20]

I recall my frustration and anger twenty years ago at the behavior of a senior nurse in a Michigan hospital emergency room where I had taken my teenage son, Stephen, who was suffering the excruciating pain of peritonitis. As we waited interminably after he had been examined for someone to tell us what was wrong, I picked up his chart to see what the intern had written. "That's not for you to read," snapped the nurse, snatching it from my hand. "Doctor will speak to you when he's ready." Sadly, almost all of us have had similar experiences of being treated as incompetents by the medical establishment. Our defined role as patients excludes the exercise of independent judgment and initiative.

It is unhealthy to persuade people that they are incapable of caring for themselves.

A second possible lesson can be gained from the collapse of health among colonial peoples. As we enter the twenty-first century we witness the devastations of new plagues. At the same time collective confidence in the validity of our beliefs about the world and in the efficacy of our social institutions and technologies is faltering in the West. There is widespread apprehension about the future. As in colonial societies whose cultural values were undercut, might not there be a relationship between the current health crisis and our civilization's fundamental uncertainties?

An instructive parallel is to be found in the plague that swept the globe at the end of the First World War: the 1918 influenza pandemic. With an estimated 30 million deaths, this was the greatest natural disaster of modern times—perhaps of all time. Significantly, mortality was most severe among adults aged eighteen to forty-five. It is an age group that typically survives flu, but in 1918 this generation, having borne the brunt of a decade of unimaginably brutal war and revolution, feared that the very foundations of civilized life were imperiled.

Healing of the Soul

The colonial situation offers us a third lesson to be learned: humility. Obviously, we in the West understood little of what we were doing when we bulldozed the healing systems of other cultures. Fortunately, many of those systems proved more resilient than expected, and though tattered and torn, they survive as reservoirs of wisdom. It is not too late for us to acknowledge that the West does not have all the medical answers and to ask what other cultures may have to teach us.

As noted earlier, the emphasis of these systems—classical and folk—is on harmony and balance, relationship and interconnectedness. They all point us back to holistic understandings and practices. For our civilization at the end of the millenium, spiritually adrift and so out of touch with the natural world that we fear we may be inadvertently killing it, the most valuable lessons may come from the oldest of all the healing traditions: shamanism.

The shamans, in common with healers of other non-Western systems, have a fund of practical knowledge of curative plants, animal extracts, minerals, and waters. In this material domain at least, the Western scientific community has finally acknowledged there is valuable information to be gleaned, and this has spurred American and European pharmaceutical companies to fund searches for medicinal plants as a source of "new" drugs.

But this is not the heart of the shaman's work. As Alberto Villoldo was told by a Peruvian teacher: "You are trained to focus on objects, on things. The world of the shaman happens in the spaces in between things."[21] Shamans are healers of physical ailments, to be sure, but their work is less with the body than with the spirit/mind/body connection. They believe that illness is not about germs or genetic defects but rather about loss of soul. Shamans lead us to places where we can recover and heal our souls.

Sandra Ingerman gives a dramatic account from her shamanic counseling practice of a successful soul retrieval. Her help was requested by a man called David, who was in very poor physical health. He revealed that just prior to his falling ill, his girlfriend, Suzanne, had committed suicide. Journeying to the beat of a drum, Sandra sought advice from a guardian spirit, her power animal, who told her that Suzanne had stolen David's soul. Following the power animal's guidance, Sandra journeyed into a forest, where she saw David tied to a tree, weak and dispirited. Suddenly Suzanne leaped out violently from behind the tree, and the guardian spirit had to shield Sandra from her attack. Suzanne persisted vainly in trying to break through this protection until finally she exhausted herself and Sandra was able to talk to her. She asked Suzanne to release David's soul. "No," Suzanne replied, "I want him to die and keep me company here." Only with great effort was Sandra able to persuade Suzanne to let go of David so she could leave this world completely and move on into the light. Sandra returned to ordinary reality and blew the fragment of soul into David, who felt an immediate rush of energy. This was the beginning of a physical and emotional healing that was complete within a few months.[22]

"Shamanism *is* the medicine of the imagination," Achterberg comments.[23] Shamans take us on journeys where we realize our own strength, and they show us spirit allies on whom we can call for help. Allies come in many forms: humans, animals, plants, and the elemental forces of nature themselves.

Shamans also mobilize circles of people for the healing of individuals, and equally they work to sustain or restore the physical and spiritual health of entire communities. Individual and group healings are complementary, the one interlaced with the other.

Fred Eiseman, a longtime resident and astute observer of Bali, comments that on the island sickness "is almost universally viewed as the result of a state of disharmony between the individual and his surroundings." In this regard it is like other misfortunes, a symptom of a breakdown of ordered relationship, at its core a spiritual problem for which the best help can come from a spiritual healer, a *balian* (shaman). Allopathic hospitals and doctors are available, and most Balinese make use of them at some time in their lives, but they find the individualistic, impersonal, hurried procedures of the allopaths alienating. By contrast, the *balian* works leisurely within a reassuring circle of friends, with all attention focused on restoring the patient to right balance. The circle includes the spirits of dead relatives, whose presence is essential to the *balian's* task.[24]

Thomas Riccio of the University of Alaska, witness to amazing shamanic healings among the Kalahari Bushmen, reports that the ceremonies are as much social gatherings as spiritual events. He notes that for the Bushmen, as for other indigenous people, "social interaction is healing, and healings are as much for the community as they are for the sick persons." A healer told him it is the power of the assembled people that brings the spirits, especially the power of the women with their singing and clapping. "It is these spirits that help me with everything I know. . . . Then I can see the sickness of the person through the darkness."[25]

It can be argued that even human healing does not reach the heart of the shaman's work. The responsibilities go further: "to the earthly web of relations in which the human community is entwined," writes David Abram. He reports that a year spent living with traditional shamans in Bali and Nepal convinced him that the shaman "is in many ways the 'ecologist' of a tribal society."

> He or she acts as an intermediary between the human community and the larger ecological field, regulating the flow of nourishment, not just from the landscape to the human inhabitants, but from the human community back to the local earth. By his or her constant rituals, trances, ecstasies, and "journeys" the shaman ensures that the relation between human society and the larger society of beings is balanced and reciprocal, and that the village never takes more from the living land than it returns—not just materially, but with prayers, propitiations, and praise.[26]

Healing of spirit, recovery of community, reconnection with the Earth—these are sorely needed by our contemporary Western world. We also need to repair our relationship with death. Our civilization, particularly our medical system, is in a state of denial about death. A consequence, as the Tibetan Buddhist master Sogyal Rinpoche points out, is environmental destruction. "Not having taken death seriously," he says, "we've become irresponsible and selfish toward life. We abuse nature as a result of it."[27]

Shamans (like Tibetan lamas, whose Buddhism is rooted in a more ancient shamanic tradition) assume special responsibilities as teachers and guides to dying and death. In fact, for most of them the path to shamanic knowledge was through "the valley of the shadow of death"— in modern terminology, a near-death experience. They have explored this other dimension, and they have techniques to lead us there and back to gain understanding for the later journey we all must take.

The literature of medical anthropology contains critical comment on what is described as the "high failure rate" of shamanic healers. Many of their patients die, it is observed. It is hard to measure these criticisms because (to the best of my knowledge) we have no statistics comparing shamanism with biomedicine or other medical systems. But in any case, this may be beside the point. Physical healing is often one of the shaman's objectives, but it is rarely the primary and never the exclusive purpose.

The shaman is first and foremost a healer of the spirit—the spirit of the community as well as the spirit of individuals. Shamans know that death is not the worst thing we can suffer. They take seriously the teaching given by the Bible, a teaching our civilization in its materialism seems to have forgotten: "What shall it profit a man, if he shall gain the whole world, and lose his own soul?" Mark 8:36

This is not to imply that shamans take death lightly. Far from it. Of all life's passages, this they recognize as the most awesome. They treat death with special concern and care—the death of animals and plants as well as of humans.

In this area as in all others, the shaman has specialized rituals to mark the sacredness of the event. With sounds, movement, colors, the burning of herbs, and the cooking of food, all the physical senses are involved in order to engage participants intensely in the ceremonies that establish a special quality of time. Shamans are keen observers of the varied rhythms of time in nature, and they know the healing qualities of human attunement to this uneven pulse. This subject of healing time will be explored more fully in the next chapter.

Are we able, as a civilization in need of healing, to pay attention to the shamans and other keepers of ancient wisdom?

Native American tradition says that ancient wisdom must be maintained "until Earth's children grow Listening Ears." The great Oglala Sioux shaman Black Elk prophesied that it was the fifth generation that would grow Listening Ears. Black Elk was born in 1863. Reckoned from that date, the time of the fifth generation is now.

6

IS THERE ANY TIME
BUT THE PRESENT?

"Time," Morgaine thought, "time runs differently in Avalon, or
perhaps it does not exist."

Marion Zimmer Bradley

Through the Looking Glass

With a gasp Lisa dropped her pen and sat bolt upright, profoundly
shocked. "Oh my God!" she said. "I can see it. They're right!"

She was an undergraduate in a class I was teaching at the University
of Michigan. The subject was Balinese time. With a jolt it had come to
her: She could see what the Balinese see. She had entered another reality; she was in Balinese time. It was a wonderful (and scary) moment
for Lisa. For me it was a moment of pure delight as I watched the cultural mirror crack to allow someone a glimpse of the other side.

To lead you, dear reader, through the looking glass is my major purpose in writing this book. When I first outlined *Other Ways of Knowing*,
Jo asked, "Why a chapter on time?" My answer: "Time—linear time—
is the linchpin of our perception of reality in the modern West. In order
to experience other ways of knowing, we must enter another time."

Time As a Line

In the modern West we make sense of reality by insisting upon linear sequence. Time for us is like that line in the middle of the roadway flashing by our car. If we look in the rear-vision mirror it is there behind us receding into the distance, and before us it stretches as far as the eye can see. The line on the road is dotted, but ahead and behind the dots appear to run together in one solid line. So too, in our perception of time we maintain two different concepts without any feeling of inconsistency: time as an unbroken line, and dotted, metrical time composed of units of even length.

Whether dotted or unbroken, time in our cultural understanding is a line, existing in only one dimension and flowing in a single direction. Events are fixed points on this line of time, and causation is understood as the sequence of events. Cause and effect are related as past and present.

As we saw in the earlier discussion of history, this perception of sequential causation in unbroken, one-dimensional, onward-flowing time is so fundamental to our civilization that we think it is natural reality. It is scientific—our truth. Other cultures' ways of understanding time, if incongruent with ours, may be attractively quaint but must be fundamentally wrong.

That's strange, because in fact we do not experience time the way it is formally described. In our day-to-day existence time is not uniform. It is neither metrically even nor qualitatively always the same. Recall the old saw "Time flies when you're having fun" and the familiar Monday morning lament "Wherever did the weekend go?" Lived time is not a smooth thread; it is a crazy quilt of fast and slow, thick and thin.

My favorite character in Joseph Heller's satire *Catch-22* is Dunbar, who plays interminable games of Ping-Pong, which he hates, and voluntarily goes to all the military's tedious health lectures. The reason? He is mortally afraid of dying and has figured out a way to live longer. When you are bored, he points out, time passes slowly!

Let me suggest a personal test of the inequality of lived time: Compare the length of a year as you remember experiencing it as a child with its length now in your adult experience. If you are like me, the years get shorter as you grow older.

David Bohm gave another familiar example:

> People who know each other well may separate for a long time (as measured by the sequence of moments registered by a clock) and yet they are often able to "take up from where they left off" as if no time had passed. What we are proposing here is that sequences of moments that "skip" intervening spaces are just as allowable forms of time as those which seem continuous.[1]

Then there is dream time, a state in which we spend perhaps a tenth or more of our entire life. Dream time is not one-dimensional and does not flow constantly in one direction. In dreams, cause and effect are not consistently related as past and present.

Time perceptions similar to dreaming are experienced in altered states of consciousness. These can be induced in a variety of ways: meditation, hypnosis, exposure to repetitive sound such as drumming or chanting, dancing or whirling in the manner of the Sufi dervishes, sensory or sleep deprivation, or the ingestion of psychedelic or psychotropic drugs. In her novel *The Mists of Avalon*, Marion Zimmer Bradley describes the priestess Morgaine in such an altered state: "Time ceased, was again transparent, something in which she moved, bathed, stepped freely."[2]

Disciplined meditators often observe that "time spent" meditating results in no "loss of time." On the contrary, a regular period of meditation "stretches" the day, enabling more rather than less to be done. Time seems to develop an elastic quality—*jam karat,* "rubber time," as they say in Malaysia and Indonesia.

Recent survey research in the United States reveals other facts difficult to reconcile with the culture's insistence upon a unidirectional time in which past, present, and future are separated. Almost half of America's adults believe they have had contact with someone who has died. Is this a form of communication with the past, or do the dead live in the present? And what of déjà vu, the feeling in a new place or situation of having experienced it before? Two-thirds of Americans say this happens to them.

The classic scientific response is that these subjective observations are unreliable. We are not encouraged in the modern West to trust our senses.

The Cheshire Cat's Grin

There is, however, evidence of time anomalies from another source that cannot be dismissed so lightly as unscientific. This evidence emerges from experiments on precognitive remote viewing conducted under rigorous research protocols at California's SRI International, Mundelein College in Chicago, and the Princeton Engineering Anomalies Research program.

A typical experiment in remote viewing proceeds as follows:

An *agent* departs from the laboratory with the understanding that at a predesignated time she will arrive at a distant target site. She carries with her several sealed envelopes, each containing the name of a different site chosen without her participation. Once well away from the laboratory, she randomly selects an envelope to open and proceeds on schedule to the site designated therein. While there she takes photographs of the site from various angles, fills in a checklist of site attributes, and writes a free-form description.

Meanwhile, back in the laboratory there is a *second participant* who has no knowledge of the agent's destination and no communication with her. His task is to focus his powers of concentration to bring to mind the place where the agent is going. Once he feels he has formed a mental image of it, he fills in the same checklist of site attributes, writes a free-form description, and draws sketches of the site from various angles if he can.

Later, *evaluators* uninvolved in the experiment to this stage are given materials produced by both agents and laboratory participants in experiments involving a variety of target locations. Without being told which laboratory visualizations belong to which target sites, the evaluators sort through the materials to find those that match.

With various modifications, this experiment has been repeated hundreds of times over the past twenty years. A statistically significant proportion of participants has described target sites accurately, even though in some cases the locations were thousands of miles distant from the laboratory.

And here's the problem for linear time: Much of this remote viewing has been precognitive. Participants have accurately described target sites *before* agents reached them and in many cases even before the agents opened the envelopes to determine the destinations.

Reporting on their experiments at Princeton, Robert Jahn and Brenda Dunne comment that "the precognitive aspects are perhaps the most striking and challenging, and also the most difficult to accommodate in any theoretical formalism." They continue:

> Of course, we might recall Einstein's and Eddington's reminders that the concepts of space and time are themselves constructions of consciousness. . . . The essential point is that various nonclassical effects of quantum wave mechanics bear useful similarities to these anomalous experiences of human consciousness.[3]

Twentieth-century physics has not been kind to linear time, although there does not yet seem to be any general comprehension of the size of the dent that has been made in the standard Western view of reality. As Annie Dillard muses:

> For some reason it has not trickled down to the man on the street that some physicists now are a bunch of wild-eyed, raving mystics. For they have perfected their instruments and methods just enough to whisk away the crucial veil, and what stands revealed is the Cheshire cat's grin.[4]

It was Albert Einstein who put the cat among the pigeons with his relativity theories. Niels Bohr, Werner Heisenberg, and their fellow quantum theorists further stirred things up with such troubling propositions as the "quantum leap" and the "uncertainty principle," which deny the existence of a subatomic arrow of time. A later generation produced John Bell and his theorem, which plays fast and loose with "locality." If separation in space does not prevent instantaneous communication, what then becomes of sequential causation?

Bell's contemporaries in physics have offered the startling possibility that there may be parallel universes with separate systems of time, and evolutionary cosmologists have suggested that the rules of the universal game are perpetually evolving—including time, we may assume. As discussed in chapter 3, the life sciences have produced Rupert Sheldrake's hypothesis of formative causation and Karl Pribram's theory of the holographic universe, both having radical implications for the understanding of time.

Time anomalies are observed from many vantage points inside and outside of science, and it is hard to avoid the conclusion that Western civilization is operating within an inadequate model of time.

This is significant and extremely interesting but not in my view a serious problem—at least not in and of itself. It becomes a problem only if we mistake the map for the territory—that is, if we disregard Einstein's sage insight that "space and time are modes by which we think, not conditions under which we live."[5]

Recall my statement in the first chapter: Linear time and sequential cause and effect are merely two of the patterns we have fabricated in order to make sense of reality. Like all such explanatory patterns they are simplifications of the universe, which in its inconceivable vastness and complexity is always threatening to overwhelm the limited capacity of the human organism to comprehend. In Loren Eiseley's words:

> One exists in a universe convincingly real, where the lines are sharply drawn in black and white. It is only later, if at all, that one realizes the lines were never there in the first place. But they are necessary in every human culture.[6]

Modern Western civilization's construction of reality, our way of knowing, is limited like that of every other civilization. It is an approximation, a crude sketch map of one section of the cosmos, and we must not mistake it for the cosmos itself. It is but a semblance of reality.

Time is a cultural construction, an agreed-upon fiction to help us get by in the world. Stephen Hawking explains:

> What we call real [time] is just an idea that we invent to help us describe what we think the universe is like. . . . a scientific theory is just a mathematical model we make to describe our observations: it exists only in our minds. So it is meaningless to ask: Which is real, "real" or "imaginary" time? It is simply a matter of which is the more useful description.[7]

Whatever explanatory system we label "time" will be somewhat, but only somewhat, useful—good for certain things but not for others. This understanding makes it easier to digest the fact that other humans (ancient, recent, and contemporary) have other "times."

On the Carousel

In its exclusive reliance on linear time, the modern West has set itself apart from many earlier civilizations. Most of our ancestors understood time as cyclical, composed of rhythmically patterned recurrences, long and short, overlapping one another in the manner of the seasons, the phases of the moon, the tides, night and day. "Round and round and round in the circle game."

Time was not metrically even, nor was it always of equal value. Full and empty time, malevolent and beneficent, was punctuated by festivals and natural calamities. For some peoples there were times when the dead and the living walked together; for others, the unborn and the dead were always with the living. As one historian has written of medieval Europe, the dead were simply "another age group."[8]

Many of our contemporaries still see time as a carousel. John Berger tells us that in French peasant villages, where he has lived and worked for many years, there is an interpenetration of past, present, and future. He explains that the gift of the past is tradition, which bestows meaning and value on peasant life. The past is consciously made present as tradition is invoked daily in the repetitive acts of work and community. The peasants' "ideals are located in the past," Berger says. They contrast their present harsh struggle for survival with a just, egalitarian order that must have existed once upon a time. The peasant's "dream is to return to a life that is not handicapped. . . . After his death he will not be transported into the future—his notion of immortality is different: he will return to the past."[9]

Maori similarly say they stand facing the past, with the ancestors, guardians of tradition, guiding them backward into the unseen future.

An inversion of that order of past, present, and future to which we are accustomed is also found in the Dreamtime of Aboriginal Australia. This is the Beginning, the time of creation in which the Ancestors were born and from which the Songlines flowed to give form and life to the land. In our terminology, Dreamtime would seem to lie "back there" in the remote past. But for Aboriginals it exists now, parallel to the present, and it can be entered in dreams, in visions, and on walkabout, when the Songs are sung anew to recreate the creation. It is into the

Dreamtime that an Aboriginal Australian hopes to die. Echoing Aboriginal speech, Bruce Chatwin wrote:

> "Many men afterwards become country, in that place, Ancestors."
> By spending his whole life walking and singing his Ancestor's
> Songline, a man eventually became the track, the Ancestor and the
> song.[10]

It is hard for us to grasp this idea of looking forward to a return to the past. It is harder still to contemplate cultures that have no concept of time. Recall Wittgenstein: "The limits of my language mean the limits of my world." Our European languages are constructed of tenses; time is woven into their very fabric. We think in time sequences. How can our minds absorb the fact that there are people who do not?

In the language of the Native American Hopi there is no reference to time. The grammatical forms that appear to correspond to our tenses distinguish not different times but different kinds of information. In Hopi ontology the major distinction is between the manifest or objective on the one hand, and the manifesting or subjective on the other. That which "has become" is distinguished from that which "is potential."

Translating this into our time-laden language, we are tempted to say that the former category comprises both past and present, while the latter is the future. But we discover that for the Hopi that which is potential or manifesting (the second category) exists in the now. We also discover that the mythic past—that past so remote it can be known only subjectively—is also included in the second category, along with all things that happen in far distant places. This is a psychological and spiritual, rather than a time, category. It embraces, as linguist Benjamin Lee Whorf wrote:

> everything that appears or exists in the mind, or, as the Hopi
> would prefer to say, in the HEART, not only the heart of man, but
> the heart of animals, plants, and things, . . . in the heart of nature,
> and . . . in the very heart of the Cosmos, itself.[11]

It Is the Mind That Moves

Exposure to concepts seemingly so bizarre reminds us that our way of knowing is the very thing that constrains our knowledge. Our systems of understanding are the constructions that enable us to have knowledge, but they also set limits beyond which we cannot know, like the horizon on the ocean, an invisible barrier to a world unseen. Human perceptions, no matter how powerful, elegant, and self-consistent, are bounded and thus bound us.

It is exceedingly difficult for us in the modern West to accept this paradox. Why? In part because paradoxes are anathema to our dualistic, either/or system of reasoning. In part because of the absolutist pretensions of modern science: our ingrained conviction that the scientific method is of a different order from all other human systems of understanding. Science is commonly held to be exempt from the limitations of other cultures' ways of knowing.

Classical science also draws a hard line between mind and matter, predisposing us as a civilization to the conviction that "mind stuff" is insubstantial, figmentary. It is now more than six decades since quantum mechanics blurred this line, and the time is long overdue for us to recognize that reality is not independent of our consciousness. Mind and matter are not distinct. With our concepts we empower particular forms and processes. We give them substance.

> *"Is it the flag that moves, or is it the wind that moves?"*
> *"No," answers the Zen master,*
> *"it is the mind that moves."*

Consciousness is the ground of being, and communications spin the web of reality. The world is not "out there," and knowledge is not confined to the individual mind. The ever-shifting interconnections that create and recreate this universe are affected and effected by perception, feeling, thought, and purpose. We must therefore be mindful of our imagery, for it shapes our world. We must be conscious of our metaphors and ask whether they are life-enhancing.

When I put linear time to this test, it fails. I believe we have severely constrained ourselves with this most pervasive of modern Western metaphors. Linear time denies lived experience and is not healthy.

The emphasis on the inexorable passage of metrically even time makes the present the least substantial of our temporal concepts. Past and future have body, but the present is a wraith—difficult to perceive, impossible to hold. "Catch it if you can," says Annie Dillard. "The present is an invisible electron; its lightning path traced faintly on a blackened screen is fleet, and fleeing, and gone."[12]

This construction of time is too narrow and confining, a source of anxiety and stress. In our daily speech we lament the oppression of time: "There's never enough time." "You're wasting my time." "We don't have time for this." "Time's running out." "I can't spare the time." "There's no time to lose." "Where did the time go?"

We feel oppressed by time, and yet we are schooled to believe that success depends upon its mastery.

> If you can fill the unforgiving minute
> With sixty seconds' worth of distance run,
> Yours is the Earth and everything that's in it,
> And—which is more—you'll be a Man, my son!
> Rudyard Kipling, "If"

Five centuries ago a civilization in the Americas offered human sacrifices to the god of time. To insure that the sun maintained its temporal cadence, the Aztec priests ripped out the hearts of living men and women and poured the sacrifical blood on the great pyramids in the valley of Mexico.

In contemporary North America we also sacrifice human hearts on the altar of time—but, unlike the Aztecs, we appear oblivious to what we are doing. Heart disease is a major killer of our day. We have a blizzard of statistics to demonstrate that stress in our lives is wreaking coronary mayhem, yet we seem determined to remain on the treadmill of our lethal time god.

A few years ago Taco Bell offered a solution for Americans suffering from the shortage of time: "Really, really fast food—the twenty-second meal." This is the classic response: gain more time by speeding up. As

Taco Bell's employees discovered to their cost, it doesn't work. Things just become more frenetic.

The Permanent Now

I propose a different approach, based on the conviction that we have all the time in the world.

Will you join me in a mind game? I want us to play with the notion that there is no time but the present. I want us to explore the possibility that the convention of a permanent now is equally as valid as linear time. The mind-play may give us a glimpse of other ways of knowing reality. We may also find that this construction—a permanent present—is more capacious, more satisfying, and healthier than the "time that waits for no man." "The present moment holds infinite riches beyond your wildest dreams," we were told by the Christian mystic Jean-Pierre de Caussade.

Aware that the test to be applied is the *usefulness* of the particular time convention we adopt, we should consider arguments against and arguments in favor of there being no time but the present. We must recognize that anomalies will persist, no matter how great the utility of the construction. Keep in mind that this is only a map, not the territory.

Memory

The first objection to a permanent present is that it denies the remembered past. If there is only the now, what are we to make of all those yesterdays that crowd our minds with nostalgia and regret? Surely it would be absurd to dismiss them as unreal?

We do have memories, but are we sure they are of the past? Could they not be generated by experiences in another dimension of the present? We may recall that there are quantum theorists who postulate the existence of parallel universes. Some non-Western cultures also tell us of a present that is multidimensional, composed of coexistent layers of time that touch and interpenetrate, or, as the Javanese and Balinese say, many circles of time that interlock in varying combinations when the circumstances are right.

But isn't this just a play on words—simply a redefinition of past and future as other dimensions of the present? I think not. These multiple, coexisting dimensions exercise an influence on one another that is interactive and ongoing. In the classic Western understanding, past, present, and future are connected by doors or valves that open only in one direction. There can be no reverse flow. The many dimensions of the present, by contrast, can be thought of as separated by thin membranes, which allow some amount of bleeding through in both directions.

Why is it then that we remember the past but not the future? If these are both dimensions of the present, why are they not equally accessible?

One answer may be cultural conditioning. In the modern West it is considered common sense that we cannot see into the future. Anthropologists caution us, however, that what is common sense in one culture is often uncommon nonsense in another. By contrast to the Irish, the Gypsies, and shamanic peoples worldwide, we do not honor those who possess "the sight," nor do we select talented children for training to develop skills in prophecy.

Despite cultural discouragement people do have precognition. There are, of course, the well-documented cases of exceptional clairvoyants like Edgar Cayce, Eileen Garrett, and Matthew Manning. But at a more humdrum level, most people can give you one or two stories from their own lives of precognitive dreams or premonitions that have proved to be startlingly accurate, as well as experiences of déjà vu. Then there is the scientific evidence of precognitive remote viewing considered earlier in the chapter.

I wrote this last paragraph at Esalen Institute in California and went to dinner immediately afterward. A woman from Argentina sat down beside me. In response to my question about what had brought her such a long distance to take a workshop, she replied it was because of a precognitive dream three months before. "I couldn't have made it up," she said. "At that stage I didn't know any of the circumstances revealed to me in the dream. It was only four weeks ago I found out that the people and objects I saw in the dream do in fact exist."

Precognition is an inexplicable anomaly in the framework of linear time but is perfectly consistent with a multidimensional present. So too are past-life remembrances, which can be understood as glimpses of current activities of other parts of ourselves in a different dimension.

The existence of a multidimensional present also makes sense of time slips, in which individuals typically find themselves among people and events of another era.

I personally experienced a time slip of a somewhat different kind. It occurred one evening at the San Francisco Asian Art Museum, where I was attending an inaugural reception for an exhibit of Indian art. I was slightly late. Most guests were already in the gallery when I entered the foyer in which a group of Indian women were performing a folk dance. They were moving in a circle that almost filled the room, and I stood in a corner to watch.

Suddenly a man and a woman carrying camera equipment hurried in the front door. They were talking animatedly to one other and inadvertently barged into the circle of dancers. Extracting themselves without apology, they went quickly into the auditorium, still lost in conversation.

As the dancers regrouped, I felt peeved at such inconsiderate behavior. Lo and behold, the next instant the same couple, still festooned with camera equipment and still engaged in conversation, came in the front door again, but this time they deftly maneuvered around the outside of the circle and entered the gallery without creating any disturbance.

I was flabbergasted! What had I seen? Two pairs of identical twins? The dancers gave no indication that they had noticed anything unusual. Could the photographers have left the gallery by a side door and reentered the foyer? Insufficient time had elapsed for that to be possible, it seemed, but nonetheless I hurried into the auditorium to see if I could find an exit door that could have been used. There was none close by.

Was I dreaming, or had I somehow created an instant replay in order to correct the couple's gauche behavior? Your guess is as good as mine. I am certain that what I experienced is inexplicable in the framework of linear time, but perhaps it makes some sense if the now is multidimensional.

Hauntings are another phenomenon that could perhaps be explained by a "layered" or multitiered present. Consider the case of the famous English psychic Matthew Manning and his family, who shared a house in the 1970s with Robert Webbe, an eighteenth-century "ghost." Manning tells the story in his book *The Strangers.*

Over a period of six years, Manning and Webbe had numerous conversations. Manning could see Webbe, though not vice versa. Webbe regularly lit the Manning household candles and gave the family presents of eighteenth-century objects. He also put some of their possessions in a hiding place, which he revealed when Manning inquired after the missing items. In their last conversation in May 1977, Webbe expressed fears for his own sanity because "I hear a voice in myne head and not in myne ears." "You frighten me," he told Manning. "Are you a ghoule of tomorrow?"[13]

In coming to terms with the idea of no time but now, I have found it helpful to visualize the present as a landscape stretching away on all sides. Some parts of this landscape are close at hand and well known, others are far off and unfamiliar. Interestingly enough, this idea seems to be implicit in the word *kal* in the languages of north India. *Kal* translates in English as "time" but also as "tomorrow" *and* "yesterday." The word seems to imply extensions of the present—those parts of the landscape of now that are farther off in one direction or another. Significantly, Indians live so much in the present that they are notorious to Westerners for their seeming disregard for future scheduling.

Every Exit an Entrance Somewhere Else

I have dealt with memory: time in the mind. But what about physical growth and decay: time in matter? How can a permanent present deal with birth, aging, and death? This is a tough one. In our culture it is axiomatic that there can be no change without time.

For starters we should recall that particle physicists have observed that this "law of nature" does not apply at the subatomic level. Down at what we have been taught in the modern West to regard as the foundation of material existence, change takes place without any observable passage of time. It is all happening in the now. "For us believing physicists," wrote Albert Einstein, "this separation between past, present and future has the value of mere illusion, however tenacious."[14]

Change is one of the constants at the subatomic level. Particles are forever appearing and disappearing in a manner so elusive and mysterious that it made the early quantum physicists at best reluctant to believe their observations. At worst it made them doubt their own sanity.

> The idea of how Universe functions that comes out of my tradition, and I hear echoes of it in other Indian traditions, is that Universe is Space which contains Energy. Energy of its nature moves. As it moves it produces Change.
>
> In the Western world we call that Change "time"—past, present, and future. But the idea is that it isn't time at all. It is Change—it was, it is, it will be.[15]

The writer is Paula Underwood Spencer, and her tradition is Native American Oneida. Theoretical physicist David Bohm believed that quantum mechanics points to the same conclusion: Change is the ground of being. It is the now.

> This view implies that flow is, in some sense, prior to that of the "things" that can be seen to form and dissolve in this flow. . . . That is, there is a universal flux that cannot be defined explicitly but which can be known only implicitly, as indicated by the explicitly definable forms and shapes, some stable and some unstable, that can be abstracted from the universal flux. In this flow, mind and matter are not separate substances. Rather, they are different aspects of one whole and unbroken movement. . . . What is implied by this proposal is that what we call empty space contains an immense background of energy, and that matter as we know it is a small, "quantized" wavelike excitation on top of this background, rather like a tiny ripple on a vast sea.[16]

This understanding that change is the ground of being is also found in Sufism and Hinduism.

> *Every moment the world is renewed, and we are unaware of its being renewed as it remains the same in appearance.*
>
> Rumi

On this Sufi teaching Seyyed Hossein Nasr comments: "The Absolute gives of Himself continuously; therefore cannot stay put."[17] For Hindus this is *leela:* the joyous, never-ceasing dance that is creation; God's play in the universe, as the universe. "I am the Dancer and the Dance."

I was blessed with a direct revelation of *leela.* One summer I lived alone for some months in the city of Simla in the Himalayan foothills. One day with the American poet Judith Kroll, a long-time resident of India, I trekked down a deep, jungle ravine below the city. After a picnic lunch we were meditating in a fern-fringed glade beside a stream when simultaneously we opened our eyes to find before us the Mother Goddess sitting naked in the yogic lotus position. The image was a hundred feet or more in height, covering the entire cliff face. Startled, we checked with each other and determined that we were seeing the same thing.

Then I looked around to discover a transformed world, radiant and in dancing motion. Everything was flowing into everything else: trees, plants, butterflies, water, earth, and myself. I knew in the very fiber of my being that there are no separations. All is one. I am nature and nature is me. I also knew in that timeless moment that there is no past and future, only the boundless present. Thus, there is no death—simply continual transformation from one form to another and back and forth between form and the formless.

The mystical traditions all testify that separations are illusory, including the separations of past, present, and future. There are non-Western societies whose cultural forms serve to reinforce this understanding in everyday life. Bali, in Indonesia, is a good example.

In Bali, according to American anthropologist Clifford Geertz, "the leading motif is the immobilization of time through the iteration of form." Geertz continues:

> Physically men come and go as the ephemerae they are, but socially the dramatis personae remain eternally the same. . . . the stages of human life are not conceived in terms of the processes of biological aging, to which little cultural attention is given, but of those of social regenesis. . . . What counts is reproductive continuity, the preservation of the community's ability to perpetuate itself just as it is.[18]

In Bali the labels by which people are identified do not draw attention to their individuality. Personal names, for instance, are seldom heard. Rather, the Balinese place them in recurring cycles. It is common to designate people by their order of birth in the family, but only four stages are recognized. Thus, while the fourth-born child will be called Ktut, the fifth must share with his or her eldest sibling the title Wayan, first-born; so too must the ninth if the family is fecund.

> For all procreating couples, births form a circular succession of Wayans, Njomans, Mades, and Ktuts, and once again Wayans, an endless four-stage replication of an imperishable form.[19]

We in the modern West are made intimately aware of the passage of time (as we understand it) because we journey in close association with unique individuals whose aging and ultimate death measure our own personal passage. For the Balinese the depersonalization of social intercourse creates (is part and parcel of, is made possible by) a permanent present, a timeless cosmic stage on which the same actors appear over and over—not the same individuals (we might point out) but the same characters (as the Balinese would emphasize). They are not always visible on stage, nor is the stage set always the same, but the old familiar characters appear again and again because the great play is forever. In search of an analogy from European traditions, one figure readily comes to mind: Santa Claus—every year the same no matter who wears the costume.

Climax, so important to satisfy the Western esthetic of purposeful linearity, is not valued by the Balinese. A concert of the *gamelan* (percussion orchestra) may seem undisciplined and directionless to an observer experienced only in a Western orchestral tradition, where the performance is neatly aligned from its crisp beginning in the hushed silence following the conductor's dramatic entry to the crescendo that signals the climactic applause. By contrast, in Bali it is difficult for the uninitiated to tell when preparations are over and the concert itself has started. Some musicians are still tuning their instruments while others are playing their pieces. Moreover, the performance seems to drift on and on without signified closure. The performers may come and go during a recital and mingle with members of the audience with an apparent casualness that blurs the distinction between "stage" and "auditorium."

Geertz comments, "Ritual often seems, as in temple celebrations, to consist largely in getting ready and cleaning up."[20] The metaphysical explanation is that the music, drama, and worship are always in existence, part of the imperishable cosmic theater (as is life itself), and their manifestions "on stage" are but "thickenings"—"for a time," as we would inappropriately express it. There can be a pulsing but no climax of the never-ending, that which is always repeating.

> *Or say that the end precedes the beginning,*
> *And the end and the beginning were always there*
> *Before the beginning and after the end.*
> *And all is always now.*
>
> T. S. Eliot

Earlier I wrote: "With our concepts we empower particular forms and processes. We give them substance. Reality is not independent of our consciousness." Different cultures construct different worlds. By focusing upon the impermanence of particular chunks of matter, we of the West plunge ourselves into a torrent of time. By focusing upon the continuity of life expressed in a repetition of familiar forms, the Balinese are able to live in a permanent present.

> Morgaine speaks. . . . "Perhaps, and I think this more as I grow older, what we speak of as time passing happens only because we have made it a habit, in our very blood and bones, to count things. . . . Within the fairy country I knew nothing of the passing of time, and so for me it did not pass."[21]

Earlier I posed this question: How can a permanent present deal with birth, aging, and death? Following the example of the Balinese, we can recognize physical growth and decay merely as "different aspects of one whole and unbroken movement."

Here is an illustration from the New Zealand bush. It has been discovered in these lush temperate rainforests that the root systems of neighboring trees are interconnected and that they exchange nutrients.

When a tree dies, its roots continue to function as part of the feeding system of its neighbors.

Or consider an apple tree. It grows and matures, changes color and shape. In some years it blossoms and bears fruit; in others it remains barren. Despite its constant change we think of it as the same tree. One of its activities is to produce apples containing seeds. Instead of classifying the resulting seedlings as separate forms, we can, if we so choose, see them as a manifestation of permanence—ongoing apple life. We can heed the wise words of that sage fellow, the Player in Tom Stoppard's comedy *Rosencrantz and Guildenstern Are Dead:* "Look on every exit being an entrance somewhere else."[22]

> *Seeds are the tickets to ride.*
> *There's one life behind them all.*
> *One Life, that the seeds grant us entry to.*
> *Seeds are the vehicles, into and through life.*
> *Body seeds. . . .*
>
> *Life was there before the body,*
> *and will be after.*
> *Bodies come and go,*
> *Life is infinite.*[23]
>
> Tony Basilio

A similar shift in perception can help us understand biological evolution in a new way. Instead of a sequence of time-bound forms advancing on a fixed line from the simple to the complex, evolution can be seen as the never-ceasing dance of life-energy shaping vital, interconnected patterns—a vivid kaleidoscope of opportunities for creative spirit in matter.

Living in the now gives humanity the opportunity it so desperately needs for reconnection with nature, which knows only the permanent present. Of this the poets sing.

> *The tree bears its thousand years*
> *as one large majestic moment.*
>
> Rabindranath Tagore

These roses under my window make no reference to former roses or to better ones; they are for what they are; they exist with God today. There is no time for them. There is simply the rose; it is perfect in every moment of its existence. But man postpones or remembers; he does not live in the present, but with reverted eye laments the past, or heedless of the riches that surround him, stands on tiptoe to foresee the future. He cannot be happy and strong until he too lives with nature in the present, above time.

Ralph Waldo Emerson

The Pattern That Connects

Another question arises: In the permanent present, where do we locate causation? If there is no sequence in time, how can a reason be found for any particular occurrence?

This is not an easy proposition for us to wrap our minds around. How can things possibly work except as "one damn thing after another"? As John Berger observes, we Westerners experience severe discomfort when we attempt to come to terms with any time system other than the unilinear: "It creates a moral vertigo since all [our] morality is based on cause and effect."[24]

An explanatory system that relies wholly upon sequence to understand causation is unable to accommodate simultaneity. Unlike cultures that recognize a multidimensional present, we have no way of explaining the mutual influence of simultaneously occurring events. Despite more than a half century of experimental evidence from particle physics indicating that the theory of sequential causation is insufficient to explain the behavior of subatomic matter, it is still a fixed tenet of our culture that there must be a past cause for any present effect.

In striking contrast, it is not sequence but simultaneity that has explanatory power for peoples who understand the present to be multidimensional. In these cultures, coincidental occurrences mark out significances. For instance, in Indonesia the word for "coincidence," *kebetulan,* also means "truth."

In the last section I used the word *timeless* in discussing Balinese culture. This is not strictly accurate. To speak of "timelessness" is right for Bali only in the sense that flow and direction are absent, not in the sense of time as never changing. In fact, the Balinese have excruciatingly intricate calendars to reckon time, but "they don't tell you what time it is; they tell you what kind of time it is."[25] It is the quality of time, its varied texture, that concerns them.

Think of a patterned fabric, one of those beautiful batiks for which Bali is famous. It is all of one piece, but in some places its pattern is rich and thick, in others meager or plain. So too with time. Though it is all "now," its texture is varied. Just as we will delight in those places where the pattern in the fabric is dense, so do the Balinese derive delight and awe from densely textured times: "thick time," *ruwat*. Significantly, *ruwat* has the double meaning of "liberation," for in thick time, with its many coincidences, truths are revealed. This is the time of conjunctures between the worlds of humans, spirits, and gods.

One of the best-known stories in the Western tradition, the Christmas story, can help us understand thick time. The star that lit the sky over the stable in Bethlehem, striking awe into the hearts of shepherds and guiding wise men of the east to the cradle of the newborn Messiah, sends rational scientific minds to astronomical calendars to find an explanatory comet. No such difficulty for the Balinese. A season that combined a flight from a king driven by doomful prophecy to slaughter his own people, a virgin birth in a strange bedchamber, a great heavenly light, and a pilgrimage of devotees from a far place could be nothing other than thick time, a time of powerful spiritual significance.

For people like the Balinese who understand the present to be multidimensional, the "thickening" of time explains why things happen. Explanatory power lies not in a sequence of means and ends but in the patterned whole: *ruwat,* the combination of textures. In the permanent now, it is not order in time but correct order in relationships that answers the question: How can it be the way it is?

To illustrate this, let's take an example from another culture, that of the Trobrianders, who live in the Solomon Islands in the western Pacific. In their language there is only one tense: the present. The cultural focus of this people is on being rather than becoming. Sequence in time is of negligible importance to their explanations of how things happen. Conversely, proper patterning is highly valued. It is truth, Trobriand science.

Here's how the Trobrianders explain human conception: Pregnancy occurs, they say, when a preordained combination is achieved. That combination must include the presence in the womb of the spirit of an ancestor, gift giving by male to female, and sexual intercourse. No one element is the prime cause, nor is it the sequence that explains conception.

From the Western scientific viewpoint this explanation is insufficient because it fails to locate the act of sexual intercourse in time. Our science "knows" there are only a few days in the female menstrual cycle when the egg can be fertilized.

A convincing rebuttal of Trobriand belief? Not really. In the first place, what is advanced as scientific fact—that conception occurs as a result of intercourse during ovulation—is a statement of probability, no more. No scientist knows for certain why pregnancy happens at some times and not others. Might not consciousness play a role: the Trobrianders' sense of the fitness of things because of a proper gift given? Moreover, the Trobriand account addresses the not inconsequential question of the origin of the human soul, something to which Western science turns a blind eye.

For peoples who understand the present to be multidimensional, I said, the "thickening" of time explains why things happen. Here is another illustration of this from the Pacific. On February 14, 1779, Captain James Cook was fatally stabbed at Kealakekua Bay on the island of Hawaii. His death has baffled historians. Why did people who welcomed the great navigator like a conquering hero in January, single him out from his officers and men for a brutal attack when he returned in February? The answer, I believe, is that unwittingly Cook became the lead player in a tragic drama of thick time.[26]

By "coincidence," Cook's two vessels, *Resolution* and *Discovery*, arrived off Hawaii at exactly the point in the annual Hawaiian ritual calendar when the image of the fertility god Lono was carried around the island. Offshore, Cook made the same circuit as the image, of which he knew nothing, and arrived at its destination, Kealakekua ("The Path-of-the-God"), at precisely the same time. Some 10,000 Hawaiians from every quarter of the island had gathered to participate in this most miraculous event, the manifestation of the god Lono in the flesh.

The British mariners received a welcome far exceeding anything they had experienced in ten years of Pacific voyaging, with men offering lavish gifts of food and women eager for sexual intercourse. Priests wrapped the captain in the red *tapa* cloth of a temple image and led him to the temple with cries of "O Lono." Still innocent of the significance of events, Cook allowed his arms to be held outstretched, while sacrifices were made before him. He became the image of Lono, a duplicate of the wooden crosspiece icon that is the god's form.

Cook was also honored by the king, even while the king and his chiefs watched warily for any signs that the newcomers, divine or otherwise, had ambitions to usurp power. The aristocrats were reassured by several coincidental acts by the British that seemed to indicate they knew their correct and limited symbolic role. The most astounding coincidence of all was the British choice to depart on a day appropriate for closure of the season of Lono.

Once the fertility god had left as he did every year, the people resumed farming and fishing—*tapu* (forbidden) activities during the preceding month. They were therefore shocked to see the British ships sailing back into Kealakekua Bay on February 11, forced to return because a mast on the *Resolution* had snapped in a storm.

Immediately it was evident to the British that the social climate had changed. The Hawaiians believed that Cook as Lono had come back to overthrow their chiefs and seize power. Tension reached a climax when a ship's boat was stolen, and Cook decided to take the king hostage until it was returned. When the attempt was made, the king's courtiers fell on Cook, stabbing him repeatedly with iron daggers.

Cook was a victim of thick time. A series of coincidences had transformed him unawares into a god. He died because his chance return disturbed ritual order, thereby endangering the political system. The aristocracy feared he was there to seize their land. In a strange way, they were right. Cook's voyages had opened the Pacific for European and American imperialism, and within a century the Hawaiian chiefs would lose their power. They too were tragedians in a drama of thick time beyond their comprehension.

In a permanent present, explanatory power lies in the combination of right textures, the pattern that connects. Carl Jung called this pattern synchronicity, "namely, a peculiar interdependence of objective events among themselves as well as with the subjective (psychic) states of the observer or observers."[27]

> It seems, indeed, as though time, far from being an abstraction, is a concrete continuum which contains qualities or basic conditions that manifest themselves simultaneously in different places through parallelisms that cannot be explained causally.
>
> Synchronicity is no more baffling or mysterious than the discontinuities of physics. It is only the ingrained belief in the sovereign power of causality that creates intellectual difficulties and makes it appear unthinkable that causeless events exist or could ever occur.[28]

Present Mindfulness

Today we know that time is a construction and therefore carries an ethical responsibility.

Ilya Prigogine and Isabelle Stengers

We've looked at a variety of philosophical objections to a permanent present, but there remains an ethical concern that merits attention. Living completely in the now, it may be argued, implies a selfish neglect of the future.

Certainly this construction of time like any other can be lived self-indulgently, but that is not an inevitable consequence of present-mindedness. Indeed, I believe it offers fewer "easy outs" than linear time, where we can conveniently dump our unresolved problems on the past or the future.

Let me give examples. The creation of the United States of America in the eighteenth and nineteenth centuries involved enslavement of Africans and genocide of Native Americans. We customarily say these are "things of the past," and this enables us (if we are not ourselves Native or African American) to turn a blind eye to the resultant racial discrimination, deprivation, and suffering that continue. These are present problems that are dumped on the past.

Another example: When nuclear technologies were developed in the 1940s and 1950s, there was no known way to dispose of the radioactive toxins produced, but the scientists and engineers of the day assured themselves and others that by and by something would be devised. They simply dumped this present problem on the future. Sadly but significantly, in the 1990s it is to Native American reservations that the nuclear and other toxin-producing industries have looked to find disposal sites for their lethal wastes.

Such avoidance is made possible by the segmentation of time. "Our culture encloses us in a tiny compartment of time, increasingly cut off from past and future," observes deep ecologist Joanna Macy.

> But we can reclaim our birthright and inhabit broader reaches of time by sensing the companionship of those who have gone before. They are with us. . . . They who loved and tended this Earth bequeath you the strength and wisdom you will need now to do what must be done, so their journey may continue.
>
> Just as the life that pulses in our bodies goes back to the beginnings of the Earth, so too does that heartbeat carry the pulse of those to come after. . . . Given the power of the life that links us, it is plausible to me that these future generations want to lend us courage for what we do for their sake.[29]

I call this "present mindfulness": the awareness that future and past are in the present. It is here and only here that we can act. "The point of power is in the present," as Seth told us.[30]

Our task? To enrich and enliven the creative present, encouraging diversity so that our organic communities may have alternative ways to grow in that continuing, unbroken present that carries us down the stream of generations through which life survives and prospers.

Be here now. Work with the present. This is far more demanding than devising imaginary futures, which too often prove to be no more than projections of narrow slices of the past. It is also far more rewarding. "Experiencing the present purely is being emptied and hollow," says Annie Dillard. "You catch grace as a man fills his cup under a waterfall."[31]

Is There Any Time but the Present?

how fortunate are you and I
whose home is timelessness we
who have wandered down from
fragrant mountains of eternal now
to frolic in such mysteries as birth
and death a day
(or maybe even less)

e. e. cummings

7

THE MAHATMA AND THE SHREWD PEASANT

Spiritual Politics

We have two tasks: To learn what's needed and to act. As Will Rogers said, "Even if you're on the right track, you'll get run over if you just sit there." To create the world we want in the twenty-first century, we must have an effective politics. The other side of the coin: For the next century to be livable, you and I must participate in the reshaping of politics as a life-enhancing endeavor.

What are the elements of such a politics?

1. A recognition that consciousness makes reality, that our politics is a manifestation of the state of our individual and collective awareness.
2. A recognition that politics shapes consciousness. As we act, we learn. Therefore, political symbols and processes must be ennobling, teaching us love, empathy, and compassion.
3. Means and ends must be congruent: "There is no way to peace. Peace is the way."
4. Our politics must encompass transformative economics and a just social order.
5. Politics must respect and empower the feminine.

6. Politics must cherish and nourish diversity.

7. Acknowledging that our perceptions are limited and changing, our politics must make room for different truths and different histories.

8. Politics must enhance consensus and harmonious community rather than intensifying antagonisms and divisions.

9. While valuing and encouraging creative leadership, politics must be alert to the lusts of power and restrain them. Rather than fostering "power over," politics must nourish "power-from-within"—the self-empowerment of individuals and groups.

10. Recognizing the psychic need for courageous engagement, politics must be the path for the hero's and heroine's journey.

11. Ours must be a politics of welfare for all beings, not just humans, expanding democracy to "biocracy," as Tom Berry calls it.

12. It must be a politics of sacred limits, spiritual politics.

Surely a tall order? Indeed, but we don't have to start from scratch. This political agenda already has been applied successfully in this century, and from that we can take courage. What's more, it was devised and applied for the first time by a nobody who rode out, like Don Quixote, with what seemed ridiculously high ideals.

> I am told that religion and politics are different spheres of life. But I would say without a moment's hesitation and yet in all modesty that those who claim this do not know what religion is.[1]
>
> Mahatma Gandhi

A Nobody Who Changed the World

The image of Mahatma Gandhi that photos, movies, and sculpture have made most familiar is of a skinny, knobby-kneed, middle-aged man wrapped in a *dhoti,* wire-rimmed glasses perched on nose, setting forth in sandals with just a walking stick for assistance on a mammoth trek through village India. It is an apt image, for it captures the brilliant absurdity of his political strategy.

The year is 1930, and Gandhi is leading the Dandi salt march. The world is mired in economic depression, and on every continent demagogues are offering violent solutions. In Europe, fascist and Marxist thugs break heads and spread terror in the name of competing ideologies. In the Soviet Union, the Stalinist purges are under way, and the Ukrainians are being starved systematically so the resources of their rich land can serve as capital for Russian industrialization. In Europe's African and Asian colonies, the efficacy of the airplane as an instrument of civilian coercion is being tested. Imperial Japan's military are preparing to launch the first assaults on mainland Asia, and in India itself, paramilitary organization, uniforms, and swaggering slogans have gained popularity in party politics.

Yet here is this little man leading a great national movement with watchcries of truth, love, self-suffering, abstinence, and nonviolence. Surely anomalous watchcries for the twentieth century with its emphasis on revolution and violent confrontation?

"Creative maladjustment" was recommended in the 1960s by Gandhian disciple Martin Luther King Jr. in a speech to students at Berkeley as a highly desirable character trait. To understand Gandhi's creative maladjustment we should look at his life.

Mohandas Karamchand Gandhi was born in 1869 in an isolated corner of northwestern India, where he was raised in an environment of orthodox Hinduism. His was an educated family, which understood the importance of English-language competence for aspiring members of the new generation. Gandhi was put into that most favored of professions for the nineteenth-century Indian elites, the law, and as few Indians in that century could hope to do, he was sent to Britain in 1887 for extended legal education.

Still a teenager, he was lonely, cold, and uncomfortable in his first months in London, as his stiff, unsmiling photographs of the period suggest: flannel suit, starched shirt, Victorian high collar, and all. Not until he dropped out of his legal studies and began to associate with a vegetarian, pacifist group did he discover some warmth and friendship in that alien city. In this company he rubbed shoulders with such European minds as Robert Owen and Leo Tolstoy, and the Americans

Emerson and Thoreau. The mixed metaphor of shoulders and minds is appropriate, for Gandhi does not appear to have gained a deep understanding of these thinkers. They influenced him, but mainly by reinforcing established beliefs. The basis of his philosophy is to be sought within Indian traditions.

In 1891, having belatedly resumed his legal studies and passed the bar examinations, Gandhi returned to Bombay, where he was an instant and spectacular flop as a barrister. Rising in court to plead his first case, he found himself at a loss for words and as a result was swiftly demoted to office work. In 1893 the firm received a lucrative but routine request for legal counsel from a member of the Indian community in the Transvaal, South Africa, and the diligent but apparently inconsequential M. K. Gandhi was dispatched to attend to the matter.

The experience in South Africa, though humdrum in origin, was to work a transformation in Gandhi's life so spectacular that it might be compared to that of Saul on the road to Damascus. Gandhi arrived in South Africa to be met with brutal racial discrimination such as he had never experienced in India or Britain. For a time he was at a loss for a course of action, but finally, in May 1894, goaded by the imminent disenfranchisement of his compatriots in Natal, he formed the Natal Indian Congress. The inarticulate young lawyer was gone. In his place stood an outspoken and courageous crusader against racial injustice.

Satyagraha

For the next twenty years until the outbreak of the First World War, Gandhi worked in South Africa. In this land far from India, step by step he fashioned a new revolutionary technique for which he coined the name *satyagraha:* "the force which is born of truth and love." This he contrasted with "brute force."

He insisted that *satyagraha* not be equated with pacifism, for there is nothing passive about it. *Satyagraha* is nonviolent but vigorous resistance to injustice and oppression, requiring rigorous personal discipline and community training. In developing *satyagraha,* Gandhi drew on the Hindu principle of *ahimsa:* reverence for life and nurturance of its multitudinous variety. It is an active principle, which includes the avoidance of harm to all things living but goes far beyond this to embrace universal altruism.

Gandhi taught that nonviolent resistance to oppression is an imperative. "Noncooperation with evil is as much a duty as is cooperation with good." Injustice must not go unresisted. Urging his fellow Indians in South Africa to united action in defense of their communal rights, his call was "not to submit; to suffer." Again he drew on traditions of his native Gujarat in applying to politics a technique of moral suasion traditionally used there in familial and mercantile disputes. The method was for the aggrieved party to shame the adversary and win sympathetic support for the cause by a display of self-abnegation, most commonly by fasting.

With this model in mind, Gandhi devised a succession of nonviolent confrontations with the South African authorities. The issues were diverse, but always there was a common aim: to provide those in power with opportunities to demonstrate the injustice of their regime by goading them into retaliation against limited, nonviolent, symbolic acts of protest.

Gandhi achieved a surprising number of victories, but the long-term gains for the South African Indian community were negligible. The real significance of this period of his work is found in the experience it gave him as a builder of consensual community and as a political organizer, tactician, and publicist. His trips to India and Britain in search of support and finance provided enduring contacts for his later work with Indian nationalism, and the attention his movement attracted in the press assured him of fame among politically aware Indians.

His international experience was gained in a momentous period. The last quarter of the nineteenth century and the first decade of the twentieth saw the culmination of European expansion. Almost every inhabited portion of the globe was now under direct or indirect imperial control. This period also marked the triumph of the scientific-industrial revolution, with the emergence of petrochemicals, electricity, and the internal combustion engine. "Limitless progress for man" through a complete technological domination of nature was widely proclaimed as a certainty before the end of the millenium. It was a powerful tide of conviction, and there were precious few like Gandhi who had the desire or temerity to swim against it. But swim he did.

Return to India

Gandhi left South Africa following the outbreak of the First World War in 1914 after achieving one of his more notable successes against the Union government. His opponent of many years, the distinguished Minister of the Interior, General Jan Smuts, breathed a sigh of relief. "The saint has left our shores," he wrote. "I sincerely hope for ever."[2] So it proved.

Gandhi in India had bigger fish to fry—if I may use so inappropriate a metaphor for a crusading vegetarian! He returned with a clear determination to play a role in the nationalist movement. With characteristic patience he waited for several years before choosing his own distinctive point of entry into the political arena. In 1918 he initiated a peasant *satyagraha* against British indigo farmers in a severely impoverished agricultural district. The indigo industry he attacked was uneconomic and had been maintained only by crude exploitation of the peasant cultivators. The *satyagraha* was a swift and complete success, and its publicity precipitated Gandhi into the front rank of nationalist leaders.

For him it was a dictum of politics that an unjust regime is bound to enlarge the area of conflict by its overreaction to protest. The months following the indigo movement proved him right. Disturbed by industrial as well as peasant unrest and with a weather eye on Bolshevik successes in Russia, the Government of India insisted on arming itself with legislation to extend its draconian wartime powers. Gandhi responded with a call for a nationwide general strike. In some places the jittery British retaliated brutally. In the bitter aftermath, Gandhi was able to persuade the preeminent nationalist organization, the Indian National Congress, to accept his blueprint for reorganization and his leadership of a mass campaign of noncooperation.

Political Principles

The principles that would guide Gandhi's three decades of political work in India were revealed in this campaign.

First, he proposed that all participation in the activities of British

Indian government cease and that Congressmen devote themselves to the construction of national institutions: "a government of one's own within the dead shell of the foreign government." Resistance, nonviolent and symbolic, might be offered to particular acts of British repression, but the really important work was in national reconstruction.

For the nation as for the individual, Gandhi taught, salvation could be gained only by inner transformation. Society had to be rid of its evils, especially those of dissension and exploitation. He called for religious and caste reconciliation and an end to economic oppression. The nationalist movement had to be a people's movement to benefit the mass of the people.

Gandhi insisted that Congress demonstrate its concern for the welfare of the poor by adopting a program of economic rehabilitation. Congress members should leave their urban professions and go into the villages to start cottage industries. The local manufacture of cotton cloth should be revived. The spinning wheel should become the symbol of India's revitalization, and the wearing of *khadi* (homespun, handwoven cloth) a gesture of the nation's rejection of economic and political imperialism.

Gandhi practiced what he preached. In South Africa he had formed a commune, Tolstoy Farm, where he shared with family and friends of many races and creeds the diverse labors of farming, cottage industry, and political mobilization. Similarly, in India he chose a rural base. His ashram in western India became a model for communities throughout the subcontinent in which men and women of different religions and castes worked together to raise local levels of economic well-being, education, and political organization.

As a nationalist leader Gandhi was frequently on the road, but his intense public periods were punctuated with intervals of retreat, some lasting months at a time, during which he would not permit the world's clamor to interrupt the ashram routines of manual labor, service, and meditation. His response to the viceroy, seeking a political parley on one occasion, has become a part of modern Indian folk legend: "Please tell his Excellency I can't meet him then. That is my day to sweep the village lane."

Gandhi stuck to his principles even in the thick of the fight. In its initial stages in the early months of 1921, the first noncooperation movement was a remarkable success. The unprecedented numbers participating in the agitation, Muslims as well as Hindus, raised serious alarm among British officials. To the perplexity of many of his colleagues in the Congress hierarchy, however, Gandhi seemed to value opportunities for confrontation with the government less than those for popular political education and social reform. *Satyagraha* was not merely a strategy for struggle against the British; it was a vehicle for transforming the consciousness of a nation. The conviction that too few of his followers had internalized the nonviolent principles of *ahimsa* led Gandhi to issue a sudden call in February 1922 for an end to the agitation.

He initiated two other great campaigns and a host of minor actions before India gained national independence. Always the major emphasis was on ethical considerations, with Gandhi insisting doggedly that he alone must be their arbiter. Always he was unpredictable in his tactical decisions and in his timing of the final withdrawal. As a consequence, some became exasperated with his leadership.

We need not follow Gandhi step by step through this quarter century, but we must surely ask: How could he retain his following despite such apparently eccentric political behavior? The question is the more intriguing when we realize that on several occasions he withdrew from active politics for five or more years at a time, and yet he was still able to emerge at his chosen moment to resume the leadership of the nationalist movement.

One answer is that Gandhi was a phenomenal publicist, communicator, and organizer. He also knew the value of good lieutenants. It is paradoxical that while he was not particularly responsive to criticism (being too assured of the quality of his own judgment), he was willing to tolerate strong differences of opinion among his associates. Consequently he retained the loyalty of a remarkable number of talented and forceful workers.

Another of Gandhi's personal attributes was extraordinary physical and mental stamina. Even in his later years the seemingly frail old man could outwalk, outsit, and outtalk others half his age.

> This little man of poor physique had something of steel in him,
> something rock-like which did not yield to physical powers. . . .

Consciously and deliberately meek and humble, yet he was full of power and authority. . . . His calm, deep eyes would hold one and . . . his voice, clear and limpid would purr its way into the heart.[3]

Jawaharlal Nehru's words are echoed by virtually every person who knew Gandhi. If there is anyone in this century who merits the adjective "charismatic," it is this man. He had what I can describe only as amazing mass appeal. He was known and revered by millions in urban and rural India as no other figure in historic times. Wherever he went, the news of his coming spread farther and faster than normal means of communication can properly explain.

Gandhi was a master of symbolism. Let me give an example: The aforementioned Dandi salt march of 1930 was one of his most brilliant, yet simple symbolic successes. All humans need salt, and in many places in India it can be produced with the simplest equipment or just scraped from dried pools or marshes. In order to levy a tax on salt, however, the British Indian government prohibited its unlicensed production. Obviously, an attack on this restriction would be universally popular and would serve as an indictment of a regime that taxed the basic needs of its pitifully poor colonial population.

Brilliant in conception, equally brilliant in execution: A long march through village India gathering thousands of supporters, drawing the attention of the world press to the moment by the sea when the imperial policemen would be forced to arrest the country's most revered leader and unmanageable numbers of his adherents simply for lighting a fire and heating a pan of salt water.

"My Life Is My Message"

Gandhi himself was a living symbol, his lifestyle a spiritual statement. The ideal that he held up to himself and others was that of the *sanyasin*, the holy man fearless of his environment because physical survival means little to him. With no defensiveness, there is no bluster or aggression. Although Gandhi's rejection of worldly comforts was sometimes ostentatious (a puckish disciple is credited with the comment "Ah, if the Mahatma only knew what it costs us for him to live the simple life"⁴), there can be no question but that he was sincere in his conviction that strength came through a renunciation of sensual indulgence.

Gandhi accepted traditional Indian theories of physiology and psychology, which hold that the bodily essences, which give physical, mental, and spiritual strength, are dissipated through outpourings of anger and sex. They are increased by yoga (disciplined meditation and exercise) and the intake of pure foods, particularly vegetables and milk products. Gandhi shared this belief with the vast majority of his fellow Hindus, Jains, and Buddhists. They saw that he was a disciplined *brahmachari* (celibate), and they had no difficulty understanding the source of his superior stamina and moral virtue.

He earned for himself the title *Mahatma*, "great soul." It is a title he disclaimed, as any great soul would! It is significant nonetheless, for it suggests a link with an Indian tradition of leadership transcending communal divisions. This is the tradition of the religious ascetic, combining spiritual instruction for a peasant community with its leadership in rebellion against oppressors: policemen, tax collectors, landlords, moneylenders. Gandhi could easily be understood by rural people as a great leader, a Mahatma, in this tradition of resistance.

Viewed in this light, his periodic withdrawals from national politics can be seen as essential to the sustenance of his power in this other arena. These were times for spiritual renewal. They were also times for village work, which (as he never tired of telling his fellow Congress members) was the best way to keep a healthy sense of proportion. "Think globally, act locally," the slogan of American environmentalists in the 1970s and 1980s, was the principle by which Gandhi lived more than a half century earlier. Daily toil in a village replaced abstractions with people, animals, plants, and the business of keeping alive. "To forget how to dig the earth and tend the soil is to forget ourselves," Gandhi would say.

By now it should be clear that Gandhi's main criterion for choosing a line of political action was not the prospect of gaining immediate advantage over the British. The acid test for him of any action was its spiritual fitness. In choosing he asked divine guidance.

I have taken up things as they have come to me and always in

189

trembling and fear. I did not work out the possibilities . . . I fancy that I followed His will and no other and He will lead me "amid the encircling gloom."

Although the political options Gandhi chose never evoked universal enthusiasm, the clarity of his spiritual commitment did give him moral authority. It also gave his life a significance transcending the historic time and place in which he worked. He remains a teacher for us today.

Questions for the Mahatma

As students, then, let's put some questions to the Mahatma.[5]

> Leadership based on divine guidance has a checkered history. How can authoritarianism be avoided?

"God appears to you not in person but in action," Gandhi replies. Political truth is not found in abstract, fixed principles; it is something that must be sought over and over again in particular situations. Absolute truth is certainly known to God (or, to put it another way, absolute truth is God), but humans can grasp truth only partially. Spiritual politics is not adherence to dogma. It is the unending search for truthful solutions to practical problems of conflict. This explains the title of Gandhi's autobiography: *The Story of My Experiments with Truth.*

Given that we all operate from partial truth (or imperfect understanding, if you prefer), we inevitably bring some untruth to a confrontation, no matter how "right" we may think we are. All parties in a dispute are to some degree wrong, and it is Gandhi's teaching that a primary purpose of political engagement is to provide opportunities to learn how to eradicate error—for oneself as well as for one's opponent. We must oppose the injustice of others, but just as vigilantly we must search out and oppose the wrong in ourselves.

> You are saying we should be tolerant?

It's more than that, Gandhi insists. "Tolerance implies a gratuitous assumption of the inferiority of other faiths to one's own, whereas *ahimsa* teaches us to entertain for the faiths of others the same respect as we accord our own, thus admitting the imperfections of the latter."

We all have different roles to play in this marvelously complex, interdependent world. Variety is to be nurtured. "Civilization is the encouragement of differences. Civilization thus becomes a synonym of democracy. Force, violence, pressure, or compulsion with a view to conformity is therefore both uncivilized and undemocratic."

> How then would you define the "truthful political solution" of which you spoke earlier?

The objective of any political engagement should be to heal social wounds and to establish a new basis for reconciliation and positive political action in the future, not to antagonize and polarize. "It is the acid test of nonviolence that in a nonviolent conflict there is no rancour left behind, and, in the end, the enemies are converted into friends."

A truthful solution eradicates injustice and exploitation while strengthening the sense of shared community—for the erstwhile oppressor as much as for the oppressed. What is sought is a new understanding between the parties from which evolves a new community dynamic with which all can be comfortable. The principle of *ahimsa* requires that no one be excluded or eliminated. Everyone has the right to live, and living means being in community. The proper aim of politics is not to beat out the opponent; it is to find a way that allows all to live together more harmoniously.

> But this seems inconsistent with your earlier statement that we have a duty not to cooperate with evil. Surely that means conflict?

"I like a good fight," says Gandhi, but that doesn't mean engaging in acts of vindictive retaliation. "An eye for an eye only ends up making the whole world blind." Conflict is not to be avoided. What's to be avoided is political behavior aimed at self-aggrandizement and the humiliation of opponents. "My experience has shown me that we win justice quickest by rendering justice to the other party." To ensure there is still ground for rebuilding community *after* the fight, we must never violate the spirit of our opponent. We must always leave self-respect intact.

"That action alone is just which does not harm either party to a dispute."

Isn't that hard to judge in the heat of battle?

Yes, but *satyagraha* imposes an effective restraint upon the political activist: the willingness to undergo suffering in pursuit of an objective. Rather than directing aggression outward against opponents, the *satyagrahi* must be prepared to take it upon him or herself.

> When a person claims to be nonviolent, he is expected not to be angry with one who has injured him. He will not wish him harm; he will wish him well; he will not swear at him; he will not cause him any physical hurt. He will put up with all the injury to which he is subjected by the wrong-doer. Thus nonviolence is complete innocence. Complete nonviolence is complete absence of ill-will against all that lives.

Besides, Gandhi reminds us, the struggle is as much against our own errors as against the errors of others. "We do not prove ourselves good by calling others bad."

But surely you must admit there are evil people?

People do things that have evil consequences. Regrettably, all of us are capable of that. We must, however, love our opponents as fellow humans capable also of goodness, truth, and divinity.

Gandhi acknowledges that many have found this attitude absurd and naive. For instance, his salutation "Dear Friend" in a letter of remonstration to Hitler in the late 1930s was widely criticized, but he points out that it is in common humanity that we find a meeting ground for reconciliation with opponents. What was it Christ taught?

> Ye have heard that it was said: "Thou shalt love thy neighbour and hate thine enemy." But I tell you, love your enemies and pray for them that persecute you, that ye may become yourselves children of your Father who is in the heavens; for he maketh his sun to rise upon the evil and the good, and he raineth upon the just and the unjust.[6]

"Love is the subtlest force in the world," Gandhi adds. "Love gives humans a partnership in the cares and needs of others. Hate and competition then yield to cooperation."

We shouldn't get angry?

If you have anger in your heart, there is anger in the world. Hate, and the world is more hate-filled. If you want a loving world, you must love. There is no other way.

Gandhi emphasizes the central role of consciousness in creating reality. Traditional Indian psychology, with which he was deeply imbued, does not make the hard distinctions between mind and matter, thought and action, with which we customarily operate in the West. Thought is action. We make the world in our minds. "The world will live in peace only when the individuals composing it make up their minds to do so."

All right, but it seems unrealistic to say that complete nonviolence is complete absence of ill-will against all that lives. Don't you admit, for instance, that there are noxious organisms that must be controlled?

"I want to realize brotherhood or identity not merely with the beings called human, but I want to realize identity with all life—even with such beings as crawl on earth. I do believe that all God's creatures have the right to live as much as we have. Instead of prescribing the killings of the so-called injurious fellow creatures of ours as a duty, if people of knowledge had devoted their gifts to discovering ways of dealing with them otherwise than by killing them, we would be living in a world befitting our status as humans: animals endowed with reason and the power of choosing between good and evil, right and wrong, violence and nonviolence, truth and untruth."

You are such an idealist! How can the ordinary person hope to live up to your exceptional standards? Besides, with so many overwhelming problems in the world, how can our puny, individual actions make any difference?

"Almost anything you do will be insignificant, but it's very important that you do it." Do not yield to hopelessness in the face of what appear to be vast problems. The universe is made and remade little bit by little bit, and only in that way. In Leon Trotsky's words: "At a time of great issues, small deeds, being a part of large problems, cease to be small."

"I have not the shadow of a doubt, that any man or woman can achieve what I have, if he or she would make the same effort and cultivate the same hope and faith," Gandhi tells us. "Strength does not come from physical capacity. It comes from an indomitable will."

Small Is Beautiful

Despite such exhortations, Gandhi was acutely aware of the numbing sense of futility felt by many people confronting the enormous size and complexity of the institutions of twentieth-century urban, industrial society. In his lifetime, individuals and groups throughout the world had been made increasingly dependent upon the distant decisions of incomprehensible, faceless bureaucracies. "India," he said, "is being ground down, not under the British heel, but under the heel of modern civilization."

It was with the aim of reversing this pernicious, global trend toward mass disempowerment that Gandhi worked to strengthen local community and regional economic self-sufficiency. What must be encouraged, he said, is "production by the masses rather than mass production."

Today we can recognize him as a pioneer in sustainability with his advocacy of community building, appropriate technology, and ecological awareness. During his lifetime, however, his views on these matters were his least respected. George Orwell spoke for the majority of educated opinion in India as elsewhere when he wrote shortly after Gandhi's assasination in 1948: "His medievalist program was obviously not viable in a backward, starving, over-populated country."[7]

Well before Gandhi died, the Indian National Congress under Jawaharlal Nehru's leadership had made a commitment to rapid industrialization with centralized economic planning on the Soviet model. Enamored by modernization theory, the government of newly independent India expanded the state apparatus—civil, police, and military—bequeathed by the British. Far from promoting the development of autonomous "village republics," as Gandhi urged, official policy encouraged the transfer of technologies from the West "to bring India's peasant masses rapidly into the twentieth century."

The Mahatma's socioeconomic ideals, however, were not lost or forgotten. Gandhian *ashrams*, with their rural development projects, survived in many parts of India as an inspiration and model for community-based initiatives elsewhere. One of Gandhi's closest associates, Vinoba Bhave, walked the length and breadth of the country encouraging land gifts to the poor. A. T. Ariyaratne, a Bhave disciple from Sri Lanka, carried Gandhian teaching back to that country in the form of *Sarvodaya Shramadana,* a village self-help movement that has since spread to other parts of the Buddhist world and beyond.

With a twist of fate that must tickle the fancy of Gandhi's ghost (for the Mahatma loved to chuckle at the ironies of history), it was a Western development expert imported to eliminate Asian backwardness who gained a global audience for Gandhian principles. This was Fritz Schumacher, author of the profoundly influential book *Small Is Beautiful: Economics As If People Mattered.*

Schumacher's life is another testament to the value of "creative maladjustment." He was a German educated in the United States and the United Kingdom who as an anti-Nazi spent most of his working life in Britain. A well-respected if controversial socialist economist, he had a spiritual awakening in his early forties when exposed not only to the teachings of Gurdjieff and Eastern mystics but also to organic gardening. The two, he said, were linked: It was working with the soil that opened him to spirit.

A short time later, in 1955, he was invited to Burma as an economic advisor to the government. His experience in this Asian culture crystalized criticisms of Western economic development that had been forming in his mind in the postwar years. He had been one of the first to denounce as irresponsible the breakneck consumption of nonrenewable natural resources, particularly fossil fuels. He now declared it the height of folly to encourage the development of similar economies in non-Western countries. While the long-term effect of living in this way off capital rather than income must inevitably be global economic impoverishment, the immediate impact of "modernization" was the spiritual impoverishment of non-Western peoples.

To tout Western material achievements as the epitome of the "advanced" and the "progressive," he said, was to undermine the faith of non-Western peoples in themselves. The objective of the economic development advocated by Western advisors, as Schumacher saw it, was the encouragement of heightened materialist desires among the people of Burma and similar countries—desires that could never be satisfied and that were fundamentally incompatible with indigenous spiritual principles.

Schumacher held up for emulation the Buddhist precept of "the middle way," moderation in all things. "Economic 'progress' is good only to the point of sufficiency, beyond that, it is evil, destructive, uneconomic."[8] Of all twentieth-century thinkers, he declared, Mahatma Gandhi alone had developed a system of economics compatible with spirituality.

To the discomfort of the Burmese government and the riled amusement of his fellow economists, Schumacher suggested that the first task for Western technical "experts" was not to advise but to *learn from* the people among whom they had come to work. "You cannot help a person if you yourself don't understand how that person manages to exist at all."[9] His slogan became "Find out what the people are doing and help them to do it better."[10]

The Shrewd Peasant

It is good advice that we should follow. The majority of people in the Third World (indeed a majority of *all* the world's people) are peasants, and one characteristic of "what these people are doing" is their stolid resistance to development. This is not universal, given the lure of the West's dazzling array of material possessions and the barrage of propaganda for the capitalist system that produces them. Nevertheless, peasant hesitations about deserting traditional ways have been so widespread and sustained as to spell ruination for many of the grand improvement projects of the modernizers. "Don't run away from anything," says a Russian peasant proverb, "but don't do anything."

We in the West belong to a civilization that has been led by "the people of the forward stampede," as Fritz Schumacher called them—people who, when they sense they are doing the wrong thing, redouble their efforts. "They are stampeding us into greater and greater violence."[11] Standing at century's end amid the ecological and cultural devastation wrought under this leadership, we would do well to look to the wisdom of those who have refused to be stampeded.

"Peasant life is a life committed completely to survival," John Berger informs us.[12] With the very survival of life on Earth threatened, the peasant way of knowing is precious. Moreover, it gives us a touchstone against which to test the value of our civilization's compulsive drive for "economic growth" through the exploitation of "natural resources."

In my days as a card-carrying academic historian, I spent several years studying a large peasant family in eastern India through nine generations from the mid-eighteenth to the mid-twentieth centuries. This research gave me insights into peasant motivations. It also acquainted me with the cross-cultural frustrations suffered by technical advisors trying to modernize agriculture in Third World countries. In their writings on rural development, I found these recurring complaints about peasant "economic irrationality":

- Peasants will not work harder "to make the extra buck."
- When they do have some additional income, they blow it on unproductive feasting or ceremony, instead of using it as capital to make more money.
- Their parochialism makes them perennially suspicious of outsiders.
- They are infuriatingly resistant to the adoption of improved technologies.
- They do not respond consistently to market opportunities.
- They retain on their land unproductive animals and uneconomic labor.

Sustainability

Is there wisdom in peasant "stubborness"? I believe so. Take the first complaint: their apparent lack of commercial drive.

We must recognize that the crucial resources for peasants are the land they till and the animal and human labor available to work that land. These must be husbanded. Much of the land on which peasants live has been worked to a low but balanced level of productivity. In some places in India and China, for example, five thousand years and more of continued occupation has seriously depleted soil fertility. Agriculture is sustained by a cautious application of inherited knowledge with an extremely limited technology that has been fully tried and tested in that exact locality.

According to the American farmer and ecophilosopher Wendell Berry, the great tests of wisdom in agriculture are "knowing what not to do and knowing when to stop."

> Invariably, at some point, the reach of human comprehension becomes too short, and at that point the work of the human economy must end in absolute deference to the working of the Great Economy. This, I take it, is the practical significance of the Sabbath. To push our work beyond that point, invading the Great Economy, is to become guilty of hubris, of presuming to be greater than we are. We cannot do what the topsoil does, any more than we can do what God does or what a swallow does.[13]

Similarly, there must be attunement to the seasonal rhythms. It is Earth and sky, rather than human reason, that dictate the labor of peasants. At times in the annual cycle there will be little to do on the farm. At other times there will be so much to do that even without sleep there will be scarcely enough human and animal shoulders to meet the demand. Adding tasks during off-seasons, as well-meaning outsiders sometimes recommend in the interest of "efficiency," makes sense only if this does not result in a requirement for additional labor at peak times. Given the organic cycle, that is rarely the case.

To repeat: Peasant agriculture is sustained by the application of inherited knowledge and technology fully tried and tested in the locality. The test they have passed is the only one that truly matters: They have enabled these peasant families to survive generation after generation.

To change is to put life itself at risk. Peasants are inveterate conservatives because there is no margin for risk in most peasant economies. Often this is not evident to outsiders who visit the community only periodically. They are likely to see the village in the good years, which outnumber the bad. But villagers themselves know that no matter how good things are now, lean years will come again. This has been their own experience and the experience of all their ancestors. The margin for survival in the lean years—sometimes lean decades—is wafer thin. If peasants are to survive, their land and their human and animal power must not be strained in the intervening good times, no matter what cash lures may be dangled before them as an incentive to gamble. Gandhi spoke from the peasant gut when he said, "Earth provides enough to satisfy every man's need, but not every man's greed."

Community
What then is the explanation for peasant behavior when there is a surplus: the "profligate" feasting and ceremonial of which the development economists complain?

One answer is the need to foster community, and in this peasants are not fundamentally different from the rest of us. To illustrate, let me put a question to those who celebrate Christmas: Knowing that prices in the stores drop substantially after the New Year, why do you persist in buying gifts and the provisions for holiday feasts in November and December? Wouldn't it be economically rational to delay expenditures a few weeks and personally celebrate the holidays, let's say, in mid-January? Because it would spoil Christmas, right? The point of the celebration (costly though it may be) is to get together with family and friends at a special time of year, a time that for many of us is sacred.

The peasant world is a world of small community. The memories, understandings, and rituals shared by community members give meaning to life, and the mutual assistance of community members makes livelihood possible. To feast and celebrate together when times are good is a sound investment in community building. Besides, what could be more fun?

For most peasants, we should also remember, the community is not limited to the present generation nor exclusively to humans and animals. It is a spiritual community in which the dead consort with the living and in which a multitude of spirits are ever present. The feasts and ceremonials—sacred time—are as much for these entities as they are for flesh-and-blood humans.

Trust

There is a second reason for conspicuous consumption: It is better to eat the windfall than have it snatched away. There is a long history of exploitation of the rural masses by non-peasants in all traditional societies. Seared into folk memory is the lesson that if you attempt to accumulate movable wealth, you stand a fair chance of being robbed of it by landlords, moneylenders, police, military and civilian officials, priests, or brigands. If you cannot hide it or convert it into land, you had better eat it. You will then have both the gift of its joy and at least for a time, its strength.

Peasants have an ingrained distrust of non-peasants. This seems like paranoia to the well-intentioned souls who wish to help them, but as we used to say in the United States in the radical sixties: "Just because you're paranoid, it doesn't mean they're not out to get you!"

It's not simply that peasants have repeatedly been exploited by outsiders; they also experience most non-peasants as ignorant and unreliable—ignorant not in a generalized sense, for peasants recognize that non-peasants know more than they do about the wider world that threatens their existence, but ignorant of what is most important: the intimate life of the village and its complex organism of survival.

Non-peasants are unreliable in that few are as endangered by the lean times as are the peasants. How can you rely on people who will not be with you when the struggle for survival gets truly grim? One of the reasons Gandhians have been able to gain the confidence of Indian villagers is that they have lived with the peasants for long periods at the same subsistence level and have stuck with the work through the bad times.

This problem of the "untrustworthiness" of outsiders is a dilemma for peasants because they are aware of their need for intelligence about the powerful wider world that impinges upon them so painfully. Their difficulty in knowing who and what to believe provides part of the explanation of their observed resistance to the adoption of new technologies and also their caution in responding to new market opportunities.

Self-Sufficiency

The peasant response to innovation is not, of course, universally obstructive. As with all else in village life, it is affected by personal considerations. A central question will be: Is the person recommending this new technique or gadget someone we have reason to trust? The decision to accept advice to change the way you farm is a huge decision—nothing less than putting your own life and the lives of present and future generations of your family in someone else's hands.

After years living in a French village and working in its peasant fields, John Berger writes:

> When a peasant resists the introduction of a new technique or method of working, it is not because he cannot see its possible advantages—his conservatism is neither blind nor lazy—but because he believes that these advantages cannot, by the nature of things, be guaranteed, and that, should they fail, he will then be cut off alone and isolated from the routine of survival.[14]

Peasant villages are never self-sufficient, but the ideal for most peasants is for the village to be as self-sufficient as possible in order to minimize dependency on the outside world. The difficulty with most new technologies (and by this I mean new systems of agriculture as well as tools) is that they increase dependency.

For example, if you adopt new high-yielding hybrid seed grains, you discover that the crop does not (unlike your old strains of wheat or rice) give seed for the following year's planting. You must go back each year to a commercial supplier or the government for the laboratory-produced hybrids. You are also likely to discover that the new grains are not as resistant to local insects and diseases, so your farming will become dependent on petrochemical pesticides and herbicides. The result? The village economy is now vulnerable to world fluctuations in oil prices.

Surely there are always the old ways to fall back on? Not necessarily. The insect and other organic balances in the fields will have been disturbed by the new grains and the newly introduced pesticides and fertilizers. As a consequence, the old crops may no longer do as well.

Tibet provides a tragic case in point. In 1959, economic cadres with the occupying Chinese forces decided that acreage traditionally planted with *chingko,* Tibetan hill barley, should be converted to Chinese winter wheat, which they believed would give higher yields. A massive campaign of peasant "reeducation" was undertaken, and the planting of winter wheat was made obligatory. The results were disastrous. Within two decades, soils in many areas had been drained of nutrients, and as crops failed there were insect invasions of huge proportions. Thousands of Tibetans starved to death.

There is also what Fritz Schumacher called "the law of the disappearing middle." Less sophisticated techniques abandoned in favor of higher technologies are frequently not recoverable. Sometimes it is a loss of skills. At other times it is the destruction of an alternative infrastructure that is too costly for the peasants to restore.

I personally witnessed an example in eastern India. Dams for new centralized irrigation schemes silted faster in the 1960s than engineers had projected, seriously reducing the flow of water to farmlands. The government's agricultural workers urged the peasants to use again the local ditches and tanks (artificial ponds) that had been dug over the centuries, only to discover that many had been filled in to provide additional rice paddies in the preceding decade, when reliance on the new irrigation channels had been encouraged. And remember, it is not engineers or agricultural advisors who die from mistakes like this; it is peasants.

Ecosystem Diversity

Responding to new market opportunities is beset with similar pitfalls. Are the outsiders who bring the news to be trusted, or are they motivated primarily by commercial self-interest? Will the market hold, and if not, will it then be possible to return to the old crops? Deeper involvement with external markets means greater dependence on the cash economy with its fluctuating prices. Frequently it is subsistence crops that must give way to the cash crop, which forces the peasants into the vulnerable position of having to buy food.

To make the move to cash cropping economically viable, it is often necessary for a peasant to devote all of his or her land to the new crop. Sometimes the whole village must make the shift. The change to monocropping can be the most perilous of all, for it disturbs the fragile balances that sustain the life of the land—what Wendell Berry calls the "community of living creatures."[15]

Most peasant villages are complex microecosystems, growing a remarkable variety of plants and animals to ensure that villagers always have a little bit of a lot of different things. This contributes to self-sufficiency. It is insurance against periodic failures of one or another crop. It makes possible crop rotation, whereby the fertility of the land can be maintained without artificial fertilizers. It ensures the diversity of wild bird, animal, insect, and microorganism populations, thereby sustaining checks and balances between predators and prey. It is frequently the source of a balanced diet for the human population as well. For instance, good nutrition in a village may depend on a small pond producing snails, frogs, and miniscule fish as sources of protein. The health of the pond in turn will depend on the preservation of the surrounding vegetation and clean drainage.

Life and Livelihood

One of the complaints of the rural development advisors, as noted earlier, is the peasant tendency to keep unproductive animals. From my own observations in several countries, this would seem to result less from affection for animals, as we pet lovers understand it, than from the gut feeling that all forms of life have been put on Earth for a purpose. This helps to explain the discomfort with monocropping. Peasants, to their credit, appear to be less certain than development economists that they know for sure what is "unproductive" in the long run. They are certain that the *long run* is what counts.

The associated complaint is that peasants retain uneconomic labor on their farms. Here we are at the crux of the divergence of Western economic reasoning from peasant values. In the former scheme of things, the aim is to maximize profit. In the latter it is to provide the means for right livelihood for everyone in the household: "Economics as if people mattered." To the peasant, possession of land is precious because it is the source of good work for the whole family and its dependents. Work has value in and of itself—spiritual value. As Schumacher wrote:

> . . . the modern economist has been brought up to consider "labour" or work as little more than a necessary evil. . . . From a Buddhist point of view, this is standing the truth on its head by considering goods as more important than people and consumption as more important than creative activity. It means shifting the emphasis from the worker to the product of the work, that is from the human to the subhuman.[16]

Which brings us back to Gandhi's observation: "To forget how to dig the earth and tend the soil is to forget ourselves."

Destruction of Alternatives

My broad characterization of the peasant stereotype is offered as a cautionary tale. To learn that millions upon millions of those who dig the earth and tend the soil are not enamored of our breakneck Western dash to overturn old ways should give us pause.

Peasants, says John Berger, have generally been scorned by modern urban people as "backward, a relic of the past." He cautions that this is a mistake:

> To dismiss peasant experience as belonging only to the past, as having no relevance to modern life, to imagine that the thousands of years of peasant culture leave no heritage for the future . . . is to deny the value of too much history and too many lives. . . . .
>
> The peasant suspicion of "progress," as it has finally been imposed by the global history of corporate capitalism and by the power of this history even over those seeking an alternative to it, is not altogether misplaced or groundless.[17]

We must be under no illusion. The destruction of other forms of economic organization and with them other cultures, other ways of knowing, has been pursued systematically to further economic growth—something that has been labeled in the modern West a good thing, even a necessity.

In order to generate a "demand" for new products and a tolerance for more elaborate organizational combinations, capitalist corporations have made systematic use of the media, the marketplace, and the educational system to influence and manipulate individual behavior. Reliance on high energy usage has been encouraged, while control over the transmission of that energy and the fossil fuels from which most of it is derived has been jealously guarded by a handful of corporations and governments.

Internationally, the same forces have operated to encourage the interdependence of national economies to the profit of those who control the high technology that we all, rich and poor of the world alike, have been taught to regard as the symbol of the advanced and progressive. The maintenance and innovative development of independent technologies have been discouraged because the elimination of alternatives (seen as competition for the corporate product or technique) is a principle of this system.

The progressive destruction of alternatives in almost every sphere has been the consequence of modern Western civilization's drive to use its technological and organizational power to dominate. In our determination to dominate nature, from which conceptually we set ourselves apart, we destroy other life forms. Monocropping produces more bushels per acre, so we put vast acreage into a single variety of one crop, disregarding the basic ecological precept that variety provides a species with the best chances for survival in a perpetually changing environment. Our vulnerable monocrops then require technological rescue missions, and we wipe out further species with agricultural toxins.

Distasteful though it may be to recall, historically we have done the same when other humans have stood in our way. Armed with industrial technology and the bureaucratic state, Europeans cleared the North American and Australian continents of huge numbers of their native occupants in the last century, just as today for corporate convenience the world's rain forests, with their rich diversity of indigenous life forms, are being razed and their peoples displaced or killed.

We have had no time for "primitives" or peasants who lack our high technology and bureaucracy. Western languages are replete with words that characterize them as our inferiors. We have not valued their cultural difference from us and from each other. We have been as little concerned with sustaining human cultural variety—alternatives for response to a changing environment—as with maintaining variety in nature. Western civilization is most dangerous because, in the interest of economic growth (as anthropologist Marshall Sahlins warns us),

> it does not hesitate to destroy any other form of humanity whose difference from us consists in having discovered not merely other codes of existence but ways of achieving an end that still eludes us: the mastery by society of society's mastery over nature.[18]

A Loving Economy

"The sickness of our age is unlike that of any other," wrote Martin Buber many decades ago. "Shall we have to follow this path all the way to the end, to the test of the final darkness?" In the answer he gave, we find both hope and the inspiration to act: "But where there is danger what saves grows, too."[19]

From all around us come indications that what saves *is* growing. The peasant way of knowing seems to be trickling upward. The spread of ecological awareness has been dramatic in the 1990s. In corporate boardrooms, presidential cabinets, parliaments, political platforms, university lecture halls, Madison Avenue slogans, and media stories, the language of environmentalism is now familiar and respectable: renewable resources, energy conservation, recyclables, organic agriculture, alternative technology, biodiversity, species protection, interdependency of life forms, sustainability. A change of consciousness is under way.

Most significantly, there is a growing realization of the critical importance of scale. Something that may be innocuous or even beneficial when done by a few can have monstrously negative consequences when multiplied by ten thousand or a million. Increases in the amount of things and speed of processes can result in sudden "state changes" in ecological and social systems. The critical point at which a change of state will occur is unpredictable, and its results are behaviors and interactions that are not explicable in terms of the old system.

The importance of scale seems a simple and obvious point, but our civilizational fixation on "bigger as better" and "faster as more efficient" blinded us to it until we experienced a declining quality of life—our own and that of our nature companions. Discomfort has prompted us to acknowledge the wisdom of the old spiritual teachings of moderation: the Golden Mean, the Middle Way, the Tao. In place of the lust for maximization, we are offered the gentler principle of optimization: the search for the point of balance between not enough and too much.

Thank God for creatively maladjusted souls like M. K. Gandhi and E. F. Schumacher, twentieth-century guardians of this spiritual principle, who kept harping on the peasant virtues of small community and technology on a human scale.

New voice is given to this refrain by Wendell Berry. With his vision of "a loving economy," he shows us the intimate relationship between a sense of place, good work, and community in the health of both human culture and nature:

> In the recovery of culture *and* nature is knowledge of how to farm well, how to preserve, harvest, and replenish the forests, how to make, build, and use, return and restore. In this *double* recovery, which is the recovery of our humanity, is the hope that the domestic and the wild can exist in lasting harmony. . . .
>
> Harmony is one phase, the good phase, of the inescapable dialogue between culture and nature. In this phase, humans consciously and conscientiously ask of their work: Is this good for us? Is this good for our place? . . .
>
> Those of us who see that wildness and wilderness need to be preserved are going to have to understand the dependence of these things upon our domestic economy and our domestic behavior. If we do not have an economy capable of valuing in particular terms the durable goods of localities and communities, then we are not going to be able to preserve anything. . . .
>
> I would call this a loving economy, for it would strive to place a proper value on all the materials of the world, in all their metamorphoses from soil and water, air and light to the finished goods of our towns and households, and I think that the only effective motive for this would be a particularizing love for local things, rising out of local knowledge and local allegiance.[20]

The Journey Home

We started this chapter with a search for a transformed politics for the twenty-first century, and we are ending with a love for local things— loving community. It is a journey of return.

You may recall from the movie *Gandhi* a scene of the middle-aged Mahatma standing by the sea wall at his birthplace, Porbandar, saying wistfully, "I have traveled so far, and all I've done is to come back home." Significantly, we find parables of this journey of exile and return in all the great spiritual traditions: the seeker's long and arduous path, at last leading home to discovery of the real treasure.

We shall not cease in our explorations,
and the end of our exploring
will be to arrive where we started
and to know the place for the first time.

T. S. Eliot

Western civilization's journey in the new millenium will be the journey of spiritual return.

8

WHOLE EDUCATION
FOR A WHOLE WORLD

*The language of the lips is easily taught, but who can teach the
language of the heart?*

Mahatma Gandhi

What is the purpose of education? Not in the abstract, but for right
now when the world seems to be coming apart at the seams?

First and foremost, education must give people a sense of meaning
and inspire them with purpose and hope. An individual life can seem
worth while only when the world at large makes sense. And it does
make sense. People—young people in particular—need to be shown
that.

They also need to be given a feeling of belonging. Education to be
worth its salt must build community, for it is caring community that
gives an individual a sense of self-worth.

I look up from my writing to see two hummingbirds outside my window, suspended on shimmering wings above the dark red foliage of a
plum tree, accelerating in an instant into the ascending, intertwined
spiral of their mating dance. Life is relationship. It is vibrant, it is beautiful, it is the mysterious purpose of this universe. And love is its power.

Mysteries

> I feel like I'm on a road at a huge intersection with thousands of streets yet I'm at a loss. There is no one to tell me the way, no "411" in the real world. You can't just call up and say, "Hey I need a destination, I need a place to go." Even if someone did tell me where to go, I wouldn't listen. Sometimes I feel like I'm going nowhere. Sure I'm on the Santa Monica freeway, but where am I going in life?

> I often wonder what lies behind our solar system, galaxy. A white light? A healing power? What will become of my life? What will happen to my girlfriend and I?

> Why have we ruined our earth? And why do we continue to ruin the thing that none of us could live without?[1]

The writers are teenagers at Crossroads School for Arts and Sciences in Santa Monica, California. They were asked to describe their personal "mysteries," the things about which they are curious, worried, wondering, or fearful. Their concerns and those of hundreds of their schoolmates over the past decade are the basis of an innovative program called *Mysteries*.

A required course for students in both middle and upper schools, *Mysteries* meets once a week for an hour and a half with teachers trained in adolescent development, active listening, group building, creative visualization, self-esteem methods, and the use of art, movement, and play. Students and teachers actually have fun together in class! Using the simple but age-old community practice of sitting in a circle and taking turns to speak, students learn to listen deeply to one another as they unravel the joys, perplexities, and pains of growing up in a society in upheaval. They also learn to share meditative silence.

Former *Mysteries* program director Shelley Kessler says this:

> Crossroads recognizes spiritual development in the adolescent. "Health education" is returned to the original meaning of health— "to make whole." Health is defined as the integration of mind, body, spirit and heart. *Mysteries* provides an opportunity to explore meaning or purpose in life, to discover the mystery of non-

ordinary experience and to feel a deep connection to the wholeness of life.[2]

Aware that actions speak louder than words, the leadership at Crossroads has worked hard to ensure that California's ethnic diversity is represented in the school's student body and faculty. Human diversity and other ways of knowing are cherished and celebrated in the *Mysteries* program. Outside the classroom, students are given the physical and emotional challenges of adventure-based learning, such as ropes courses and wilderness retreats. Ceremonies and rituals drawn from native traditions are used. Learning from the wisdom of the ancestors reaches a climax toward the end of the senior year, when students spend a week camping out in the rugged Los Padres Mountains. A sweat lodge and other ceremonies, guided by Native American teachers from the Ojai Foundation, provide them with a rite of passage to adulthood.

> I went to Ojai a few weeks ago. It was an amazing experience for me. . . . it changed my view of looking at things, looking at people, looking at nature, and other things. Especially, I learned to look at people's true being—their hearts, their souls—not their outward being. I think almost everybody puts on some kind of cover to cover their true heart. I could see that through the fellowship with people during the trip, especially through the sweat lodge, where people opened up their deepest hearts. People who I never expected would open up, opened up. That night was just indescribably beautiful.[3]
>
> Mi Kyoung Shin

"Touchy-feely" is the pejorative label sometimes slapped onto programs like *Mysteries*. The criticism leveled at this sort of education is that it lacks "academic content." I would reply that it is not an either/or proposition. Affective education versus content-based education is a false dichotomy. Conversely, in educational programs that do not encourage the expression of feelings, nurture self-esteem, or foster community, students find it hard, at best, to reach their full academic potential. And there are much darker possibilities. Given the hazards youngsters face today in a society where alcohol and other drugs, sexually transmitted diseases, dysfunctional families, and violence are widespread, the absence of such supportive programs places them at risk of becoming digits in the appalling statistics of attempted or successful youth suicide.

Self-Trust

"The goal of education is to teach self-trust," Emerson said. I was blessed with many teachers who believed this, my own parents foremost among them.

In graduate school I had two contrasting educational experiences: one good, one not so good. My doctoral studies provided the good experience. I went to the Australian National University, which in those days was a small research institute. Everyone—student and faculty member alike—was treated as a grownup. We were all doing research, and we were all provided with the needed resources, including offices. Everyone, from the eminent head of the school to the newest junior arrival, was expected to give a work-in-progress report each term, and everyone showed up for this weekly seminar. Beyond that, we were trusted to use our good sense in going to whichever seminars were useful for our work. Or we could get together a cross-disciplinary group to organize a discussion series that met our mutual needs.

My field was modern India, and I had the good fortune to be dropped down among highly intelligent scholars who shared my passion for the field, but who (as far as India was concerned) were greenhorns like myself. It was good fortune because as a consequence I was not subjected to the weary condescension that so often characterizes the "old hand" in academe. We were all starting out fresh and eager, and we were keen to give each other a leg up. Together for the next several years, we had lots of fun and helped each other learn a great deal. The most precious gift was self-trust.

My contrasting experience was during my M.A. work in New Zealand. The head of my department was of the fixed opinion that academic standards in the country were deplorable, and he was determined to raise them, single-handed if need be. For starters, he gave notoriously low grades. Moreover, he treated with skepticism and scarcely concealed scorn any student like myself who harbored an ambition for advanced graduate study. I was petrified by the man. The increasingly frequent need to run the gauntlet of his sardonic questioning as my career proceeded gave me a stomach ulcer by the age of twenty-two.

For him the acid tests of quality (forgive the pun) were meticulous attention to detail, complete accuracy, and a strictly logical presentation. His view of education was what Brazilian educator Paulo Freire has characterized as the "banking concept": putting information into the student like money deposited in a bank, then using examinations to measure how much is in the account.

> In the banking concept of education, knowledge is a gift bestowed by those who consider themselves knowledgeable upon those whom they consider to know nothing.[4]

This is not the way to encourage a desire to learn or to create independent, self-confident, whole people.

Regrettably, not all educational practice has independence as its objective. Many teachers, though they might not admit it, value the opportunity provided by the classroom and lecture hall to demonstrate their superiority. Indeed, we have a phalanx of institutions in our society (schools and universities prominent among them) intended to demonstrate that someone is above someone else, or that someone knows more than someone else.

When the classroom is an arena for the demonstration of superordinate and subordinate roles, what is being taught is deference and dependency, not self-trust. Deferential attitudes and dependent behavior prop up hierarchical institutions. This seems to be the aim of too much of our education: maintaining the established inegalitarian structures by producing young people who are carbon copies of the preceding generation—appropriately smudged and slightly inferior! They should "know their place."

Is this what is needed in a world undergoing rapid and profound change? Little wonder that our universities seem increasingly irrelevant, or that so many children and their parents feel short-changed by their schools. Listening to apologists describing the latest tinkering with the system gives me the uncomfortable feeling of sitting beside Alice at the Mad Hatter's tea party, with the March Hare lamenting that the watch doesn't keep good time, even though he used the very best butter to fix it!

A World Turned Upside Down

When I was in high school forty-five years ago, I had a geography teacher who hung a huge globe at the front of his classroom. It was suspended at head height upside down with Antarctica at the top. There for once was our New Zealand surrounded by its vast oceans, right where we could see it without having to peer under the bottom. Now it was North America and Europe that disappeared around the underside. This pleased and amused us. It also prompted us to look at things in a new way.

The world *is* turning upside down. Like so much else in contemporary Western civilization, however, our maps reflect an older, outmoded reality. Most still show the Western Hemisphere as the center of the world and relegate the lands of the Pacific rim to the periphery—this despite the fact our world is now multicentric and united in a way that makes nonsense of the concepts "center" and "periphery."

Recent geopolitical and geoeconomic shifts have been immense. Millions of people in the last three generations have been torn from their roots by warfare, the collapse of empires, and associated dislocations in economic systems. This has led to an ethnic and cultural mixing of a scale and speed almost certainly unprecedented in human history. In just the last decade, integrated telecommunication and electronic information technologies have further accelerated the erosion of economic, political, and cultural divisions.

The current era has unique demographic characteristics. For one thing, our species is now so numerous. It is estimated that more people are alive today than the total of all who have lived and died in the 150,000 years since *Homo sapiens* evolved.

Age disparities between human populations in different parts of the world have become marked. Most industrialized countries, including Japan, are becoming top-heavy with old people. By contrast, in the Third World the majority of people are children and teenagers. The demographics of the family also have changed. Many households in North America, for example, now have only one adult, reflecting (among other things) altered gender relations.

Another profound change of the past two decades has been the attitude to "advanced" technology. Once thought to be life-enhancing, even relatively recently, many of the industrial technologies that have shaped our century are now regarded as life-threatening. The electrical revolution, the petrochemical revolution, and the nuclear revolution are seen as mixed blessings at best. Many people are apprehensive that the planet's ecosystem is incapable of withstanding the assault of the complex technologies that sustain exploding human populations. As our species overpopulates its habitat it invades and destroys the habitats of other life forms.

On the other side of the coin, the electronic revolution appears to offer hopeful new opportunities for decentralization and democratic communication. Potentially, with microelectronics and the harnessing of solar energy, we need be tied no longer to the centralized power sources and bureaucratic structures that have dominated the past 250 years of the industrial age.

At the same time as new postindustrial technologies are emerging, there are new understandings in the natural sciences. Gone is the classical assumption that we can observe nature without affecting it. Gone is the certainty that mind and matter are distinct. We have operated for the past hundred years with a model of nature as a hostile, competitive environment. Now there is a new, persuasive understanding emerging from the life sciences that this is a world of symbiosis, of altruism—a natural world of purpose and meaning.

A natural world, moreover, where the whole sends messages to the parts. From its beginnings in the seventeenth century, modern science has rested on the assumption that the way to understand causation is to work from the little things (such as genes) to the big things (such as the whole organism). Now the suggestion is being taken seriously that the little things are guided by the big ones. Perhaps planet Earth sends messages to our gene chains to sustain the purpose of the whole?

As this fundamental rethinking occurs, we are facing a loss of confidence in some of the social institutions that have been most admired. Consider, for example, the precipitate decline over the last decade in the esteem rating of the American medical profession. Biomedicine, for most of this century considered proof positive of the superiority of the scientific method, is now under a cloud. People are no longer certain it promotes health.

Science is in doubt, and this has prompted a profound search for meaning reflected in a worldwide spiritual resurgence, some of it scarred by the ugly extremes of fundamentalism.

Many more examples could be given. Suffice it to say that we are in an unsettling moment in world history. We are also in what environmentalist Hunter Lovins calls a "teachable moment." There are many, many people who feel like the youth from Santa Monica: lost on a fast freeway without signposts. With so many seeking new direction, it is a moment of great opportunity for the encouragement of transformative change in our civilization.

We should not be surprised or dismayed to discover, however, that most institutions conduct business as usual. For instance, the universities, where we might have hoped to find innovative responses, remain doggedly committed to highly specialized, separatist disciplines that equip students for service in those industrial, techno-bureaucratic structures that are fast being undermined.

Despite the fact our world is turning upside down—perhaps *because* of that fact—most people resolutely maintain established routines. They seek refuge in habit from growing uncertainty. It's a natural response, but it won't work.

What Is a Teacher to Do?

It's not an easy time to be a teacher, but it's an exciting one—and there is the place to start. Teach what you're excited about. Teach what you can make come alive. If you are not yourself alive—excited, passionate, awake—forget it! Find another career; don't be a teacher.

There's nothing like visible passion for a subject to turn others on. You don't have to be an expert on what you teach. You do need a burning desire to know more, and into this desire you can gather your students to become co-explorers with you. If you reveal your passions, they will reveal theirs, and that opens more territory for them to explore, led by their excitements.

Looking back on my own schooldays, I realize I learned most from the teachers who let me see who they really were. We teach by what we do and who we are rather than what we say. We must walk our talk if we expect our students to do so. If we tell them that learning is precious, then we must show that we ourselves are eager to learn. "Everyone is ignorant, only on different subjects," quipped Will Rogers. It's true, and we do our students a service by being grownup enough to invite them to teach us stuff they know and we don't. If we are open to learning from them, they will be open to learning from us.

It is one of Paulo Freire's dictums that teacher and student both must be learners, their roles interchangeable. You must not prescribe to people, for that puts them in an inferior and dependent position. "Liberating education," Freire writes, "consists in acts of cognition, not transferrals of information."[5] People learn best when they are encouraged to see how much they already know and to build on it. From this comes self-trust.

The teacher's job is to open a space in which people can explore, learn, and grow. This does not imply passivity on the teacher's part. She must give leadership in defining clear purposes, processes, and norms to guide interactions. For example, she should monitor the tendency of competetive male dialogue to drown out female voices. Openness is a challenging teaching style. It requires keen sensitivity of when to give direction and when to let things flow. It requires vulnerability in the teacher, because not all the agendas can be hers. It requires the acknowledgment of varying styles of expression and learning.

Different people learn at different speeds and in different ways. One of the many gifts of feminist scholarship has been to draw attention to this fact, encouraging us to expand and enrich the forms we use to communicate knowledge. There are truly many ways of knowing, and they are not equally accessible to all.

For example, the abstract statement above will go in one ear and out the other for many people unless there is a story to illustrate it. (Note the word *illustrate*, connoting something pictured.) Here's the story:

Raoul and Marvin bought sailboats at about the same time. To prepare for life on the ocean waves, Raoul read every how-to manual he could get his hands on, and he took boat-handling and navigation classes at the local community college. His boat was parked in the driveway until he felt competent to go to sea. By contrast, Marvin simply put his boat in the bay at the nearest slip and started puttering around in it. He sailed close to shore to get the feel of things, and when he faced something he couldn't figure out, he asked other boat people for advice. His neighbor, Raoul, questioned this unscientific approach. Marvin explained that he could never retain much from books. He had to get his hands on something before it made sense to him. What worked for Raoul did not work for Marvin. They had different learning styles.

For many people a story does what an abstract statement cannot do: it allows them to make a connection to their own life experience. This is the *connected knowing* of which feminist educators—Mary Belenky and others—have written. They contrast this with *separate knowing*, "the game of impersonal reason."[6]

> Connected knowers develop procedures for gaining access to other people's knowledge. At the heart of these procedures is the capacity for empathy. Since knowledge comes from experience, the only way they can hope to understand another person's ideas is to try to share the experience that has led the person to form the idea.[7]

By opening space in our classrooms for connected knowing, we acknowledge the value of personal experience and we nurture empathy. We honor the feminine. We encourage caring and cooperative learning. We respect different ways of comprehending and expressing knowledge. We allow for the expression of different feelings about the process of learning. We prize the richness of texture that diversity brings to a community of knowledge.

This is the appropriate educational form for a multicultural society in which people of both sexes and of all ethnicities, classes, and sexual preferences can be empowered. This is an education that respects and enriches the life of the whole person, not simply the life of the mind.

The effectiveness of education that honors connected knowing is demonstrated by New Zealand's *kohanga reo*. In the past decade and a half, these "language nests" have been developed nationwide by the Maori community in a successful effort to reverse a precipitous decline in knowledge of the Maori language. Preschoolers are the primary target, but unlike traditional kindergartens, *kohanga reo* encourage parents to come to class with the children. Elders and other community members drop in to share songs, games and crafts, knowledge of foods and healing, stories from their own lives and the lives of ancestors, and nuggets of spiritual tradition. The "nests" are like family gatherings with as much doing as talking. Language learning flows from the exchange of practical experience and cultural wisdom.

In Touch

Knowledge does not refer simply to the intellect. We all have "inner knowing." Our bodies have knowledge. They know how to be born, they know how to breathe, they know how to grow, they know how to heal, they know how to love, they know how to give birth, they know how to die. Deep wisdom is available to us if we will but listen intently to our bodies.

As teachers we must encourage students to trust their gut understandings, their intuitions. Here is the wellspring of imagination and creativity.

> Reason sets the boundaries far too narrowly for us, and would have us accept only the known—and that too with limitations—and live in a known framework, just as if we were sure how far life actually extends. As a matter of fact, day after day we live far beyond the bounds of our consciousness.[8]

It was Carl Jung who taught of the power of archetypes, which carry condensed information from the collective unconscious. The existence of universal archetypes, which surface in dreams, daydreams, meditations and altered states, explains the emotive power transcending cultural boundaries of fables and fairy tales, poetry, music and dance, sculpture and painting. We must have the imagination and courage in our teaching to carry students into this potent symbolic realm.

> *Work of sight is done; now work on the pictures within you.*
>
> Rainer Maria Rilke

We learn from words. We learn more forcefully from forms (images, colors, smells, tastes, sounds, movements) that engage more than our intellects and involve more than one of our senses. We remember best what we do, rather than what we read or are told. Effective education, therefore, must have a large experiential component.

The Crossroads School *Mysteries* program is a good model. Along with adventure-based learning it incorporates group problem solving, conflict resolution, role playing, theater games, mask making, mime, expressive dance, song, art, guided visualization, meditation, and ceremony. As we saw with the seniors' rite of passage, significant stages in the lives of students are marked ceremonially. To assist life transitions and acknowledge their sacredness with ritual was a practice followed by our ancestors for millenia, and it is customary still in non-Western cultures.

So too are rituals to mark the transitions of the seasons, nature's rites of passage. We should take a leaf from the calendar of the Onondaga Indian School in Nedrow, New York. During the time of the midwinter ceremonials, when the Dancing Stars (the Pleiades) stand high in the sky, the school provides a vacation. At the traditional thanksgiving to the maple trees when the sap is gathered in March, the school holds a maple festival. When it is time to dig wild onions, a group of students and teachers goes out with celebration into the surrounding fields to harvest them.

Given the current critical imbalance between humans and other species, a primary area of experiential education should be nature. Students and teachers should spend time in wild places to restore direct awareness of the intricate interconnections that sustain the life of this vibrant organism, planet Earth. A principle of Aboriginal Australian education is that a thing should be touched before it is named. This suggests to me that we should balance the abstractions of our classrooms with experiences of the wholeness of living, growing, wild things. Interestingly, we use the terms *grounded* and *in touch* approvingly, but rarely do we acknowledge the connection to the Earth of which they speak.

> To forget how to dig the earth and tend the soil is to forget ourselves.
>
> Mahatma Gandhi

Chapter 4 described the paths of return to the place where we can hear again nature's voices. We must lead our students down these paths, away from the elaborate constructions of our cities, and out again into our natural home. Quiet time spent there reminds us that we are nature, that what grows around us grows also within us. We are part of a more expansive organism, possessed of consciousness, spirit, and purpose. It grows us.

Writing about his experience with a group of Athabascan Indians in Alaska, Richard Nelson says:

> If I have understood Koyukon teachings, the forest is not merely an expression or representation of sacredness, nor a place to invoke the sacred; the forest is sacredness itself. Nature is not merely created by God; nature is God. Whoever moves within the forest can partake directly of sacredness, experience sacredness with his entire body, breathe sacredness and contain it within himself, drink the sacred water as a living communion, bury his feet in sacredness, touch the living branch and feel the sacredness, open his eyes and witness the burning beauty of sacredness.[9]

Gregory Bateson wrote of "the pattern which connects." Our education must strive to reveal the relationships between things: "the dance of interacting parts" that makes up the whole and the context that gives meaning.

When a New Zealand Maori stands to introduce himself on the *marae*, the sacred ground of community, he acknowledges the presence of spirit and the breath of life expressed in bird song and in his own voice. He greets the ground on which he stands; the meeting house; and all those present, living and dead, "people of the four winds." In order he then names his mountain; his river, lake, or sea; the canoe in which his people voyaged to these islands; his tribe and the ancestor from whom he traces his descent; his home place; and where he now lives. Finally he gives his name. He has acknowledged the pattern which connects—"the community of all our relations," as the Lakota Sioux say.

It is important to bring into the classroom living examples of this kind from other cultures. A gift to education of our electronic age is visual and aural access to expressions of other ways of knowing. We are no longer confined to the images and sounds of the West. Already on video, and no doubt soon to be available more directly to students through multimedia software on desktop computers, are the totemic cave and bark paintings of the Aboriginal Gagudju of northern Australia, the mask dances of Tibetan lamas, the ritual costumes of the Tlingit of the southeastern coast of Alaska, and the visionary divinations of the Kogi priests of Colombia, to cite just a few examples.

If our students are primarily of European descent, it is equally important to show them that the contemporary non-Western belief in the interconnectedness of all life was an outlook shared by their own ancestors.

> The European shamans visioned a web of fibres that flow through the entire universe, linking absolutely everything—each person, object, event, thought, and feeling. This web is so sensitive that any movement, thought or happening—no matter how small—reverberates throughout the entire web.[10]

The writer is Brian Bates, a University of Sussex scholar of Anglo-Saxon and ancient Celtic cultures, who points out that the image of the all-encompassing web is a recurring motif in early European literature and art. The spinners of the web were spider spirits, whose aid shamans (or sorcerers, as they were called in old English) could enlist to enter other realities. "The spirits enable the sorcerer to traverse the webs that lead into all worlds: of the gods, Middle-Earth and the dead."[11]

Bending the Corners of Reality

> And honey you had best take care
> The world is made of spider webs.
> The threads are stuck to me and you.
> Careful what you're wishing for
> 'Cause when you gain you just might lose,
> You just might lose your spider web,
> Spider web.[12]
>
> Joan Osborne, "Spider Web"

Spider spirits guiding journeys to the other world? Surely it demands too much of teachers to ask them to peddle this sort of weirdness in their classrooms? And risky? In some ways it may be. But we have to take risks and venture into strange places to shake ourselves and our students into the realization of the immensity of what is happening in this era. Besides, rock musicians, video artists, and computer-game designers are way ahead of us.

To repeat an earlier statement: We are undergoing a scientific revolution as profound as that which ushered in modern Western civilization three hundred years ago. This is no time for timidness in the classroom. The alternative is to continue to dish up the myth of a segmented universe of separated objects. The damage wrought by the sciences, technologies, and social systems spawned by reductionism can be seen on every side. We need to teach indivisible wholeness. The time is long overdue for us to heed the wise words of Tolkien's old wizard, Gandalf: "He that breaks a thing to find out what it is, has left the path of wisdom."

The path of wisdom is a tortuous one, and to point the way a teacher has to stretch. Our immodest aim is the expansion of consciousness. The most treasured comment I have received about my own teaching is one made by a California Institute of Integral Studies student, Roxana Wales: "You have a way of teaching that bends the corners of 'reality,' so that those who are with you can see through to an infinity of possibilities."

Making possibilities visible—enriching possibilities—that's the thing to aim for. I see us opening windows through which people can gaze, and doors through which they can walk, in order to piece together—as each of us must do—an integrated life. The French existentialists talk of life as a project. That's what it is. We're all working on a project: to piece together a wise and joyful way of being in the world.

"Living on purpose—discovering what really matters and finding the courage to risk living it." This is the precept Peter and Trudy Johnson-Lenz offer adult learners on their innovative educational computer network "Awakening Technology." "We encourage participants to use their inner sense of what is most appropriate for them, and then to act in the world in ways that will make a difference."[13]

Whole education addresses ethical concerns and encourages moral engagement. It calls upon us (in Joanna Macy's words) "to sustain the gaze"—to look horror and injustice full in the face and to name them for what they are. At the same time it demands compassion and a sense of humor. A sense of humor saves us from being too hard on ourselves; compassion saves us from judging others too harshly. Together they may prevent us from taking ourselves and our moral pronouncements too seriously.

Along with an encouragement to commitment, whole education must provide training in the disciplined examination of evidence. My emphasis on affective and experiential education in no way implies a denigration of the value of factual knowledge or the tools of critical analysis. I do not agree with Ronald Reagan that "facts are dumb." I imagine I am also in disagreement with him in my belief that education must foster open consideration of diverse viewpoints, no matter how uncomfortable or unpopular.

Whole education must encourage diversity, for with diversity our organic communities have alternative ways to grow. The price of diversity is periodic disagreement and contention. We should not be afraid of contention at the level of face-to-face interaction. It is yeast to the social dough. It also gives us a "practicum" to use for the training of students in techniques of conflict resolution, so sorely needed in our society. We should invite Mahatma Gandhi and Martin Luther King, Jr., to our classrooms.

Contention should be balanced by mutual caring. The aim of education should be the creation of caring community. I believe that the rebuilding of community is a critical task in the contemporary Western world. Schools can serve as practical models of humane, participatory communities. We need a life in our schools that is not a jumble of segments but a supportive life together, to encourage all of us to grow and change—and I mean everyone in the institution, not just students and teachers. I would emphasize that I regard the administrative and the educational as one and the same. Administrative structures and processes—the behavior of administrators—must model our educational ideals. We teach through what we do outside the classroom as much as inside.

If we want humane, participatory communities, we should pay attention to the effects of scale. Our educational institutions must be kept to a reasonable size, and they must be organized internally into meaningful subgroupings. If our schools are scaled to comprehensible human dimensions, the people in them can have a sense of belonging.

In this regard I saw a sad contrast between my own high school experience and that of my children and stepchildren. My public high school in New Zealand had eight hundred students when I entered in the late 1940s and a thousand by the time I graduated. This growth was already prompting concern but the increased numbers did not erode the "school spirit," as our sense of community was always described. It is a measure of my feeling of belonging that to this day the school colors—royal blue and black—carry a happy emotional charge for me.

Even though my kids grew up in the Michigan university centers of Ann Arbor and East Lansing, towns smaller than my home city, the high schools they attended in the 1970s and 1980s were four thousand-student gargantuas. A visit to an administrator or counselor at these schools left one convinced that Franz Kafka had designed the curriculum and supervised personnel recruitment! Once I tried to find one of my stepsons at school but nobody had the slightest idea where he might be. In fact, he had not been at school for more than a week—and no one had paid any attention. How could a kid have a feeling of belonging in a place where few people seemed aware of his existence? There was no sense of community in these teenage wastelands, where simple trips to the lockers and bathrooms required the youngsters to resist drug pushers and periodically run the gauntlet of mean gang members. My children left with little affection for these dispirited places.

The heart of caring community is spirit, and life in community is the ground for spiritual practice, as Martin Buber tells us.

> God is in all things, but he is realized only when individual beings open to one another, communicate with one another, and help one another. . . . The true place of realization is community, and true community is that in which the godly is realized between people.[14]

Our schools must become once again spiritual communities. We must restore to education not religion, not dogma, but spirituality: the awareness that the moving force in the universe, that which makes life possible and gives purpose, is spirit. It has many names—Love, Great Spirit, Earth Mother, God—and is unnameable. It is the Mystery of mysteries and will remain that way despite all our scholarship and scientific research.

> *Knowledge does not vanquish mystery, or obscure its*
> *distant lights.*
>
> Annie Dillard

Let us encourage our students to delight in the permanence of the unknowable and to sit in reverence and awe before the majesty of the mysterious: *Yielbongura*, "the thing that knowledge can't eat," as the Dagara of West Africa say. Though the mysterious cannot be unraveled with the intellect, it can be entered into in silence. We must bring meditative silence into our classrooms. "In silence is learned what cannot be taught," the Zen masters tell us.

At the heart of mysticism lies the paradox that this is both an inexplicable universe and a purposeful one. Here is the good news we can give our students: Spirit is at work in the world, and spirited consciousness is a powerful force for good. When we work with love in our hearts, we have unseen allies. "Believe in the simple magic of life, in service in the universe," exhorts Buber.[15]

In the knowledge that "love is a cosmic force" lies the hope that today's young people need above all else. As teachers this is our pre-eminent task.

> *I know you cannot live on hope, but without it life is not*
> *worth living. And you, and you, and you, have to give them*
> *hope.*
>
> Harvey Milk

The wonderful thing about hope—like love and so much else in this universe of reciprocity—is that the more you give away, the more you get for yourself.

CONCLUSION:
LOVE IS A COSMIC FORCE

These are the days of miracle and wonder
This is the long-distance call.
The way the camera follows us in slow-mo,
The way we look to us all.
The way we look to a distant constellation
that's dying in a corner of the sky.
These are the days of miracle and wonder,
And don't cry baby, don't cry, don't cry.

Paul Simon, *Graceland*

Days of Miracle and Wonder

We live in strange times—amazing and scary. We are bombarded with bizarre and unfamiliar images, and the interpretations we are given are contradictory and confusing.

One set of voices speaks with supreme optimism of evolutionary advance and the unfolding of boundless human potential. There is evidence of a bright future, we are told, in today's technological breakthroughs, which hold incalculable promise for the improvement of the human condition. From the opposite corner a chorus chants a dirge of environmental disaster: Human overpopulation and overconsumption are destroying the Earth. We are done for if we go on like this.

What are we to believe? The doom-and-gloom school is hard to stomach, but the rosy vision of the evolutionists seems to fly in the face of facts. Those advances in scientific knowledge, intended to give "man" control over the forces of nature, seem to have left us disempowered in the wake of their devastating effects on the natural environment.

Are the doomsayers right? If so, what went wrong? Is there anything we can do, or is it already too late? Is there no hope left?

Of course there is! Things are bad, but they are not hopeless. We must understand what happened and what needs to happen. Let's start with the conundrum of the increasing impotence of our "powerful" science.

Science with No Holds Barred

The initial impact of science and the technologies it spawned was like a tidal wave. The source? Science's disregard for all limitations. Nothing was off limits to its probing. As a consequence, science overwhelmed self-restrained cultures, those that imposed sanctions against human intrusion into realms deemed sacred.

The mastery of nature was stated baldly as the central purpose of classical science. This provided justification for the domination by "rational man" of not only other natural species but also nonscientific or "natural man." In the name of progress, other ways of knowing had to yield to science. Violent conquest was elevated to the status of natural law by the Darwinian precept of the survival of the fittest, which won general acceptance by educated Europeans and Americans in the Victorian era.

Science as the one truth became the clarion call of a civilization. This immodest claim was lent credibility by the apparent incapability of nonscientific cultures to offer a contest. The fact that scientists believed their own propaganda—that they and they alone were on the path to truth—resulted in a laser-like focus of energy upon this narrow shaft of knowledge. Moreover, the vast material resources skimmed off by Europeans as their navies, armies, and administrative bureaucracies swarmed across the globe in the eighteenth and nineteenth centuries permitted the fabrication of technological marvels that seemed to confirm that scientific man had subdued nature.

But classical science bore the seeds of its own destruction. A consciousness that conceives an indifferent, spiritless machine universe of which the basic constituents are senseless chunks of matter locked in interaction by random, purposeless energies is profoundly unhealthy for humans, critters, and the very Earth itself.

With the best of intentions, scientists were prevented by the specialization of their disciplines from comprehending the full extent of their impact on the Earth. They had hefted a boulder into a pond, as it were, and in their single-minded concentration on its descent to the mud, they were oblivious to the waves that rolled out to every shore. With a segmented picture of nature and the corresponding compartmentalization of knowledge, they were only dimly aware of the seamless, integrated whole. Reductionism—the belief that it is the parts that govern the functioning of the whole—ill-prepared them for systemic reactions. They knew that the boulder affected the pond; they didn't expect the pond to retaliate. The Earth as a self-nurturing organism was bound ultimately to react to correct the imbalances generated by a science that had forgotten the principle of reciprocity.

To change the metaphor: Scientists whose prime purpose was to establish universal, immutable natural laws found it hard to perceive that the rules of the game—even perhaps the shape of the playing field—might change in response to their activities. Nor was it easy for them to accept that "man" was not the only player. Persuaded that none but humans are possessed of self-reflective consciousness, our scientific civilization was unprepared for purposeful initiatives taken by the "lower creatures." Consider as a case in point the disarray into which medical science has been thrown by the recent ingenious behaviors of viruses and carcinomas.

A Paradoxical Universe

Fortunately, as Eastern traditions teach, everything contains its opposite. Each great advance in scientific knowledge has revealed unexpected mysteries. When the physicists split the atom and threw open the door they believed would finally disclose the fundamentals of existence, they found themselves gazing upon a surreal landscape disturbingly similar to the alchemical vision on which their seventeenth-century precursors had so resolutely turned their backs. When the chaos theorists harnessed microelectronic computing to power up mathematics, they found that their nonlinear equations clouded the certainty of dualistic oppositions on which much of classical scientific reasoning rests: simple/complex, order/disorder, random/determined.

For the "new science" that has emerged, subscribing as it does to Werner Heisenberg's dictum that "every process of observation produces a large disturbance,"[1] there can no longer be simple, absolute certainties. For the new scientists, the visual symbol that typifies their craft is the mind-bending fractal image on the chaos mathemetician's computer display—a maze without end. The new scientists stand in awe of the sublime mysteries they confront. With Annie Dillard they muse:

> What do I make of all this texture? What does it mean about the kind of world in which I have been set down? The texture of the world, its filigree and scrollwork, means that there is the possibility of beauty here, a beauty inexhaustible in its complexity, which opens to my knock, which answers in me a call I do not remember calling, and which trains me to the wild extravagant nature of the spirit I seek.[2]

A wild, extravagant universe in which everything contains its opposite is a paradoxical universe. As we piece together our jigsaw puzzle, we must begin with paradox. Once we accept paradox, we see that we are not constrained by the absolutes of classical science.

Consider objectivity. Objectivity requires an ability to stand apart—but there is no "apart." We are inescapably of the universe. Here in the belly of the beast we cannot step back to draw perfectly proportioned pictures. But where in the heavens is it written that disengagement is a requirement for understanding? Because we are of the universe—"stars thinking," as Sister Miriam MacGillis says—its knowledge is patterned into our very cells. There's no better place than the belly of the beast to feel its life force. This may not be scientific knowledge, but it is knowing, nonetheless.

A universe in which everything contains its opposite is a universe of interconnectedness, of interpenetration. Ancient traditions, Western as well as Eastern, teach that the appearance of the separateness of things is illusion, *maya*. Again, a paradox: The existence of "the many things" is the source of much delight and beauty (*vive la différence*, as the French say of gender). This is what the Hindus call *leela*, the joyous play of life force in matter. They warn us, however, not to become so entranced by the *maya* of separateness that we forget that the reality is connectedness. If in our consciousness we empower separateness, we are all too likely to ignore the fact that what we do to "the other" we do to ourselves. If we pollute the stream, we pollute our own bodies, made as we are from the water we drink.

If this is a world of connectedness, it is also a world of impermanence. Here is another way to understand *maya*. Rather than saying that separate objects are illusory, we can say that their appearance of permanence is illusory. Form is not fixed. Things assume particular shapes for a time and then change into other shapes. Diversity of form allows the world to be known (experienced) in diverse ways.

A Collaborative Work in Progress

From native peoples we learn that the path of wisdom lies in opening ourselves to these other forms—"*Mitakuye oyasin*" (To all my relations), as Lakota Sioux say with reverence: the four-leggeds, the eight-leggeds, those that crawl and those that swim, our feathered friends and green relatives, the waters and the winds, Grandfather Sky and Grandmother Earth.

Indigenous traditions also teach that boundaries between forms are not as impermeable as they may seem. By "shifting shapes" to enter the eagle's keen eye, the bear's great strength, or the flame's searing heat, the shaman shows us passageways to the spirit wisdom of every natural form.

The great good news the shamans bring is that we are not alone. On a planet that is everywhere alive, conscious, and inspirited, humans have many wise allies for counsel and aid. We should lay to rest our exaggerated fears that we do not have the resources to keep this show going.

Equally we must learn humility. The hubris of *Homo sapiens* in claiming superiority over all other species has been the source of severe damage. Humanity is merely one spirit form among countless billions.

> *As the crickets' soft autumn hum*
> *is to us,*
> *so are we to the trees*
> *as are they*
> *to the rocks and hills.*[3]
>
> Gary Snyder

In this age there is no greater imperative than for humans to open to the wise consciousness of our spirit companions. We must learn to truly see and hear. We must wake up. The shaman's path is but one of a myriad of age-old disciplines (yogas) of body and mind that open clear channels of imagery, intuition, and the senses to allow these sounding boards to resonate with the harmonies of spirit.

The path of awakening begins in silence, for it is in silence that the busy chatter of the mind can be stilled. Too often the pattern of our thoughts is stuck in old, habitual ruts. When the Native American teacher Rolling Thunder says "all pollution begins in the mind," he encourages us to engage in the mental spring cleaning of spiritual discipline.

He also reminds us of the immense power of consciousness, which by now you know I consider to be central. The universe is conceived in the mind. Matter is thought made manifest. I once saw an electronics company billboard along the Massachusetts Turnpike that expressed this with surprising poetry: "Dreams taken seriously become realities." We find the same teaching in Mahatma Gandhi's simple but exacting dictum: If you want a loving world, you must love everybody and everything unconditionally—your enemies included.

Given that the world is made in the mind, every thought has an effect. But we do not make the world alone. This is a cocreated universe, a brilliant, multicolored fabric woven of the myriad strands of consciousness of all beings. As the ancient European shamans understood, there is "a web of fibres that flow through the entire universe, linking absolutely everything—each person, object, event, thought, and feeling.

This web is so sensitive that any movement, thought, or happening—no matter how small—reverberates throughout the entire web."[4]

The world is forged in relationship. We live in community with human and nonhuman companions, and our world is an ongoing cocreation. The statement that consciousness is fundamental is not a prescription for individual disengagement. Significantly, Gandhi, a man who placed great emphasis on the power of thought, was one who insisted equally upon engagement with others. "God is found in action," he said. Truth (synonymous with God in Gandhi's view) emerges from the struggles required to build and sustain community.

The universe is an ongoing creation, a collaborative work in progress. Here we come face to face with the most intriguing paradox of all. We make up the world as we go along, and yet the outcome is not happenstance. Though this is not a determined universe, it is a purposeful one. We have freedom of choice and yet we are part of the weaving of a vast intended pattern. Recall Martin Buber's words:

> Fate and freedom are promised to each other. Fate is encountered only by him that actualizes freedom. . . . this free human encounters fate as the counter-image of his freedom. It is not his limit but his completion; freedom and fate embrace each other to form meaning.[5]

It is also Martin Buber who tells us that "love is a cosmic force." Believe him, and take heart. This is a loving, nurturing universe. Living in it is not a cakewalk. You and I came here in this time to do a job of work, and acquiring the experience we need has its inevitable trials and tribulations. Life is suffering, say the Buddhists. Equally, life is joy. Both will pass. What will never pass—and this is the ultimate gift of this universe of love—is life itself. Life everlasting is a fact.

Notes

Introduction

1. C. G. Jung, *Memories, Dreams, Reflections*, 302.

Chapter 1: Dancing with the Past

1. C. V. Wedgewood, *William the Silent, William of Nassau, Prince of Orange* (London: Jonathan Cape, 1944), 35.
2. Quoted in Croswell Bowen and Shane O'Neill, *The Curse of the Misbegotten: A Tale of the House of O'Neill* (New York: McGraw Hill), 315–316.
3. Bernard S. Cohn, "The Pasts of an Indian Village," 241–249.
4. Jane Roberts, *The Individual and Mass Events* (Englewood Cliffs: Prentice Hall, 1981), 68.
5. *Encyclopedia Americana* (New York: Americana Corporation, 1978).
6. Boyce Richardson, *Strangers Devour the Land*, 45.
7. Hans-Georg Gadamer, *Philosophical Hermeneutics*, 58.
8. Lewis Thomas, *The Medusa and the Snail*, 74.
9. Gadamer, 54.
10. Loren Eiseley, *All the Strange Hours*, 105.
11. Quoted in Fritjof Capra, *The Tao of Physics*, 27.
12. Ludwig Wittgenstein, *Tractatus Logico-Philosophicus* (Translated by D. F. Pears and B. F. McGuiness. New York: Humanities Press, 1961), 115.
13. Michel Foucault, *The Birth of the Clinic*, xix.
14. Foucault, *The Order of Things*, xi.
15. John Berger, *Pig Earth*, 201.
16. Robert Graves, *The White Goddess: A Historical Grammar of Poetic Myth* (London: Faber & Faber, 1959), 448.
17. This account is based on Richardson, *Strangers Devour the Land*.

18. Marcia Langton, *Age* (Melbourne, Australia, February 13, 1981).
19. Stanley Keleman, *Living Your Dying,* 97.
20. W. K. Hancock, *Attempting History* (Canberra: Australian National University, 1969), 35.
21. Langton.
22. Lecture by Seyyed Hossein Nasr, "Mysticism and Rationality in Islam," Geist und Natur Conference (Hannover, May 24, 1988).
23. Claude Lévi-Strauss, *Tristes Tropiques,* 43.
24. Annie Dillard, *Pilgrim at Tinker Creek,* 147.
25. Richardson, 46.

Chapter 2: The Frail Hero and the Small Demon

1. A. L. Becker, *Beyond Translation,* 52–53.
2. David Bohm, *Wholeness and the Implicate Order,* xiv, 113.
3. James Gleick, *Chaos: Making a New Science,* 3.
4. Becker, 34, 40.
5. Thomas S. Kuhn, *The Structure of Scientific Revolutions,* 111.
6. James Spedding, Robert Leslie Ellis, and Douglas Devon Heath, eds., *The Works of Francis Bacon* (London: Longmans Green, 1870), Vol. 4, 115.
7. Ibid., Vol. 3, 222.
8. Quoted in A. Vartanian, *Diderot and Descartes* (Princeton: Princeton University Press, 1953), 47.
9. René Descartes, "Discourse on Method," in E. S. Haldane and G. R. T. Ross, eds., *The Philosophical Works of Descartes* (New York: Dover, 1955), Vol. 1, 85.
10. Quoted in Gary Zukav, *The Dancing Wu Li Masters,* 29.
11. Niels Bohr, *Atomic Physics and Human Knowledge,* 72.
12. Irene Born and Max Born, eds., *Correspondence between Albert Einstein and Max Hedwig Born, 1916–1955* (New York: Walker, 1971), 91.
13. Quoted in Rushworth M. Kidder, "Making the Quantum Leap," *Christian Science Monitor* (Boston, June 15, 1988).
14. Stephen W. Hawking, *A Brief History of Time,* 68.
15. Lecture by Gordon Kane, "Interpreting the Recent History of Particle Physics" (University of Michigan, Ann Arbor, April 13, 1983).
16. Hawking, 13.
17. Ibid., 56.
18. Ibid., 156.
19. Rupert Sheldrake, *The Presence of the Past,* 13, 37–38.
20. Gregory Bateson, *Mind and Nature,* 8.

21. Werner Heisenberg, *Physics and Philosophy,* 107.

22. Ibid., 81.

23. Bohm, 7.

24. Dillard, *Pilgrim at Tinker Creek,* 206.

25. Bohm, 9, 11.

26. Bateson, 41.

27. Quoted in Gleick, 314.

28. Ilya Prigogine and Isabelle Stengers, *Order Out of Chaos,* xxix.

29. Ilya Prigogine, *From Being to Becoming: Time and Complexity in the Physical Sciences* (San Francisco: W. H. Freeman, 1980), 215.

30. Becker, 34, 40.

31. Berger, 202.

32. Becker, 34, 40.

Chapter 3: The Legend of the Green Earth

1. Lecture by Raimundo Panikkar, "Mythos and Logos—Mythological and Rational World Views," Geist und Natur Conference (Hannover, May 24, 1988).

2. C. G. Jung, *Dream Symbols of the Individuation Process* (Zurich: privately printed, 1937), 43.

3. Loren Eiseley, *The Firmament of Time,* 136, 140.

4. Quoted in John Gliedman, "The Quantum Debate," *Science Digest,* 91, no. 6 (June 1983), 76.

5. Ludwig Wittgenstein, *Philosophical Investigations* (translated by G. E. N. Anscombe, Oxford, B. H. Blackwell, 1953), Vol. I, 129.

6. Lecture by Raimundo Panikkar, "Mythos and Logos—Mythological and Rational World Views," Geist und Natur Conference (Hannover, May 24, 1988).

7. From the reconstruction of Chief Sealth's (Seattle's) 1854 speech by Ted Perry quoted in John Seed et al., *Thinking Like a Mountain,* 68, 70, 71.

8. Quoted in Loren Eiseley, "Science and the Sense of the Holy," 70.

9. Dillard, *Pilgrim at Tinker Creek,* 141–142.

10. Quoted in James Cameron, *An Indian Summer* (London: Macmillan, 1987) 29.

11. Prigogine and Stengers, 306.

12. Starhawk, *Dreaming the Dark,* 3–4.

13. Martin Buber, *I and Thou,* 82.

14. All selections from Rabindranath Tagore's poems are from his *Lekhan.*

15. Gleick, 24.

16. Buber, *I and Thou*. These two sentences are translators' variants of the German original, respectively, Ronald Gregor Smith (New York: Charles Scribner's Sons, 1958), 16; and Walter Kaufmann (Edinburgh: T. & T. Clark, third edition 1970), 67. All other *I and Thou* references are from Kaufmann's translation.

17. Robert Ornstein and David Sobel, *The Healing Brain*, 12.

18. Thomas, 14.

19. Buber, 69.

20. Stephen Mitchell, *Tao Te Ching*. All references to the *Tao Te Ching* in this chapter are from Mitchell's translation.

21. Buber, 59.

22. Gleick, 103.

23. Ibid., 304.

24. Sheldrake, *The Presence of the Past*, 225–226.

25. Quoted by Renée Weber, *Dialogues with Scientists and Sages*, 38.

26. Peter Tompkins and Christopher Bird, *The Secret Life of Plants*, 23.

27. Ibid., 80.

28. Research conducted by Pennsylvania State University botanists, reported on TV program, "The Nature of Things" (October 30, 1986).

29. Tompkins and Bird, *The Secret Life of Plants*, 1–31, and Larry Dossey, *Healing Words*, 149.

30. Robert G. Jahn and Brenda J. Dunne, *Margins of Reality*, 148.

31. Alan Ereira, *The Heart of the World*, 115–118.

32. This account is drawn from Bruce Chatwin: *Songlines*, 18.

33. Quoted in Ken Wilber, *Quantum Questions*, 184.

34. Quoted in Flora Courtois, "Mahayana Buddhism and the Growing Perceptual Revolution," 53.

35. Bohm, 172.

36. Ibid., 9.

37. Ibid., 186–187.

38. Ibid., 11.

39. Quoted in Weber, 39.

40. Ibid., 41.

41. Sheldrake, *Presence of the Past*, xviii–xix.

42. Ibid., xvii.

43. Quoted in Weber, 83.

44. Karl Pribram, "What the Fuss Is All About," *The Holographic Paradigm and Other Paradoxes* (ed. Ken Wilber), 30.

45. Ibid., 32.

46. Ibid., 34.

47. Quoted in "A New Perspective on Reality," *The Holographic Paradigm and Other Paradoxes* (ed. Ken Wilber), 8.

48. Chatwin, 179.

49. Erwin Shroedinger, *What Is Life and Mind and Matter?* (London: Cambridge University Press, 1969), 137.

50. Dillard, *Teaching a Stone to Talk*, 40.

51. Quoted in "A New Perspective on Reality," *The Holographic Paradigm and Other Paradoxes* (ed. Ken Wilber), 8.

52. Bohm, 7.

53. Prigogine and Stengers, 312.

54. Quoted in Wilber, *Quantum Questions*, 101.

55. Quoted in Evelyn Fox Keller, *Reflections on Gender and Science*, 165.

56. Eiseley, "Science and the Sense of the Holy," 69–74, 104–107.

57. Ibid., 107.

58. Quoted in Weber, 208.

59. Hawking, 210.

60. Bede Griffiths, quoted in Weber, 176–177.

61. Ibid., 169.

62. Gleick, 98, 115.

63. Thomas, 16.

64. Buber, 102, 108–109.

65. Quoted in Gleick, 251, 314.

66. Albert Einstein, *The World As I See It*, 5.

67. Quoted in Wilber, *Quantum Questions*, 107.

68. Lecture by Stephen Jay Gould, 1987 Rochester Conference on Creation (University of Rochester, New York).

69. Dillard, *Teaching a Stone to Talk*, 69–70.

70. Gary Snyder, "By Frazier Creek Falls," from *Turtle Island*, reprinted in *No Nature*, 234.

Chapter 4: All That Exists Lives

1. Karl Marx, *Manifesto of the Communist Party* (Moscow: Foreign Language Publishers, 1965), 47.

2. Lecture by Thomas Berry (California Institute of Integral Studies, San Francisco, November 11, 1988).

3. Chatwin, 70.

4. Joseph Needham, "Human Laws and Laws of Nature in China and the West," *Journal of the History of Ideas* 12 (1951), 250.

5. J. R. R. Tolkien, *The Lord of the Rings*, part 1, 143.

6. Barry Lopez, *Arctic Dreams*, 279.
7. "Australia's Twilight of the Dreamtime," National Geographic documentary, 1987.
8. Richardson, 5.
9. Ibid., 6.
10. Ibid., 6.
11. Ibid., 9.
12. Willis Harman, "The Need for a Restructuring of Science," 15.
13. Lecture by Joachim-Ernst Berendt, "The Idea of Listening," Geist und Natur Conference (Hannover, May 25, 1988).
14. Quoted in Buber, 146, note 9.
15. William Barrett, "On Returning to Religion," 34.
16. Geoff Park, *Nga Uruora*, 134.
17. Jim Nollman, *Animal Dreaming*, 93.
18. Richardson, 9.
19. Michael King, *Te Puea*, 163.
20. Richard Nelson, *The Island Within*, 44.
21. Ibid., 52.
22. Dillard, *Pilgrim at Tinker Creek*, 193–205.
23. Barrett, 35–36.
24. Ibid., 35–36.
25. Satish Kumar, "To the Deep North: A Sacred Journey, III," *Resurgence* 121 (March–April, 1987), 14.
26. Chatwin, 14, 52.
27. Richardson, 8–9.
28. Nollman, *Animal Dreaming*, 146–151.
29. From the movie *Haa Shagoon* (Chilkoot Tlingit Nation, 1983).
30. Malidoma Patrice Somé, *Of Water and the Spirit*, 17–18.
31. Michael J. Roads, *Talking with Nature*, 37–47.
32. Findhorn Community, *The Findhorn Garden*, 81.
33. Roads, 27–30.
34. Barry Lopez, *Crossing Open Ground*, 62–63.
35. Dossey, 112.
36. Machaelle Small Wright, *Behaving As If the God in All Life Mattered*, 114–115.
37. Dillard, *Teaching a Stone to Talk*, 69–70.
38. Stanislav Grof, *The Adventure of Self-Discovery*, 53.
39. Ibid., 59–61.
40. Ibid., 118.
41. Jeanne Achterberg, *Imagery in Healing*, 24.

42. Sandra Ingerman, *Soul Retrieval*, 33.

43. Nelson, 37–38.

44. Roads, 82.

45. Nicholas and Helena Roerich, *Leaves of Morya's Garden: Book One—The Call* (New York: Agni Yoga Society, 1953), 96–97.

Chapter 5: Our Medicine, Their Medicine

1. This account draws on Paul Starr, *The Social Transformation of American Medicine*.

2. Thomas McKeown, *The Modern Rise of Population*, 162.

3. Thomas McKeown, *The Role of Medicine*, xiii.

4. Erwin Ackerknecht, *A Short History of Medicine* (New York: Ronald Press Company, 1968), 49.

5. Andrew Weil interview with Joan Smith, *San Francisco Examiner* (July 19, 1992).

6. Letter to author, December 19, 1996.

7. Thomas, 14.

8. McKeown, *The Role of Medicine*, 45.

9. Poole, *The Heart of Healing*, 114–117; and Daniel Goleman and Joel Gurin, eds., *Mind/Body Medicine*, 233–257.

10. Goleman and Gurin, 259–275.

11. Achterberg, 3–4.

12. Ibid., 10.

13. Dossey, 106.

14. Jalaludin Rumi, "When Grapes Turn to Wine," trans. Robert Bly, in *The Enlightened Heart: An Anthology of Sacred Poetry*, ed. Stephen Mitchell (New York: Harper and Row, 1989), 53.

15. Michael Murphy, *The Future of the Body*, 274–283.

16. Achterberg, 158–159.

17. Poole, 133.

18. Goleman and Gurin, 331–332.

19. Illich, *Medical Nemesis*, 274.

20. Ibid., 114.

21. Alberto Villoldo and Erik Jendresen, *Dance of the Four Winds*, 126.

22. Ingerman, *Soul Retrieval*, 104–108.

23. Achterberg, 6.

24. Fred B. Eiseman, *Bali*, 135–145.

25. Thomas Riccio, "Today We Sing!" 47–49.

26. David Abram, "The Ecology of Magic," 31.

27. Mark Matousek, "Death's Secrets: Interview with Sogyal Rinpoche," *Common Boundary*, 10, no. 5 (September–October 1992), 37.

Chapter 6: Is There Any Time but the Present?

1. Bohm, 211.
2. Marion Zimmer Bradley, *The Mists of Avalon*, 174.
3. Jahn and Dunne, 280–281.
4. Dillard, *Pilgrim at Tinker Creek*, 206.
5. Quoted in David Park, Kala (Time) Seminar (New Delhi, November 21, 1990).
6. Eiseley, *All the Strange Hours*, 105.
7. Hawking, 139.
8. André Varagnac, *Civilisation Traditionelle et Genres de Vie* (Paris: A. Michel, 1948), 211, 244.
9. Berger, 200–201.
10. Chatwin, 179.
11. Benjamin Lee Whorf, *Language, Thought and Reality*, 59–60.
12. Dillard, *Pilgrim at Tinker Creek*, 80.
13. Quoted in Michael Shallis, *On Time*, 162–163.
14. Quoted in Arnold R. Beisser, *Flying without Wings*, 13.
15. Paula Underwood Spencer, "A Native American Worldview," 19.
16. Bohm, 11, 191.
17. Lecture by Seyyed Hossein Nasr, Kala (Time) Seminar (New Delhi, November 21, 1990).
18. Clifford Geertz, *The Interpretation of Cultures*, 371–378.
19. Ibid., 371.
20. Ibid., 403.
21. Bradley, 407–408.
22. Tom Stoppard, *Rosencrantz and Guildenstern Are Dead* (London: Faber, 1967), 20.
23. Tony Basilio, "Seeds Are the Ticket to Ride," *Noetic Sciences Review* 16 (Autumn 1990), 24–25.
24. Berger, 201.
25. Geertz, 393.
26. This account is based on Marshall Sahlins' brilliant "Captain James Cook; or The Dying God," *Islands of History*, 104–135.
27. Jung, *Psychology and Religion, West and East* (translated by R. F. C. Hull, *Collected Works*, Vol. 20, New York: Bollingen Foundation, 1958), 592.
28. Jung, *Memories, Dreams, Reflections*, 388–389.

29. Joanna Macy, "What's So Good about Feeling Bad?" 35–36.

30. Jane Roberts, *The Nature of Personal Reality*, 435.

31. Dillard, *Pilgrim at Tinker Creek*, 82.

Chapter 7: The Mahatma and the Shrewd Peasant

1. Direct quotations from M. K. Gandhi are from my personal collection of his sayings gathered over almost forty years from published and unpublished sources.

2. Quoted in W. K. Hancock, *Smuts: The Sanguine Years, 1870–1919* (London: Cambridge University Press, 1962), 345.

3. Jawaharlal Nehru, *An Autobiography* (London: Bodley Head, 1942), 129.

4. Sarojini Naidu, quoted in James Cameron, *An Indian Summer* (London: Macmillan, 1987), 93.

5. The following "dialogue" with Gandhi was inspired by Mark Juergensmeyer's "Conversations in the Mind" in his *Fighting with Gandhi*. I am grateful to him for the idea.

6. Matthew 5:43–45.

7. George Orwell, *Shooting an Elephant*, 94.

8. Quoted in Barbara Wood, *E. F. Schumacher*, 248.

9. Quoted in George McRobie, *Small Is Possible*, 2.

10. Quoted in Wood, 326.

11. Quoted in McRobie, 7.

12. Berger, 196.

13. Wendell Berry, *Home Economics*, 66.

14. Berger, 208.

15. Berry, 66.

16. E. F. Schumacher, *Small Is Beautiful*, 54–56.

17. Berger, 211–212.

18. Marshall Sahlins, *Culture and Practical Reason*, 221.

19. Buber, *I and Thou*, 105.

20. Berry, 142–144.

Chapter 8: Whole Education for a Whole World

1. Shelley Kessler, *The Mysteries Sourcebook*, iii–iv.

2. Ibid., ii.

3. Ibid., appendix.

4. Paulo Freire, *Pedagogy of the Oppressed*, 58.

5. Ibid., 67.

6. Mary Field Belenky, et al., *Women's Ways of Knowing*, 104.

7. Ibid., 113.

8. Jung, *Memories, Dreams, Reflections*, 302.

9. Nelson, 52.

10. Quoted in Janet Allen-Coombe, "Weaving the Way of Wyrd," 20.

11. Brian Bates, *The Way of Wyrd*, 115.

12. Joan Osborne, "Spider Web," from the album *Relish*, 1995.

13. Peter and Trudy Johnson-Lenz, "Humanizing Hyperspace," *In Context*, 23 (Winter 1990), 55.

14. Quoted by Maurice S. Friedman, *Martin Buber*, 43.

15. Buber, *I and Thou*, 67.

Love Is a Cosmic Force

1. Werner Heisenberg, *The Physicist's Conception of Nature*, 15.

2. Dillard, *Pilgrim at Tinker Creek*, 142.

3. Gary Snyder, "Little Songs for Gaia," in *Axe Handles*, reprinted in *No Nature*, 287.

4. Brian Bates, quoted in Allen-Combe, 20.

5. Buber, 102.

Bibliography

Abram, David. "The Ecology of Magic." *Orion* (Summer 1991).

Achterberg, Jeanne. *Imagery in Healing: Shamanism and Modern Medicine.* Boston and London: Shambhala, 1985.

Allen-Coombe, Janet. "Weaving the Way of Wyrd: An Interview with Brian Bates." *Shaman's Drum* 27 (Spring 1992).

Arrien, Angeles. *The Four-Fold Way: Walking the Paths of the Warrior, Teacher, Healer and Visionary.* San Francisco: Harper San Francisco, 1993.

Barlow, Cleve. *Tikanga Whakaaro: Key Concepts in Maori Culture.* Auckland: Oxford University Press, 1991.

Barrett, William. "On Returning to Religion." *Commentary* 62, no. 5 (November 1976).

Bates, Brian. *The Way of Wyrd: Tales of an Anglo-Saxon Sorcerer.* San Francisco: Harper San Francisco, 1992.

Bateson, Gregory. *Mind and Nature: A Necessary Unity.* New York: E. P. Dutton, 1979.

Becker, A. L. *Beyond Translation: Essays Toward a Modern Philology.* Ann Arbor: University of Michigan Press, 1995.

Beisser, Arnold R. *Flying without Wings: Personal Reflections on Being Disabled.* New York: Doubleday, 1989.

Belenky, Mary Field; Blythe McVicker Clinchy, Nancy Rule Goldberger, and Jill Mattuck Tarule. *Women's Ways of Knowing: The Development of Self, Voice, and Mind.* New York: Basic Books, 1986.

Berendt, Joachim-Ernst. *The Third Ear: On Listening to the World.* Shaftesbury, England: Element, 1988.

Berger, John. *Pig Earth.* New York: Pantheon Books, 1980.

Bergson, Henri. *Creative Evolution.* London: Macmillan, 1911.

Berry, Thomas. *The Dream of the Earth.* San Francisco: Sierra Club Books, 1988.

Bibliography

Berry, Wendell. *Home Economics: Fourteen Essays.* San Francisco: North Point Press, 1987.

Bohm, David. *Wholeness and the Implicate Order.* London & Boston: Routledge & Kegan Paul, 1980.

Bohr, Niels. *Atomic Physics and Human Knowledge.* New York: John Wiley, 1958.

Boone, J. Allen. *Kinship with All Life.* San Francisco: Harper San Francisco, 1976.

Bradley, Marion Zimmer. *The Mists of Avalon.* New York: Ballantine Books, 1984.

Breeden, Stanley, and Belinda Wright. *Kakadu: Looking after the Country—The Gagudju Way.* Brookvale, Australia: Simon & Schuster Australia, 1989.

Broomfield, John H. "High Technology: The Construction of Disaster." *Alternative Futures* 3, no. 2 (Spring 1980).

———. "The Lethal Meccano." *Australian Journal of Politics and History* 27, no. 1 (July 1981).

———. "Gandhi: A Twentieth-Century Anomaly?" *World History. Vol. II, 1500 to Twentieth Century.* Edited by David McComb. Guilford, Ct.: Dushkin Publishing Group, 1988.

Brown, Joseph Epes. *Animals of the Soul: Sacred Animals of the Oglala Sioux.* Rockport, Mass., & Shaftesbury, England: Element, 1992.

Buber, Martin. *I and Thou.* Translated by Walter Kaufmann. Edinburgh: T. & T. Clark, third edition 1970.

Campbell, Joseph. *Historical Atlas of World Mythology. Vol. I, The Way of the Animal Powers.* San Francisco: Harper & Row, Alfred van der Marck editions, 1983.

Capra, Fritjof. *The Tao of Physics: An Exploration of the Parallels Between Modern Physics and Eastern Mysticism.* Boston: Shambhala, second revised edition 1985.

———. *The Turning Point: Science, Society and the Rising Culture.* New York: Simon and Schuster, 1982.

Chatwin, Bruce. *The Songlines.* New York and London: Penguin Books, 1988.

Cohn, Bernard S. "The Pasts of an Indian Village." *Comparative Studies in Society and History* 3, no. 3 (March 1961).

Cornell, Joseph. *Listening to Nature: How to Deepen Your Awareness of Nature.* Nevada City, Calif.: Dawn Publications; Watford, England: Exley Publications, 1987.

Courtois, Flora. "Mahayana Buddhism and the Growing Perceptual Revolution." *The Eastern Buddhist* new series 14, no. 2 (Autumn 1981).

245

Dillard, Annie. *Pilgrim at Tinker Creek.* New York: Bantam Books, 1975.

————. *Teaching a Stone to Talk.* New York: Harper & Row, 1982.

Dossey, Larry. *Healing Words: The Power of Prayer and the Practice of Medicine.* San Francisco: Harper San Francisco, 1993.

Dudley, Michael Kioni. *Man, Gods, and Nature.* Honolulu: Na Kane O Ka Malo Press, 1990.

Einstein, Albert. *The World As I See It.* New York: Citadel Press, 1979.

Eiseley, Loren. *All the Strange Hours: The Excavation of a Life.* New York: Charles Scribner's Sons, 1975.

————. *The Firmament of Time.* New York: Macmillan, 1966.

————. "Science and the Sense of the Holy." *Quest 2,* no. 2 (March-April 1978).

Eiseman, Fred B. *Bali—Sekala and Niskala: Vol. I, Essays on Religion, Ritual, and Art.* Singapore: Periplus Editions, 1990.

Eliade, Mircea. *Shamanism: Archaic Techniques of Ecstasy.* Translated by Willard R. Trask. Princeton, N.J.: Princeton University Press, 1972.

Ereira, Alan. *The Heart of the World.* London: Jonathan Cape, 1990.

Findhorn Community. *The Findhorn Garden.* Edited by Shoshana Tembeck. New York: Harper & Row, 1975.

Foucault, Michel. *The Birth of the Clinic: An Archaeology of Medical Perception.* Translated by A. M. Sheridan Smith. New York: Vintage Books, 1975.

————. *The Order of Things: An Archaeology of the Human Sciences.* New York: Vintage Books, 1973.

Friedman, Maurice S. *Martin Buber: The Life of Dialogue.* New York: Harper & Row, 1960.

Freire, Paulo. *Pedagogy of the Oppressed.* Translated by Myra Bergman Ramos. New York: Continuum, 1970.

Gadamer, Hans-Georg. *Philosophical Hermeneutics.* Berkeley: University of California Press, 1976.

Geertz, Clifford. *The Interpretation of Cultures: Selected Essays.* New York: Basic Books, 1973.

————. *Local Knowledge: Further Essays in Interpretive Anthropology.* New York: Basic Books, 1983.

Gilligan, Carol. *In a Different Voice: Psychological Theory and Women's Development.* Cambridge, Mass., and London: Harvard University Press, 1982.

Gleick, James. *Chaos: Making a New Science.* New York and London: Penguin Books, 1988.

Gold, Peter. *Navajo and Tibetan Sacred Wisdom: The Circle of the Spirit.* Rochester, Vt.: Inner Traditions International, 1994.

Goleman, Daniel, and Joel Gurin, eds. *Mind/Body Medicine: How to Use Your Mind for Better Health*. Yonkers, N.Y.: Consumer Reports Books, 1993.

Griffiths, Bede. *The Marriage of East and West*. Springfield, Ill.: Templegate Publishers, 1982.

————. *Universal Wisdom: A Journey through the Sacred Wisdom of the World*. New York: Harper Collins, 1994.

Grof, Stanislav. *The Adventure of Self-Discovery: Dimensions of Consciousness and New Perspectives in Psychotherapy*. Albany, N.Y.: State University of New York Press, 1988.

————, ed. *Ancient Wisdom and Modern Science*. Albany, N.Y.: State University of New York Press, 1984.

Harman, Willis. "The Need for a Restructuring of Science." *Revision* 11 no. 2 (Fall 1988).

Harman, Willis, and Jane Clark, eds. *New Metaphysical Foundations of Modern Science*. Sausalito, Calif.: Institute of Noetic Sciences, 1994.

Harner, Michael. *The Jívaro: People of the Sacred Waterfalls*. Garden City, N.Y.: Doubleday/Natural History Press, 1972.

————. *The Way of the Shaman*. San Francisco: Harper San Francisco, tenth anniversary edition 1990.

Hawking, Stephen W. *A Brief History of Time from the Big Bang to Black Holes*. New York: Bantam Books, 1988.

Heisenberg, Werner. *The Physicist's Conception of Nature*. Translated by Arnold J. Pomerans. New York: Harcourt Brace, 1958.

————. *Physics and Philosophy: The Revolution in Modern Science*. New York: Harper & Brothers, 1958.

Illich, Ivan. *Medical Nemesis: The Expropriation of Health*. New York: Pantheon Books, 1976.

Ingerman, Sandra. *Soul Retrieval: Mending the Fragmented Self*. San Francisco: Harper San Francisco, 1991.

————. *Welcome Home: Following Your Soul's Journey Home*. San Francisco: Harper San Francisco, 1994.

Jahn, Robert G., and Brenda J. Dunne. *Margins of Reality: The Role of Consciousness in the Physical World*. New York: Harcourt Brace Jovanovich, 1987.

Jonas, Hans. "Toward a Philosophy of Technology: Knowledge, Power, and the Biological Revolution." *Hastings Center Report* 9, no. 1 (February 1979).

Juergensmeyer, Mark. *Fighting with Gandhi*. San Francisco: Harper & Row, 1984.

Jung, C. G. *Memories, Dreams, Reflections*. Recorded and edited by Aniela Jaffé. Translated by Richard and Clara Winston. New York: Random House, 1961.

Kaiser, Jon D. *Immune Power: A Comprehensive Healing Program for HIV.* New York: St. Martin's Press, 1993

Keleman, Stanley. *Living Your Dying.* New York: Random House; and Berkeley, Calif.: Bookworks, 1974.

Keller, Evelyn Fox. *A Feeling for the Organism: The Life and Work of Barbara Mc-Clintock.* San Francisco: W. H. Freeman, 1983.

———. *Refiguring Life: Metaphors of Twentieth-Century Biology.* New York: Columbia University Press, 1996.

———. *Reflections on Gender and Science.* New Haven: Yale University Press, 1985.

Kessler, Shelley. *The Mysteries Sourcebook.* Santa Monica, Calif.: Crossroads School, 1990.

King, Michael. *Being Pakeha: An Encounter with New Zealand and the Maori Renaissance.* Auckland: Hodder & Stoughton, 1985.

———. *Te Puea: A Biography.* Auckland: Hodder & Stoughton, 1977.

Kuhn, Thomas S. *The Structure of Scientific Revolutions.* Chicago: University of Chicago Press, second enlarged edition 1970.

Lawlor, Robert. *Voices of the First Day: Awakening in the Aboriginal Dreamtime.* Rochester, Vt.: Inner Traditions International, 1991.

Lévi-Strauss, Claude. *Tristes Tropiques.* Translated by John and Doreen Weightman. New York and London: Penguin Books, 1992.

Lewis, David. *The Voyaging Stars: Secrets of the Pacific Island Navigators.* Sydney: Fontana/Collins, 1980.

Lightman, Alan. *Einstein's Dreams: A Novel.* New York: Pantheon Books, 1993.

Livingston, John A. *One Cosmic Instant: Man's Fleeting Supremacy.* New York: Dell, 1974.

Lopez, Barry. *Arctic Dreams: Imagination and Desire in a Northern Landscape.* New York: Charles Scribner's Sons, 1986.

———. *Crossing Open Ground.* New York: Vintage Books, 1989.

Macy, Joanna. *Dharma and Development: Religion As Resource in the Sarvodaya Self-Help Movement.* West Hartford, Conn.: Kumarian Press, revised edition 1985.

———. "What's So Good About Feeling Bad?" *New Age Journal* (January-February 1991).

———. *World As Lover, World As Self.* Berkeley, Calif.: Parallax Press, 1991.

Masson, Jeffrey Moussaieff, and Susan McCarthy. *When Elephants Weep: The Emotional Lives of Animals.* New York: Dell, 1996.

McKeown, Thomas. *The Modern Rise of Population.* New York and San Francisco: Academic Press, 1976.

————. *The Role of Medicine: Dream, Mirage, or Nemesis?* London: The Nuffield Provincial Hospitals Trust, 1976.

McRobie, George. *Small Is Possible.* New York: Harper & Row, 1981.

Merchant, Carolyn. *The Death of Nature: Women, Ecology and the Scientific Revolution.* San Francisco: Harper & Row, 1983.

Metzner, Ralph. *Opening to Inner Light: The Transformation of Human Nature and Consciousness.* Los Angeles: Jeremy P. Tarcher, 1986.

————. *The Well of Remembrance: Rediscovering the Earth Wisdom Myths of Northern Europe.* Boston: Shambhala, 1994.

Mitchell, Stephen. *Tao Te Ching: A New English Version.* New York: Harper & Row, 1988.

Murphy, Michael. *The Future of the Body: Explorations into the Further Evolution of Human Nature.* Los Angeles: Jeremy P. Tarcher, 1992.

Neihardt, John G. *Black Elk Speaks: Being the Life Story of a Holy Man of the Oglala Sioux.* New York: Pocket Books, 1972.

Nelson, Richard. *The Island Within.* New York: Vintage Books, 1991.

Nollman, Jim. *Animal Dreaming.* New York: Bantam Books, 1987. [The second edition, also published by Bantam Books in 1987, was retitled *Dolphin Dreamtime.*]

————. *Spiritual Ecology: A Guide to Reconnecting with Nature.* New York: Bantam Books, 1990.

Orbell, Margaret. *The Illustrated Encyclopedia of Maori Myth and Legend.* Christchurch, New Zealand: Canterbury University Press, 1995.

————. *The Natural World of the Maori.* Auckland: David Bateman, second edition 1996.

Ornstein, Robert, and David Sobel. *The Healing Brain: Breakthrough Discoveries about How the Brain Keeps Us Healthy.* New York: Simon & Schuster, 1988.

Orwell, George. *Shooting an Elephant.* New York: Secker & Warburg, 1950.

Palmer, Parker J. *To Know As We Are Known: A Spirituality of Education.* San Francisco: Harper & Row, 1983.

Park, Geoff. *Nga Uruora—The Groves of Life: Ecology and History in a New Zealand Landscape.* Wellington, New Zealand: Victoria University Press, 1995.

Poole, William, and Institute of Noetic Sciences. *The Heart of Healing.* Atlanta: Turner Publishing, 1993.

Prigogine, Ilya, and Isabelle Stengers. *Order Out of Chaos: Man's New Dialogue with Nature.* New York: Bantam Books, 1984.

Riccio, Thomas. "Today We Sing! Healing Rituals of the !Xuu and Khwe Bushmen." *Shaman's Drum* 42 (Summer 1996).

Richardson, Boyce. *Strangers Devour the Land.* Post Mills, Vt.: Chelsea Green, 1991.

Roads, Michael. *Talking with Nature: Sharing the Energies and Spirit of Trees, Plants, Birds, and Earth.* Tiburon, Calif.: H. J. Kramer, 1987.

Roberts, Jane. *The Nature of Personal Reality: A Seth Book.* Englewood Cliffs, N.J.: Prentice-Hall, 1974.

Sahlins, Marshall. *Culture and Practical Reason.* Chicago: Chicago University Press, 1976.

———. *Islands of History.* Chicago: Chicago University Press, 1985.

Schumacher, E. F. *Good Work.* New York: Harper & Row, 1979.

———. *Small Is Beautiful: Economics As If People Mattered.* New York: Harper & Row, 1975.

Seed, John, Joanna Macy, Pat Felming, and Arne Naess. *Thinking Like a Mountain: Towards a Council of All Beings.* Philadelphia: New Society Publishers, 1988.

Shallis, Michael. *On Time: An Investigation into Scientific Knowledge and Human Experience.* Harmondsworth, England: Penguin Books, 1983.

Sheldrake, Rupert. *A New Science of Life: The Hypothesis of Formative Causation.* Los Angeles: Jeremy P. Tarcher, 1981.

———. *The Presence of the Past: Morphic Resonance and the Habits of Nature.* New York: Times Books, 1988.

———. *The Rebirth of Nature: The Greening of Science and God.* Rochester, Vt.: Park Street Press, 1994.

Skolimowski, Henryk. "The Participatory Universe and its New Methodology." *Frontier Perspectives* 5, no. 2 (Spring-Summer 1996).

Snyder, Gary. *No Nature: New and Selected Poems.* New York & San Francisco: Pantheon Books, 1992.

Somé, Malidoma Patrice. *Of Water and the Spirit: Ritual, Magic, and Initiation in the Life of an African Shaman.* New York: Jeremy P. Tarcher/Putnam Books, 1994.

Spencer, Paula Underwood. "A Native American Worldview." *Noetic Sciences Review* 15 (Summer 1990).

Spradley, James P., and David W. McCurdy, eds. *Conformity and Conflict: Readings in Cultural Anthropology.* Boston: Little Brown, 1971.

Starhawk. *Dreaming the Dark: Magic, Sex and Politics.* Boston: Beacon Press, second edition 1988.

Starr, Paul. *The Social Transformation of American Medicine.* New York: Basic Books, 1982.

Tagore, Rabindranath. *Lekhan*. Calcutta: Visva Bharati, 1961.

Thomas, Lewis. *The Medusa and the Snail: More Notes of a Biology Watcher.* New York: Viking, 1979.

"Time and Presence." *Parabola* 15, no. 1 (February 1990).

Tolkien, J. R. R. *The Lord of the Rings.* Boston: Houghton Mifflin, second revised edition 1965.

Tompkins, Peter, and Christopher Bird. *The Secret Life of Plants.* New York: Avon Books, 1974.

———. *Secrets of the Soil: New Age Solutions for Restoring Our Planet.* New York: Harper & Row, 1990.

Uberoi, J. P. S. *Science and Culture.* Delhi: Oxford University Press, 1978.

Villoldo, Alberto, and Erik Jendresen. *Dance of the Four Winds: Secrets of the Inca Medicine Wheel.* Rochester, Vt.: Destiny Books, 1995.

Weber, Renée. *Dialogues with Scientists and Sages: The Search for Unity.* London & New York: Routledge & Kegan Paul, 1986.

Weil, Andrew. *Natural Health, Natural Medicine: A Comprehensive Manual for Wellness and Self-Care.* New York: Houghton Mifflin, 1990.

Wheeler, J. A. "The Universe as Home for Man." *The American Scientist* 62, no. 6 (November-December 1974).

Whorf, Benjamin Lee. *Language, Thought, and Reality: Selected Writings.* Edited by John B. Carroll. Cambridge, Mass.: M. I. T. Press, 1956.

Wilber, Ken, ed. *The Holographic Paradigm and Other Paradoxes: Exploring the Leading Edge of Science.* Boulder, Colo., and London: Shambhala, 1982.

———. *Quantum Questions: Mystical Writings of the World's Great Physicists.* Boulder, Colo., and London: Shambhala, 1984.

Wood, Barbara. *E. F. Schumacher: His Life and Thought.* New York: Harper & Row, 1984.

Wright, Machaelle Small. *Behaving As If the God in All Life Mattered: A New Age Ecology.* Jeffersonton, Va.: Perelandra, 1987.

Zukav, Gary. *The Dancing Wu Li Masters: An Overview of the New Physics.* New York and Toronto: Bantam Books, 1980.

Index

252

For information on John Broomfield's
international workshops and tours contact

The Eagle Connection
Private Bag
Havelock
Marlborough
New Zealand
Fax: 64-3-576-5148
E-mail: John@eagle.nelson.planet.org.nz